Re

Reimagining Ireland

Volume 93

Edited by Dr Eamon Maher,
Technological University Dublin – Tallaght Campus

Brian Lucey, Eamon Maher
and Eugene O'Brien (eds)

Recalling the Celtic Tiger

PETER LANG
Oxford • Bern • Berlin • Bruxelles • New York • Wien

Bibliographic information published by Die Deutsche Nationalbibliothek.
Die Deutsche Nationalbibliothek lists this publication in the Deutsche Nationalbibliografie; detailed bibliographic data is available on the Internet at http://dnb.d-nb.de.
A catalogue record for this book is available from the British Library.

A CIP catalog record for this book has been applied for at the Library of Congress.

ISSN 1662-9094
ISBN 978-1-78997-286-3 (print) • eISBN 978-1-78997-287-0 (ePDF)
eISBN 978-1-78997-288-7 (ePub) • eISBN 978-1-78997-289-4 (Mobi)
DOI 10.3726/b16190

Cover image: Copyright Paul Butler

Cover design by Peter Lang Ltd.

Published by Peter Lang Ltd, International Academic Publishers,
52 St Giles, Oxford, OX1 3LU, United Kingdom
oxford@peterlang.com, www.peterlang.com

This publication has been peer reviewed.

Printed in Germany

Brian: I would like to dedicate this book to my wife Mary, a never-ending font of good advice, love and support, and my son Sam, whom I hope grows up in a society as calm and wonderful as he is.

Eamon: I would like to dedicate this book to Liz and our three wonderful children.

Eugene: I would like to dedicate this book to my very supportive family: Áine, Sinéad, Dara and Eoin.

Contents

Acknowledgements xix

BRIAN LUCEY, EAMON MAHER AND EUGENE O'BRIEN
Introduction 1

CONSTANTIN GURDGIEV
100% mortgages 7

KARL DEETER
Accidental Landlords 9

PATRICIA MEDCALF
Advertising 11

SEAN BARRETT
Ahern, Bertie 13

CONSTANTIN GURDGIEV
Anglo Irish Tapes 17

CONSTANTIN GURDGIEV
Ansbacher Accounts 19

NEIL DUNNE
Auditors 21

CHARLES LARKIN
Bailout 23

LORCAN SIRR
Balanced Regional Development 25

JOE BRENNAN
Bank Lending Policies in the 2004– 2010 Period 27

FRANCES COPPOLA
Bank Regulation 31

FRANCES COPPOLA
Bank Solvency Crisis 35

STEPHEN KINSELLA
Banking Culture 39

EOGHAN SMITH
Banville, John 41

CHARLES LARKIN
Barrett, Sean 43

SEAMUS COFFEY
Black Economy 45

BRIAN LUCEY
Bondholders 49

CHARLES LARKIN
Bord Snip Nua 53

EUGENE O'BRIEN
Browne, Vincent 55

KARL DEETER
Buy-to-lets 59

CHARLES LARKIN
Cardiff, Kevin 61

CHARLES LARKIN
Chopra, Ajai 63

RUTH BARTON
Cinema and the Celtic Tiger 65

BRIAN MURPHY
Coffee Culture 69

LORCAN SIRR
Commission on the Private Rented Sector 73

BRIAN O'NEILL
Communications 75

SHAEN CORBET
Contracts for Difference (CFD) 79

SUSAN BOYLE
Craft Beer 81

STEPHEN KINSELLA
Credit Crunch 83

STEPHEN KINSELLA
Credit Default Swaps 85

SHAEN CORBET
Credit Rating Agencies 87

SARAH KELLEHER
Cross, Dorothy 89

EOIN FLANNERY
Debt 93

JOHN O'CONNOR
Design and the Celtic Tiger 95

MÁIRTÍN MAC CON IOMAIRE
Dining Out 97

FINOLA KENNEDY
Divorce: 'Till Debt Do Us Part' 101

MEGAN GREENE
ECB 103

MEGAN GREENE
Economists 105

JOHN MCDONAGH
Electric Gates in the Celtic Tiger 107

MEGAN GREENE
Emergency Liquidity Assistance (ELA) 111

CONSTANTIN GURDGIEV
Entrepreneurship 113

DARRAGH FLANNERY
ESRI 115

DAVID BEGG
Euro 117

STEPHEN KINSELLA
Euro: Cause and Consequences 121

EUGENE O'BRIEN
Fianna Fáil 123

MAURA ADSHEAD
Fianna Fáil and Social Partnership: The Boom 127

MAURA ADSHEAD
Fianna Fáil and Social Partnership: The Bust 131

EUGENE O'BRIEN
Fine Gael–Labour Government 2011–2016 135

STEPHEN KINSELLA
Free Market 139

JOHN MULCAHY
Gastro-tourism 141

ROB KITCHIN
Ghost Estates 143

EAMON MAHER
Golf Clubs 145

MARTINA FITZGERALD
Harney, Mary 147

VIC MERRIMAN
Higgins, Michael D. 151

SARAH KELLEHER
Hillen, Sean 155

MEGAN GREENE
Honohan, Patrick 159

EUGENE O'BRIEN
Howard, Paul 161

NA FU
Human Resource Management 165

NEIL DUNNE
IAS 39 167

SARAH KELLEHER
IMMA 169

CHARLES LARKIN
Independent Politicians 173

DAVID BEGG
International Context 175

CHARLES LARKIN
International Monetary Fund 179

CATHERINE MAIGNANT
Internet 181

SEAMUS COFFEY
Irish Fiscal Advisory Council 185

AOIFE CARRIGY
The Irish Pub 189

BRIAN LUCEY
Kelly, Morgan 193

STEPHEN KINSELLA
Liquidity Crisis 195

KATE SHANAHAN
Media and the Celtic Tiger: The Watchdog that Didn't Bark 197

MARTINA FITZGERALD
Merkel, Angela 201

EUGENE O'BRIEN
Mobile Technology 205

KARL DEETER
Mortgages 207

JOHN LITTLETON
Murphy Report 209

SEAMUS COFFEY
National Accounts 213

CONSTANTIN GURDGIEV
National Treasury Management Agency (NTMA) 217

DARRAGH FLANNERY
Neary, Patrick 219

DARRAGH FLANNERY
Negative Equity 223

LORCAN SIRR
Neoliberalism 225

DEREK HAND
Novels of the Celtic Tiger 227

SEAN BARRETT
Nyberg Report 229

SEAN BARRETT
Oireachtas Joint Committee Report 233

FABRICE MOURLON
Peace Process: A French Perspective 239

MICK FEALTY
Peace Process and Anglo-Irish Relations 243

JUSTIN CARVILLE
Photography 245

SHAEN CORBET
PIIGS Countries 249

EOIN FLANNERY
Poetry 253

CHARLES LARKIN
Political Economy 257

NA FU
Professional Service Firms 259

CONSTANTIN GURDGIEV
Progressive Democrats 261

CONSTANTIN GURDGIEV
Property Boom 263

PASCHAL DONOHUE
Public Finances in the Celtic Tiger 265

BRIAN LANGAN
Publishing 267

CHARLES LARKIN
Quinn, Sean 271

DEIRDRE FLYNN
Referendums 273

CONSTANTIN GURDGIEV
Regling-Watson Report 275

KARL DEETER
Repossessions 277

HARRY WHITE
Riverdance 279

EAMON MAHER
Ryan, Donal: *The Spinning Heart* 283

CATHERINE MAIGNANT
Ryan Report 285

SHAEN CORBET
Saint Patrick's Day Massacre of Shares 289

CONSTANTIN GURDGIEV
Second Houses 291

IDA MILNE
Shopping Trips to New York 293

SHAEN CORBET
Short Selling 297

CONSTANTIN GURDGIEV
Single Currency 299

LORCAN SIRR
Social Housing 301

SHAEN CORBET
Sports 303

CONSTANTIN GURDGIEV
SSIA 307

EOGHAN SMITH
Suburban Literature 309

FRANCES COPPOLA
Target2 Balances 311

EIMEAR NOLAN
Texting and the Celtic Tiger 313

VIC MERRIMAN
Theatre of the Celtic Tiger 315

RAYMOND KEARNEY
Tourism 319

NA FU
Trade Unions 321

CHARLES LARKIN
Troika 323

EUGENE O'BRIEN
U2 325

CONSTANTIN GURDGIEV
Unemployment 329

LORCAN SIRR
Unfinished Estates 331

PADDY PRENDERGAST
Universities 333

CONSTANTIN GURDGIEV
'We all partied' 335

BRIAN MURPHY
Wine Culture 337

SHARON TIGHE-MOONEY
Women and the Church 339

DEIRDRE FLYNN
Women in the Celtic Tiger 341

MARY O'DONNELL
Women Writers 345

Notes on Contributors 349

Acknowledgements

The editors would like to sincerely thank the large number of contributors to this collection, many of whom did multiple entries, for their hard work and cooperation. The enthusiasm with which they accepted our invitation to be involved and their willingness to accept editorial guidance where necessary, speaks volumes as to their professionalism and dedication. We would also like to thank the Commissioning Editor at Peter Lang, Tony Mason, for seeing the potential of this collection from the outset and for the courteous and helpful way he assisted us at each stage of its development. Finally, we are immensely grateful to Paul Butler for providing us with such a beautiful cover image and to all the staff at Peter Lang Oxford for bringing this book out in a timely and professional manner.

BRIAN LUCEY, EAMON MAHER AND EUGENE O'BRIEN

Introduction

There has been a lot written and said about the periods of Irish history known collectively as the Celtic Tiger. Indeed, 'history' is probably the incorrect term as we are still living through this period, with its cycle of boom-and-bust economics. For a number of years, starting in the mid-1990s with an export-led boom, and resuming in the early noughties with a credit boom, Ireland roared ahead. Each year, national income rose, Ireland became a net importer of people as immigrants from Europe flocked to come and work in Ireland, the price of property rose and rose, and consumer spending ballooned every year. The export-led Celtic Tiger having been seemingly revived by the Credit Celtic Tiger, saw Ireland being touted as a role model for other economies, and there was a sense that Ireland, having been for so long a closed and pre-modern society and economy, had now bypassed the slow, accretive progress associated with modernity, and had transported itself into a postmodern society and model neoliberal economy. Financial services, technology, and property were the drivers of this ongoing economic phenomenon, and the standard of living across the country rose as consumer goods became an index of the increasing levels of wealth and credit flowing in the economy.

Shiny new buildings, business and retail parks, which channelled the American 'mall' concept, designer stores, gallerias and plazas became familiar sights and commercial experiences. Arts centres and theme parks sprang up all over the country, as did hotels, golf complexes and housing estates, as people with now significant disposable income sought easy ways in which to spend it. Ireland had become a consumer-driven, multi-ethnic and multiracial economy almost overnight, it seemed, and there was a great sense of pride in being Irish. Culturally and politically, this was also the case as the Good Friday Agreement, which brokered an historic peace in Northern Ireland, brought Irish Taoiseach Bertie Ahern to the world stage. Traditional Irish music and dance also enjoyed a period of sustained success, a success that is undoubtedly best encapsulated by the *Riverdance* phenomenon. Irish actors such as Colin Farrell, Saoirse Ronan, Cillian Murphy and Liam Nelson became important figures in Hollywood, while U2 and The Script were carving out a musical legacy, as Maeve Hinchey and Cecelia Ahearn (to cite just two novelists who really emerged at this time) were similarly achieving a worldwide reputation.

Many of our novelists, poets and playwrights were at the zenith of their careers, chief among them Seamus Heaney, being awarded the Nobel Prize for Literature in 1995. One began to wonder if Ireland had finally taken its place among the nations of the earth. The country was seen as the poster-child for an open economy, whose main attributes were portrayed as having an English-speaking and well-educated population. It seemed that a history of colonisation and the loss of a native language in favour of a global one had paid dividends, and that our location in Europe, allied to our cultural and linguistic connections with the United States, ensured that we were ideally located to benefit from commerce with both these hugely significant markets.

Bank credit was freely available, loans were given for various projects (many of which we now know to have been dubious), and new buildings and housing estates were appearing all over the country. Internet access (still a bone of contention when it comes to easy access to broadband in parts of rural Ireland), and increasing availability of mobile phones meant that business was now being transacted in new ways and, once again, Ireland appeared to be very much at the heart of these developments with hi-tech companies being attracted here due to the young educated work force and the low corporation tax (another still contentious issue, especially with our European partners). Instead of going abroad to build other nations' infrastructures, the Irish were now going abroad to buy buildings and companies in Britain and the USA. Generations of poverty-driven emigration were being replaced by acquisition-driven emigration. There had been a sea change in the perception of Ireland and the Irish at home and abroad. Bertie Ahern and his Fianna Fáil-led governments basked in the glow of continued and seemingly endless economic prosperity; social partnership ensured that there was very little disruption by the trade unions, whose members were kept happy by a steady raft of generous pay increases. Ireland's banks and financial centres were the envy of the developed world, as they doled out incredible sums of money to a vast array of developers, companies and individual clients. Seen as a European version of the Asian Tiger economies, the governing powers in the state, financial and business sectors were seen as architects of a new way of doing business.

The openness of our economy, which had been a causal factor in the influx of investment, meant, however, that Ireland was similarly vulnerable to world trends, and the financial crisis around the collapse of Lehman's and the beginning of a worldwide credit crisis led to a collapse of the Irish economy that was even more spectacular than its rise. The massively over-extended banks convinced the political leaders that they were undergoing a crisis of liquidity, which was soon revealed to be a crisis of solvency. In the meantime, however, the banks' debt became sovereign debt, with the government guarantee proving to be a costly mistake (that said, there was no silver bullet to solve Ireland's chronic problems at this time, and the guarantee was viewed as the least bad option).

Meanwhile, under severe pressure from the European Central Bank's President Claude Trichet not to 'burn the bondholders', the government was bounced into the Troika bailout programme in 2010. From a period of unparalleled prosperity, therefore, Ireland as a nation suddenly descended into a period of grim austerity, with emigration replacing immigration, repossession replacing property acquisition, and bank debt replacing bank credit. It was a time when verbal truisms like 'You can never lose money in bricks and mortar', or 'As safe as money in the bank', were undermined by actuality, and it became clear that these old certainties were no longer true. The junk mail from banks and building societies assuring us that we could afford to build that extension, or buy that new car, and that we *did* deserve to have that foreign holiday and that they, in their goodness, were only too happy to loan us the money for these luxuries, was replaced by curt demands for payment of outstanding loans and solicitors' letters advising us of legal consequences for not paying mortgages and debt.

This was a sudden shock to the system, especially the grim and frightening discovery that the banks, estate agents, auctioneers and those who oversaw the financial and property markets (and who seemed to bestride that market like the Masters of the universe in Tom Wolfe's famous novel, *The Bonfire of the Vanities*), were completely out of their depth. An appearance on TV by the Financial Regulator, heretofore a man and role unknown to the vast majority of the population, was generally agreed to be a key turning point, the regulator seemingly both insouciant and out of touch. The results are well known to anyone with even a passing interest in Irish affairs: Ireland slipped into a sharp depression from which it appeared to re-emerge slowly after more than a decade of deep cuts and austerity measures which ruined lives, broke up families and led to utter despair for many. Unemployment soared, along with tax increases, and empty semi-developed housing and commercial building sites became the concrete manifestation of an economy that was not experiencing the promised 'soft landing', but rather a startling crash-landing into recession. The mourning period had its own associated terminology, when terms like 'senior debt', 'bondholders' and 'haircuts', became part of colloquial vocabulary. The Fine Gael–Labour coalition, which replaced Fianna Fáil and the Greens, in spite of all their promises to reverse the compliant policies of their predecessors, in the end merely implemented more cuts, which inevitably hit the most vulnerable in society. In the run-up to the 2016 election, the Fine Gael slogan, 'Keep the recovery Going', and their promises of the abolition of the despised USC tax, were not accepted by an electorate that did not buy into the notion of a financial recovery, as they did not feel any benefits of it in their pay checks.

There have been several books dealing with the fall-out from the Celtic Tiger's demise and its aftermath. Most concentrate on the economic and political ramifications of the crash, but there are a significant number that have examined the cultural and social implications. They all provide information and opinion on the Celtic Tiger, but usually the angle chosen reflects the particular disciplines of the authors, and very often, the facts, details and information are somewhat lost in the argument that is being propounded. In this book, we are attempting to offer a more complete and representative account of what happened, who was involved and what were the consequences, and we hope to look at these from a different perspective. Our initial aim was to provide an overview, from A to Z, of the phenomenon that has come to be known as the Celtic Tiger, but that proved somewhat ambitious. Instead, we approached contributors from a vast array of disciplines who possess a skills set and insights that are unique to this study.

The topics they cover constitute a canvas that has never up until now been woven. They cover areas as diverse as economic factors, society, culture, politics, religion and people, in a way that we believe provides a comprehensive survey and analysis of how the Celtic Tiger came into being, the way it developed and the ramifications it has had, and is having, on Irish society. The passage of time is helpful certainly when it comes to teasing out such issues and we are confident that readers will find in these short reflections, each of which condenses swathes of material into what constitute in effect an indispensable overview of Celtic Tiger Ireland from its beginnings to its shuddering and abrupt end, to the difficult aftermath, the legacy of which will continue to impact generations of Irish people. With another potential economic crisis on the horizon with Brexit, the reality is that we as a nation need to be aware of the fact that, as a small island nation on the periphery of Europe, Ireland will always be subject to the volatility of world markets and events, while nevertheless having the capacity to plan for an uncertain future and not assume that the good times last forever.

Brian Lucey
Eamon Maher
Eugene O'Brien

CONSTANTIN GURDGIEV

100% mortgages

The Irish banking sector's weapons of mass destruction, 100% mortgages, were dangerously risky loans that required persistently rising property prices to sustain banks' balance sheet values and risk-weightings. As such, these mortgages reflected the endless overconfidence, at times reaching into arrogance, of the Celtic Tiger-era Irish economic policy and finance.

100% mortgages were first introduced in Ireland in 2005, near the top of the housing prices valuations, and in the heyday of the Celtic Tiger. At first, restricted to cover only the house price, these mortgages subsequently evolved, under some lenders' terms and conditions, into linked loans that provided funds not only to cover the agreed purchase price of the property, but also the stamp duty and, in rare cases, some 'holiday money'.

Originally opposed by some members of the government, the 100% mortgages were welcomed by both the Department of Finance and the Irish Financial Regulator who dismissed any concerns about the risks involved in bank-lending on residential property with zero down payment by the buyer. By doing so, the Irish Financial Regulator de facto abandoned enforcement of any loan-to-value ratios in residential mortgage lending, setting the stage for the spectacular collapse of the Irish banking system in 2008–10. 100% mortgages rapidly accelerated inflation of the property bubble in Ireland that, by 2005, was already showing signs of residential property prices over-valuation to the tune of 30–40% above fundamental values.

By mid-2006, roughly fifteen months after the new mortgage product hit the markets, over 30% of first-time buyers were borrowing 100% of their purchase price to fund house acquisitions. By the end of that year, the number rose to 35%, while 61% of the mortgages drawn down by first time buyers in the country had terms of over 30 years.

Sustaining 100% mortgages required an ongoing assumption of continuously appreciating (in real terms) house prices, and/or declining risk-weighting constraints on banks' assets. In other words, 100% mortgages were the Irish financial system's equivalent of the North Korean nukes: explosive, even if handled with care.

KARL DEETER

Accidental Landlords

You cannot become an accidental landlord any more than you can become an accidental pilot of a Boeing jet. To continue with the metaphor, what did happen was that people found themselves pilot-less in mid-air, and had to take the controls due to a variety of factors. All we hear of at the moment (late 2019) is focused on housing shortages and high prices in rents and values, whereas during the crash, it was the opposite. The combined forces of falling prices and rents meant that people who had outgrown homes due to finding a partner, having children and needing a larger home, who needed to leave the property for work, or to rent it out so that rent could help pay the mortgage due to job loss, were becoming what is known colloquially as 'accidental landlords'. They did not set out to become landlords, they just ended up that way. The accident was the shift in the ownership approach to that of 'landlord' rather than 'dweller': that home-ownership was the starting point was never in doubt.

Often people in this situation might move back in with relatives, or rent out a more suitable home while renting out their own at the same time. They were people who never intended to buy a property with a view to becoming a landlord, and therefore they came into an industry that was increasing in regulation, which was and still is subject to a brutal brand of income taxation (compared to the way we tax say, international and institutional landlords, REITS or Section 110 companies), and they often did so with the most amateur understanding of how to operate a property as a business. This has led to calls for some form of assistance, which were ignored.

A typical misunderstanding which resulted in financial hardship was where people rented out their homes, but did not cancel their TRS, which is a tax break given to owners of primary homes in Ireland. TRS stands for 'Tax Relief at Source', and Revenue did a large trawl of audits asking people to provide proof of residency, and when they could not provide this, it resulted in large fines for people who in many cases were already hard-pressed. Another issue occurred when people did not make tax returns in the belief they were not making profits. This arose where a mortgage may have cost €1,000 and the person was receiving €1,000 in rent. In those instances many believed (wrongly) that they were only breaking even, but because only a certain percentage of mortgage interest is an allowable expense, the capital repayment portion is not, so they were creating large tax bills with no corresponding cash flow gain with which to settle the liability.

As Revenue began to do a better job of collating data between different departments such as the Residential Tenancies Board (where tenancies have to be registered), this resulted in another wave of people caught for late payments, fines and penalties. Another force in the rental sector was increasing regulation, which took the form of new rules for minimum standards, requirements to register and comply with new laws and then a move towards rent control as the government introduced 'Rent Pressure Zones', which meant that landlords were curtailed in rent reviews and that rent controls passed through inter-tenancy, which is highly irregular.

These controls did not apply to a new wave of industrial landlords who were bringing new properties into the market and this further punished the accidental landlords and 'mom' 'n' pop' investors who still represent the majority of the private rented sector. Accidental landlords often had preferential finance such as tracker mortgages, and in many cases, because they did not 'own' other homes, they were given protection of a very high level, due to a condition in the rules of mortgage arrears which meant that if you only owned one home in the country, it would be considered a 'primary home' even if it was rented out to a third party.

Accidental landlords are no longer in the position of seeing values recover but many have no route into a change in position because the thing that drove them to leave the home (such as people leaving a small home when they started a family) have often not changed, and the ability to save in a rising rental market, or where they went on to have children, have reduced their capacity to borrow and leave accidental landlord-ship.

PATRICIA MEDCALF

Advertising

The years preceding the Celtic Tiger were quite unremarkable in terms of advertising activity in Ireland. Total spend by advertisers across the various media rose modestly from IR£163.8 million in 1990 to IR£223.8 million in 1994. Tony Meenaghan categorised Ireland as an 'under-advertised' economy at that stage in its development when compared to many other countries, including the UK, where advertising spend as a percentage of GDP was almost twice that of Ireland. This would change dramatically, and activity in the advertising sector perfectly encapsulates the trajectory of the Irish economy between 1994 and 2008 – steady growth, superseded by a frenetic spending spree by companies, consumers and the government, all culminating in a precipitous fall, the consequences of which are well documented.

The strengthening economy gave companies the confidence, and the finances required, to invest in advertising. At the same time, a number of media outlets were launched, thus affording advertisers more choice and better targeting opportunities. The seeds of this expansion in the media landscape were sown in 1988, a year that marked the start of the enactment of a number of broadcasting acts by the Independent Radio and TV Commission (IRTC). These paved the way for the rapid growth in licences granted to local radio stations in the nineties, all driven by a commercial imperative and funded primarily by advertising. Similarly, the television backdrop was redrawn and in 1996, TG4 commenced broadcasting, soon to be followed by the launch of TV3 in 1998. Meanwhile, the provision of television services through cable and satellite afforded viewers and advertisers even greater choice.

In the interim, the profile of advertisers changed in the early years of the Celtic Tiger as globalisation took hold. Some well-known Irish brands were taken over by more powerful, advertising-savvy global counterparts. Many brand names changed, and were consigned to history. Others remained intact, but their new owners determined their advertising strategies from then on. In 1996, Unilever acquired Lyons Tea, but due to its popularity among Irish consumers, the brand name remained. Conversely, Tesco's 1997 acquisition of Quinnsworth resulted in extinction for this highly respected Irish brand name. Diageo was created in 1997 as a result of a merger between Guinness and Grand Metropolitan. The entity owned a stable of high performing brands, which maintained their strong positions through advertising.

In 1995 advertisers placed €344 million worth of ads with various media outlets and by 2007, this figure had increased more than five-fold. Even though the seeds of the economy's decline were sown as far back as 2002, expenditure on advertising belies this. Between 2002 and 2007, it enjoyed continued rates of growth and broke through the billion euros landmark for the very first time. In 2002, levels of €1.035 billion were reached, which prefigured the beginning of the march towards a record breaking €1.822 billion in 2007, a figure that was unsustainable and has not been matched since.

Such prolific advertising activity reflected the frenzy of spending across many sectors, including the government, financial services, retail, and construction sectors. Advertisers ignored early warning signs of an overheating economy, and media outlets continued to benefit from the money that was being spent on advertising. However, one sector in particular cannot be ignored when recounting the story of advertising during the Celtic Tiger years. By 2006, the Construction/Property sector was the third biggest spender on advertising. It spent a record €143,336,641, with various media outlets, particularly on property supplements. Five estate agents/property companies were among the top 50 advertisers that year. With spend of €16,553,403, Sherry Fitzgerald outspent global marketing giant, Proctor and Gamble, and was ranked the third biggest spender on advertising. CB Hamilton Osborne King was ranked sixth. Combined spend by five estate agents/property companies was €52,356,416, something that could not be sustained.

Ominously, in 2007 Lisney dropped out of the top 50, and Sherry Fitzgerald fell to seventh place. Expenditure by property companies plummeted to €20,116,767 in 2008. Just as the Irish economy's fortunes had been built on the vagaries of the property sector, and profligate spending by consumers and the government, so too had the burgeoning advertising industry. When the spending spree stopped, so too did the boom in advertising.

SEAN BARRETT

Ahern, Bertie

Politicians associated with the Irish bank bailout paid a heavy price. The government elected in 2007 comprised Fianna Fáil with 78 Dáil seats and the Green Party with six seats. In the 2011 election Fianna Fáil secured 20 seats and the Greens none. This was an unprecedented loss of Dáil members from an outgoing government.

Two Taoisigh associated with the bank bailout gave evidence to the Oireachtas Banking Inquiry, Bertie Ahern and Brian Cowen. Their evidence given in July 2015 and their written submissions to the Inquiry provides insight into why the political odium attached to the bank bailout was so strong, even when compared to the banks themselves and the failed regulatory agencies such as the Central Bank, the Financial Regulator and the Department of Finance. The success of the auditors of Irish banks in avoiding public excoriation for the bailout is remarkable, considering the price paid by the government of the day.

Bertie Ahern was Taoiseach from June 26, 1997 to May 7, 2008. His *Witness Statement to the Banking Inquiry* on July 16, 2015 was divided into four main sections, which are listed below with Mr Ahern's observations in each case:

1. Nature and effectiveness of operational implementation of macro-economic and prudential policy. Mr Ahern's presentation emphasises the real GDP growth rate of 7.25% over the decade to 2006 at more than double that of the US and triple the average rate achieved by other Eurozone countries. The Exchequer Debt/GDP ratio fell from 63.6% in 1997 to 25.1% in 2006.
2. Appropriateness of Expert Advice. Mr Ahern states that 'the overwhelming and virtual consensus during this time was that Irish policy was moving the economy in the right direction'. He cites the ESRI Medium Term Review in 2005 that 'there is a growing aura of invincibility about

the Irish economy'. He also states that 'it can be readily seen that the crash was not foreseen by the IMF who only revised their outlook when the slowdown was well and truly at hand', while noting the complacency of the ESRI he states that 'no home grown crisis was foreseen and even an imported one would have relatively mild effects due to the fundamentally sound nature of the Irish economy'.

3. Effectiveness of Oireachtas in Scrutinising Public Policy and Associated Issues. Mr Ahern stated that 'the effectiveness of the Oireachtas in scrutinising public policy on the banking sector and the economy is good'. He stated that the report by Rob Wright entitled *Strengthening the Capacity of the Department of Finance*, 'if implemented, would result in a more effective Department in terms of guiding Government policy making'.
4. Formulation and Reaction to Crisis Simulation Exercises and the Role of the DSG (Domestic Standing Group). The DSG comprising the Department of Finance, the Financial Regulator and the Central Bank was established in 2008 to deal with crisis management issues and financial stability. Under a memorandum of understanding they 'met quarterly to consider matters of significance in relation to financial stability on the basis of an agreed annual work plan'. Mr Ahern stated that 'the severity and unprecedented nature of the events than unfolded meant that such shortcomings as existed in regulatory capacity could not have been overcome by the kind of co-ordinating and information exchange role envisaged for the DSG'.

Mr Ahern acknowledged that 'the housing boom was caused mainly by cheap credit due to low interest rates, along with rising incomes and a strong demand for housing. There is no doubt that this created a structural weakness in the economy and the international downturn ensured this has turned from s soft landing to a very hard one. I wish that this didn't happen and with hindsight, of course, I would have done things differently'. He supported the reintegration of the regulatory role into the Central Bank and the establishment of the Central Expenditure Evaluation Unit in the Department of Finance in 2006.

Mr Ahern's submission indicates that fiscal and monetary policies were not co-ordinated. The DSG was not an adequate substitute for the non-supervision of banks by the Financial Regulator, Central Bank and the

Department of Finance. It is difficult in retrospect to agree with his statement that 'the effectiveness of the Oireachtas in scrutinising public policy in the banking sector is good and compares favourably with that of other countries with democratically elected parliaments'. Mr Ahern's endorsement of the *Wright Report* reforms indicates the inadequacies of the Department of Finance prior to the crisis. On the monetary side it appears that the deficiencies noted in the *Wright Report* in the Department of Finance and in financial regulation as noted throughout the Report of the Oireachtas Inquiry presented issues in the public agencies which should have been addressed by the government. The need to do so was obscured by the period of rapid economic growth. When the downturn inevitably came, Irish institutions were inadequately prepared to respond, and the elected government paid a high price.

CONSTANTIN GURDGIEV

Anglo Irish Tapes

In June 2013, the *Irish Independent* uncovered the audio recordings of internal phone discussions between two senior executives at the Anglo Irish Bank, dating back to September 2008. This was the peak of the Global Financial Crisis, which led to the Irish State bailing out the failed bank in a sweeping guarantee that stung Irish taxpayers for tens of billions of euro, and led to the collapse of Anglo Irish, nationalisation of Allied Irish and several smaller banking institutions, and a partial nationalisation of the Bank of Ireland.

The Anglo tapes involve conversations between Mr John Bowe (Anglo's head of capital markets), and Mr Peter Fitzgerald (bank's director of retail banking). Described in the media as 'jaw-dropping', 'scandalous', and 'shocking', the tapes reveal the strategy pursued by the Anglo executives in manipulating the Irish government to extend the bank bailout money; the lamentable disarray at the Irish Financial Services Regulator; and the psychology of the bank executives caught in the maelstrom of the 2008 Global Financial Crisis. The tapes also exposed the culture of vulgarity, over-confidence, and lack of professional fitness at the top of Irish banking management elites that epitomised the later stages of the Celtic Tiger.

In one conversation, John Bowe recalled how the Irish Financial Regulator responded to the bank demand for €7 billion in funding from the State to shore up its failing wholesale funding model, quoting the alleged response by the Regulator as 'Jesus that's a lot of dosh ... Jesus fucking hell and God ... well do you know the Central Bank only has €14 billion of total investments so that would be going up 20 ... Gee ... that would be seen. Jesus you're kind of asking us to play ducks and drakes with the regulations'.

In another instance, Peter Fitzgerald asks John Bowe as to how the bank arrived at the figure of €7 billion that Anglo requested. Bowe replies: 'Just as Drummer [the then Anglo CEO David Drumm] would say, "picked it out of my arse."'

The tapes show that the Anglo management knew that the original requested bailout was not sufficient to steady the bank's finances, and that they informed the Regulator that the bank was already trading in breach of the major regulatory requirements. The combination of the severity of the bank's problems in the funding markets, and the fact that the bank continued to trade during its failure to fulfil liquidity requirements, made the bank balance sheet insolvent at the time of the bailout. Yet, subsequent to the Guarantee, the government and regulatory authorities persistently denied having any knowledge of bank solvency condition as of September 2008.

CONSTANTIN GURDGIEV

Ansbacher Accounts

Precursors to the financial engineering shenanigans of the Celtic Tiger, Ansbacher accounts were born out of the high-tax era of the 1970s and 1980s. The accounts were set up and managed by the Ansbacher Cayman Limited – a banking licence-holding firm – run by Des Traynor, a director with Guinness & Mahon Bank, and an advisor to Taoiseach Charles Haughey. Ansbacher accounts facilitated tax evasion and avoidance by Irish elites, as well as by a number of ordinary small business owners and senior private and public sector employees. The scheme facilitated lodgement of funds in Ireland with Ansbacher Cayman. After this, the deposits were first registered to Cayman Islands, and then made available for clients' withdrawals back in Ireland. By using the scheme, Irish clients were able to avoid Irish taxes. In addition to tax evasion, Ansbacher offered clients so-called back-to-back loans, which were secured by the deposits held 'offshore'. These loans were subject to fraudulently claimed tax relief, netting their recipients double-savings on tax. In many cases, Ansbacher deposits involved black market funds, breaching more than tax laws alone, and acting as a money-laundering scheme.

The Ansbacher scheme continued to operate from 1971 through the mid-1990s, and was exposed in the McCracken Tribunal in 1997 that examined private payments to former Taoiseach Charles Haughey, and former Minister Michael Lowry. Subsequent to the McCracken Tribunal, Irish Revenue Commissioners undertook investigation of the Ansbacher accounts, starting with 1999 and lasting until 2013, recovering €113 million in back taxes and penalties.

The Revenue report on Ansbacher accounts was considered for potential criminal charges by the Director of Public Prosecutions, and the then Irish Revenue Commissioner, Frank Daly warned that tax cheats will have 'no hiding place in future'. However, in a typically Irish fashion, no one was prosecuted for using the scheme.

While Ansbacher accounts were not the only scheme to defraud Irish tax authorities that operated in the tax evasion Wild West of Ireland of the 1970s and 1980s, they were perhaps the largest and the most daring one, involving anonymity, encryption of records and hundreds of millions in illicit funds. They also exemplify the very culture of regulatory and legal laxness that, over the 1990s, has migrated from the domestic tax and accounting services to the International Financial Services Centre in Dublin, and subsequently permeated the entire financial services sector, paving the way to the excesses of the 1997–2007 that laid the basis of the Irish Financial Crisis that struck in 2008.

NEIL DUNNE

Auditors

Auditing has traditionally constituted a venerable, if prosaic, calling. For many years its practitioners enjoyed relative autonomy on the understanding that they would protect the public interest. However, the banking crisis prompted a wave of public ire towards the audit profession. Although auditors were not unacquainted with condemnation (for example, in the aftermath of accounting scandals such as Enron, WorldCom and others), this time their perceived failures coincided with the collapse and subsequent State rescue of six financial institutions (Allied Irish Banks, Anglo Irish Bank, Bank of Ireland, Educational Building Society, Irish Life and Permanent, and Irish Nationwide Building Society).

The spotlight of public scrutiny shone most severely on the 'Big Four' accounting firms (Deloitte, EY, KPMG and PwC). These firms dominate the audit market, and also perform various non-audit activities such as accounting, tax, advisory, actuarial, corporate finance and legal services. Specifically, EY, KPMG and PwC had granted unqualified audit reports in respect of the rescued banks in both 2007 and 2008. 'Where were the auditors?' thus became a common refrain in the public and media discourse.

The European Commission responded to concerns surrounding the audit profession by mandating new rules regarding auditor rotation, prohibition of certain non-audit services, and banning of 'Big-Four only' clauses in financing arrangements. However, auditing's role in the Irish crisis was not publicly addressed until 2015, when the Big Four were summoned to the Committee of Inquiry into the Banking Crisis. There, they had to explain why they had granted unqualified audit opinions to subsequently distressed financial institutions.

The Big Four's response to this scrutiny was multi-faceted. First, they distanced themselves from their clients' activities. For example, in their testimony, KPMG argued that 'we don't tell airlines ... what aircraft to buy and what routes to fly. And we didn't tell AIB what loans to give'. Second, the Big Four claimed that the nature of auditing means that auditors could not have foreseen the crisis. For instance, Deloitte stated that auditing 'is not an insurance policy or a prediction of the future'. In fact, the Big Four's inquiry evidence consistently framed auditing as a restricted and backwards-looking endeavour, to the extent that a layperson could reasonably ask: what exactly do auditors *do*? The answer is that auditors determine whether financial accounts give a 'true and fair view'. True and fair view is a nebulous term that has evaded statutory definition, but one interpretation is that accounts prepared in accordance with accounting rules inherently give a true and fair view. Observers may have (erroneously) anticipated auditing's role to be broader than that, and more specifically, that auditing might provide assurance that a company would 'be okay'.

This incongruence between what auditors do and what others *think* they do is commonly referred to as the 'expectations gap'. Third, the Big Four defended themselves at the inquiry by explaining how accounting rules, and in particular the much-maligned and now-replaced International Accounting Standard (IAS) 39, had prevented them from obliging their clients to recognise expected losses on loan assets. Finally, the Big Four claimed that no one could have foreseen the extent of the banking crisis. Notably, perhaps because it relied on non-technical and thus contestable assertions, this line of defence was the one that the committee members challenged most vociferously. Specifically, the committee members responded that some observers *had*, in fact, anticipated the scale of the crisis.

Nonetheless, the inquiry's findings were relatively benign towards the Big Four. The inquiry concluded that the audits had been carried out in accordance with the prevailing rules, and that any blame for audit failure lay with the banks, regulators and IAS 39. However, although the Big Four may have emerged relatively unscathed from this parliamentary encounter, ongoing scandals mean that auditors continue to experience the glare of public scrutiny. In the UK, for example, significant changes are currently being mooted regarding decoupling the Big Four's audit and non-audit activities, and restructuring the regulatory regime pertaining to audit. Although a long-term project, the intention is to revitalise the role and supervision of auditing, in order to prevent future audit failure of the scale witnessed in the banking crisis.

CHARLES LARKIN

Bailout

Bailout is the general descriptive term given to the process of providing financial support to a financial entity, such as a bank or to a national economy, such as is done by the International Monetary Fund and other multilateral bodies. The bailout is distinct from a bail-in insofar as the administrators of the bailout are providing additional funds as opposed to imposing losses on the bank or country. In the case of a typically designed bailout, the International Monetary Fund provides a short-term 36-month structure of loans to assist the recipient country with access to global debt markets.

During that 36-month period the country will restructure its public finances to make itself more sustainable at supporting whatever existing debt burden exists. In certain cases, the initial debt burden's net present value is changed by extending the time of repayment, interest rates or reducing the principal of the loans. If the support is brought about by a currency crisis, the bailout allows time for a more robust exchange rate policy to be introduced while shoring up central bank currency reserves.

Bailout success is determined by the ability to maintain a stable currency vis-a-vis trading partners and the currency of debt denomination and/or successful reentry into the global capital markets for domestic or foreign currency-denominated public debt at the end of 36 months of programme support. Some countries will also take on a precautionary credit line with the IMF if they are unsure if there will be sufficient demand for their debt, fear an exogenous terms of trade shock or generally fear a buyer strike on the bond market. In countries with large programmes or multiple programmes, an IMF resident will be appointed to ensure progress on conditionality and programme monitoring.

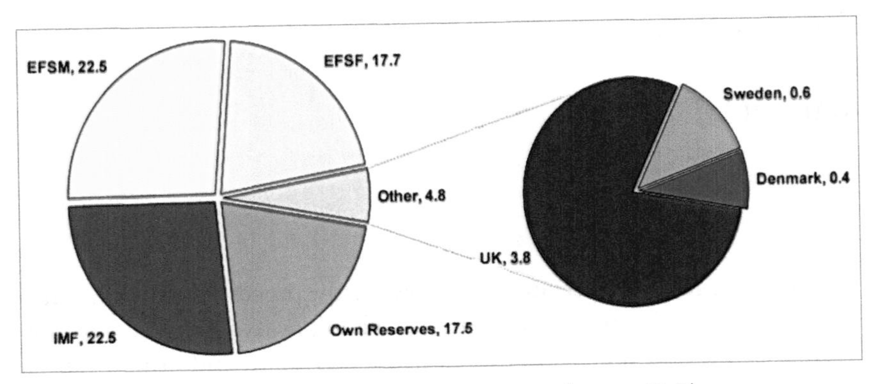

Figure 1: Ireland's funding programme (source: DoF)

LORCAN SIRR

Balanced Regional Development

The idea of not letting Dublin reap all the rewards of the Celtic Tiger was a significant driving force in the State's drive to 'rebalance' Ireland, economically at least. Politically, this 'rebalancing' was a convenient rural vote-winner with many politicians creating an artificial 'have' versus 'have not' false dichotomy between urban and rural parts the country.

Not only is this central policy thrust of 'balanced regional development' difficult to achieve, as many countries have discovered, but there was little clarity about what the term meant. BRD does not mean the equal development of every region in the country, but can mean the simultaneous development of each region. Many politicians latched onto the first component of what it does not mean as their version of reality. This inaccurate interpretation persisted both during and after the Celtic Tiger years, with the imperative of diverting economic and physical development from Dublin an important political goal.

Prior to the Celtic Tiger, Ireland already had a history of trying to reduce regional disparities by supporting (employment and wealth-generating) economic activities in different regions. Regional development policy had tended to try to achieve these objectives by means of large-scale infrastructure development and by attracting inward investment, particularly industrial (e.g. 'Advance' factories developed by the Industrial Development Authority). Past policies failed to reduce regional disparities significantly and haven't really helped individual lagging regions to catch up, despite the allocation of significant public funding, mostly as the focus of economic development has shifted from production to services (especially financial) whose preferred choice of location is urban.

Balanced regional development, this mantra of rural politics during the Celtic Tiger, aimed to redistribute investment to regions hitherto suffering from insufficient demand, despite all the evidence that showed many modern Irish industries did not want to locate in the regions. In the early 2000s, this concept of balanced regional development (BRD) took shape in policy form in the National Spatial Strategy 2002–20 (and was a key objective of the later National Development Plan 2007–13).

The National Spatial Strategy was launched in December 2002. It was the first national spatial strategy in Europe after the publication of the ESDP (European Spatial Development Perspective), and was considered best practice by other countries. It sought be inclusive in vision and was underpinned by good intentions and it promoted a planned approach to development. Unfortunately, The National Spatial Strategy 2002 (NSS) with its focus on 'balanced regional development' was almost immediately 'torpedoed' by the government's politically motivated 'decentralisation' policy introduced in the Budget of 2003 (which involved moving parts of government departments and agencies to towns and cities around the country, as industry was reluctant to move), coupled with the subsequent economic collapse and withdrawal of the €300 million 'Gateway Innovation Fund' designed to help implement the strategy.

The years of the Celtic Tiger exacerbated the social and economic differences between the different regions in Ireland, and as a result amplified calls for 'fairness' and a redistribution of economic advantages. BRD was then, and remains, both a social and economic concept and the idea of achieving 'balance' is very much a contested one. Many argue that BRD could never have worked as Ireland does not have the resources to promote every location with a 'one for everyone in the audience' approach. An historic emphasis on diverting development away from cities, particularly into regional locations, meant that Ireland never developed a network of cities with the ability to compete with Dublin. The success of the Celtic Tiger years drove that message home, and misguided attempts to thwart reality through, for example, facilitating the development of housing estates in areas with no demand leading to ghost estates, merely made matters worse.

JOE BRENNAN

Bank Lending Policies in the 2004– 2010 Period

As the National Asset Management Agency (NAMA) was preparing a decade ago to take over risky commercial property loans from the nation's banks, Scott Rankin, then an analyst with stockbroking firm Davy, took out his calculator to work out how much of a discount lenders would have to accept for their assets.

Journalists, like myself, and the wider public were hungry at the time for any clues about prices NAMA would pay to take over the loans. But Rankin – like most analysts, and NAMA itself – proved to be wildly optimistic in his projections. (The loans would end up transferring in 2010 at a 58% discount to their original value – almost twice NAMA's original estimate.)

However, Rankin did highlight one caveat – the spectre of 'phantom equity' – that stood in the way of any analyst's ability to make such forecasts. The phrase, for me, captured how banks' lax lending standards during the property boom would come back to haunt them.

While banks would point out during the heady days that they remained prudent in requiring developers to put up equity of between 40%–50% of the size of a development land deal, it often was not in hard cash. 'It was borrowed on the back of equity tied up in other sites, investment properties and interests,' said Rankin in the report in July 2009, months before he joined the Department of Finance to help its efforts to deal with the banking crisis. This equity 'evaporated' as the property market went into freefall.

The combined size of the loan books of the six lenders that taxpayers would be forced to guarantee during the financial crisis doubled in the four years through 2008, according to the 2011 report by the Commission of Investigation into the Banking Sector in Ireland, written by Peter Nyberg, a former Finnish central banker and civil servant.

The growth was fuelled by a mushrooming of the bank's property-related loans, which expanded from €46 billion in 2002 to €168 billion in 2007, according to the Nyberg report. Within that, speculative and construction property lending soared by more than 800% to €35 billion, while residential mortgage lending grew at a much slower pace of about 160% to €91 billion.

I remember at the time hearing stories from senior bankers of some of developers, rather than waiting for banks to come back to them with loan offers for projects, actually drawing up their own draft term sheets, and hawking them around the banks. It spoke of power dynamics at play as banks chased growth at all costs.

Perturbed by the extent to which Anglo Irish Bank was cleaning up on the commercial property lending front, and by claims Bank of Scotland about the business it was doing in Ireland, AIB's then chief executive, Michael Buckley, told the *Sunday Business Post* in an interview in February 2004 that he had set up a 'win-back team'. 'That's what you should do, isn't it?' he said.

One lender, Irish Nationwide Building Society (INBS), which had long abandoned its home loans roots, got increasingly involved in profit-share agreements with developers in return for offering up to 100% loan financing for development projects. Such loans, where principal and interest payments were typically put on ice until developments were completed, accounted for €6 billion of INBS's loans in 2008, an inquiry into the now-defunct lender heard in July (2019). That equated to about 60% of INBS's loan book at the time.

The fierce competition was not confined to construction and development lending either. Bank of Scotland shook up the mortgage market in 2001 when it introduced cheap mortgages linked to the European Central Bank's (ECB) main rate. By 2010, tracker mortgages made up at least half of all Irish home loans, according to Banking & Payments Federation Ireland (BPFI). These loans were loss-making at the time, as banks' funding costs shot up during the crisis.

Meanwhile, under the new ownership of Royal Bank of Scotland's (RBS) Ulster Bank, First Active came out in mid-2005 with the country's first mass-marketed 100% mortgage. Up until then, such loans were only offered by banks on a limited – and discreet – basis to top professionals. The wider industry soon followed First Active's lead.

The prevalence of high loan-to-value mortgages during the boom years would plunge as many as 314,000 home loans being in negative equity by the end of 2012 as prices slumped, according to the Economic and Social Research Institute (ESRI).

Banks' lending standards deteriorated in other ways. Morgan Kelly, an economics professor at University College Dublin, noted in a December 2009 paper that the average first time buyer mortgage had risen to eight times average earnings. The average stood at three times that of 1995, before the Celtic Tiger era.

The pendulum has since swung the other way. German investment bank Berenberg noted in an Irish property market report in July (2019) that while banks in the UK and Europe are willing to lend up to a 70% loan-to-value ratio for commercial property investment, Irish banks 'are typically unwilling to go much above 50%'.

Might Irish banks be tempted to relax these policies in the coming years, as they are struggling to rebuild their loan books following more than a decade of contraction?

Meanwhile, there are growing calls on the Central Bank to ease back on mortgage restrictions introduced in 2015. They limit most home loans to three and a half times borrowers' incomes and loans-to-values to 90% in the case of first-time buyers. The argument among some house builders and real estate agents is that the caps are affecting demand, house prices and a recovery in construction levels.

But housing supply and pricing is not a matter for the Central Bank. Its main concern must be to protect banks – and borrowers – from themselves.

FRANCES COPPOLA

Bank Regulation

The 2008 financial crisis showed how quickly bank collapses in one country could spread to others, especially when borders are open and there is free movement of capital. Although Ireland's banking collapse was mainly caused by the overblown Irish property market, its effects rippled out across Europe. Irish banks had borrowed heavily from German, French and British banks. Their failure ripped holes in the balance sheets of the banks from which they had borrowed. As these were some of the largest banks in Europe, and indeed in the world, Ireland's banking crisis threatened to bring down the European and even the global financial system.

Both the disastrous collapse of the Celtic Tiger and its bloated condition prior to the crisis were blamed on banks and their regulators. Bank regulation in Ireland underwent structural reform soon after the crisis, effectively reversing many of the changes made over the preceding decades.

Since the mid-1980s, regulation of Irish banks had been progressively eroded. Liberalisation of the Irish banking system, and relaxation of entry criteria for the Irish clearing system, encouraged the entry of foreign banks such as the UK's RBS and Germany's Depfa, both of which failed in the financial crisis.

In 2003, the Central Bank and Financial Services Authority of Ireland Act created a single financial regulator, called the Irish Financial Services Regulatory Authority (IFSRA). IFSRA and the Central Bank of Ireland were both brought under the umbrella of the newly formed Central Bank and Financial Services Authority of Ireland (CBFSAI). IFSRA was given a dual mandate to protect consumer interests and to build a regulatory framework that protected the stability of the banking sector. It also aimed to 'foster an internationally competitive banking industry in Ireland'. With hindsight, this conflict of interest was a significant cause of IFRSA's ineffectiveness as a regulator.

In 2009, IFRSA was abolished as a separate entity, and regulation of Irish banks was brought within the Central Bank of Ireland's remit. But reform of the regulatory structure itself was not sufficient. In 2010, a report by Dr Patrick Honohan, then Governor of the Central Bank of Ireland, reviewed the roles of regulators and the central bank in the crisis. It identified three regulatory deficiencies:

1. regulators had an 'excessively deferential and accommodating' attitude to financial institutions under supervision;
2. bank supervision was systematically under-resourced, forcing regulators to rely on financial institutions' own estimates of their risks;
3. regulatory response to the looming crisis was too little and too late.

Responding to Honohan's report, the Central Bank of Ireland observed that it was not so much the regulatory structure as the supervisory approach that had failed, and said it was 'reshaping our approach to banking supervision to institutionalise these lessons'.

Structural reform of bank regulation and supervision extended far beyond Ireland. The European Commission decided that European banks capable of bringing down the European financial system should be supervised by the EU's institutions, not by their own supervisory bodies. After much discussion, it was agreed that the ECB should take on the role of supervisor for the largest banks in the Euro area, including some in Ireland.

In 2014, the Single Supervisory Mechanism was born, and supervision of the largest banks in Ireland duly passed from the Central Bank of Ireland to the ECB. Smaller financial institutions remain under the Central Bank of Ireland's supervision, though the ECB keeps a watchful eye and can take over supervision at any time.

At the time of writing, six banks domiciled in Ireland are supervised by the ECB: Allied Irish Bank, Bank of Ireland, Ulster Bank (a subsidiary of the British bank RBS, which is majority-owned by the British government), Bank of America Merrill Lynch International, Citigroup Holdings Ireland, and Barclays Bank Ireland. Barclays Bank Ireland, a subsidiary of the British bank Barclays, was added to the ECB's list in 2018 due to Barclays moving assets out of the UK in anticipation of Brexit. At the same time,

Permanent TSB was removed from the list and is now supervised by the Central Bank of Ireland.

However, whether Irish banks are supervised nationally or as part of a European network of systemically important financial institutions, they are now subject to similar prudential regulations. Capital and liquidity requirements for banks had been downplayed prior to the crisis, not only in Ireland, but across the Western world. Afterwards, it was acknowledged internationally that the banks that had failed were those with the smallest capital buffers.

The Basel committee of the Bank for International Settlements (BIS) recommended new capital and liquidity standards for banks, replacing the flawed 'Basel 2' standards which had resulted in many banks' capital buffers being too low to absorb their risks. The principle behind the 'Basel 3' rules is that banks should have sufficient 'loss-absorbing capital' to protect depositors and, by extension, taxpayers if they suffer severe losses due to asset price collapse, as happened in 2008. The largest and most interconnected banks have the highest capital requirements. Banks should also have enough ready cash, or assets that can easily be exchanged for cash, to meet their expected payment obligations for the next 30 days, and their funding should come from sources that are not prone to run, such as retail deposits.

The EU took on board the Basel committee's new recommendations. In its 'Fourth Capital Requirements Directive' (CRDIV), it created a two-tier capital structure for banks. Tier 1 capital is 'going concern' capital: banks must maintain enough Tier 1 capital to stay solvent in the event of severe macroeconomic and financial shocks, such as a sharp fall in house prices and a large rise in unemployment.

Tier 2 capital, or 'gone concern' capital, consists of subordinated debt and other liabilities which can be bailed in to protect other creditors in the event of the bank becoming insolvent. In addition to this, the European Bank Resolution Directive provides for losses to be imposed if necessary on senior bondholders and, as a last resort, depositors.

At the time of writing, EU banks need to have capital of at least 8% of risk-weighted assets, of which at least 4.5% must be 'core equity Tier 1' (CET1) capital, which broadly speaking consists of shareholders' funds. Most banks exceed these minimum levels by some distance.

The way in which banks and their supervisors determine capital requirements still primarily relies on 'risk-weighted' calculations. However, these can significantly underestimate the risk of losses. So there is now an additional measure – a simple ratio of assets to equity without risk-weighting, known as the 'leverage ratio'. Regardless of whether their assets are collateralised debt obligations or houses, banks must have now enough 'own funds' to cover the risk of losing a percentage of their total unweighted asset base, not just their risk-weighted assets.

But the question is whether leverage ratios are high enough for a country in which acquiring property is a national obsession. Historically, mortgages have attracted low risk-weightings, so banks and building societies have been able to lend exorbitantly against property without having much in the way of capital buffers. Financial institutions that have a high proportion of mortgage loans on their balance sheets lobby hard for the leverage ratio to be kept low, claiming that a high leverage ratio would unfairly penalise them. So far, it appears that regulators have listened to them. Instead of imposing high leverage ratios, regulators are turning to tools which act directly on certain types of lending to reduce their risks. Loan-to-value (LTV) and loan-to-income (LTI) limits, for example, to prevent the return of mortgages of 100% or more of the property value and loans to people with no stable source of income.

The story of the Celtic Tiger shows us that regarding mortgages as 'low risk' can be a fatal mistake, and that sensible regulations can fail if supervision is ineffectual. Prior to the crisis, the IFRSA had powers to tighten capital requirements and impose lending controls (including prohibition of high-LTV, interest-only and very long maturity mortgages). But it failed to do so. Furthermore, its supervision was too lax to enforce even what standards there were: banks bypassed lending standards with impunity. When house prices crashed, therefore, banks became insolvent because existing regulations had not been applied or properly enforced.

At present, the wounds from the 2008 crisis have not yet healed: being tough with banks is still a political vote-winner even if it means people being shut out of the mortgage market. But over time, will the political desire to help people acquire property once again trump the need to ensure a safe and functional financial system? By keeping leverage ratios low and relying on banks maintaining lending standards, are regulators inadvertently setting the scene for another crisis?

FRANCES COPPOLA

Bank Solvency Crisis

Nowhere did the Celtic Tiger roar louder than in Irish banks. During the booming 2000s, supported by rapidly rising property prices, strong demand for mortgages and an increasingly dominant construction sector, the collective asset base of Ireland's six biggest lenders expanded massively, along with their profits and their market capitalisation. The share prices of the two largest banks, Allied Irish and Bank of Ireland, hit historic highs in February 2007.

However, there was trouble ahead. By the end of 2006, house prices had already peaked, but both mortgage lending and construction continued to boom, helped by increasingly risky bank lending. By mid-2007, the IMF was sufficiently concerned about Irish banks' exposure to property lending to warn about the possible economic effects of a sudden fall in house prices. In its Article IV consultation with Irish authorities, it said: 'the end of rapid house price appreciation could trigger a reassessment of the risks associated with mortgage lending, possibly leading to a tightening of lending standards, which in turn could affect domestic demand. Cross-country, historical evidence presented in the April 2003 WEO suggests that sharp increases in house prices are followed by sharp declines about 40% of the time'. However, the IMF reassuringly said that banks had 'big cushions' of capital and liquidity which should see them through a property market downturn. 'Even in an extreme scenario, involving a sharp rise in unemployment and a sharp decline in house prices, capital remains adequate at every bank. In addition, even a very substantial withdrawal of private sector deposits would not exhaust any major lender's stock of liquid assets,' it said. This assessment proved fatally flawed.

In March 2008, the failure of US investment bank Bear Sterns triggered a sharp fall in the Irish stock market, which became known in the industry as the 'St Patrick's Day Massacre'. Irish banks led the retreat, with Anglo

Irish Bank's share price falling by 15% due to concerns about its exposure to commercial property loans. For the first time, people began to wonder – could Irish banks possibly share the fate of Bear Stearns?

But the authorities remained complacent – for a few months. Then, in September 2008, the sudden collapse of the US investment bank Lehman Brothers brought the global financial house of cards tumbling down. As banks fell like dominoes across the Western world, governments and central banks embarked on extraordinary measures to bail them out and ward off a disastrous spiral of defaults and failures, and Ireland entered its worst banking crisis in nearly two centuries.

Initially, the problem appeared to be merely a shortage of funds. The fall of Lehman caused markets to freeze and funding costs to head for the moon. Unable to fund themselves in the markets, Ireland's banks turned to the Central Bank of Ireland for emergency liquidity – and depositors, spooked by rumours of bank failures, started to remove their cash from Irish banks. To nip nascent bank runs in the bud and make funding conditions easier for the banks, the Irish government provided a temporary unlimited guarantee for all debt obligations of Irish banks.

The guarantee temporarily eased the banks' funding difficulties, but it soon became apparent that their real problem was not liquidity, but solvency. The asset side of Irish banks' balance sheets consisted mainly of loans against property. As Irish property prices collapsed in the global recession that followed Lehman's failure, more and more of these loans turned sour. Writing them down progressively wiped the banks' capital buffers, rendering them insolvent. Since the government had guaranteed the banks' debt obligations, bailing in bondholders was not an option. The government had little choice but to recapitalise the banks. That guarantee was to prove extremely expensive.

The worst hit bank was Anglo Irish, Ireland's third largest lender. Anglo Irish was already in trouble even before Lehman's failure: the income statement for the year ended September 2008 reveals that impairment losses had risen to €724m, from €82m in 2007. But as the recession deepened, loan defaults dramatically increased. Only 15 months later, Anglo Irish's impairment losses totalled €14.9bn. In December 2009 it recorded a total loss of €12.709bn.

In January 2009, the Irish government nationalised Anglo Irish Bank. However, nationalising it did not solve its problems. In June 2009, the government injected another €4bn of capital. This was comprehensively wiped by the end of the year, forcing the government to inject a further €8.3bn, and rising to €10.3bn in May 2010. As Anglo Irish continued to haemorrhage money, more capital injections inevitably followed. In total, Anglo Irish Bank was bailed out four times at a total cost of €29.3bn – about 18.3% of Ireland's GDP.

Other banks were also in deep trouble. Ireland's two biggest lenders, Allied Irish Banks and Bank of Ireland, both suffered catastrophic losses on their property loan books and needed capital injections of, respectively, €7.2bn and €3.5bn. Two building societies also needed bailout: Irish National Building Society (INBS) received three capital injections totalling €5.4bn between March and December 2010, while the Educational Building Society (EBS) received a total of €0.9bn.

The total cost to the Irish State of bailing out the banks and building societies was €46.3bn, or 29% of Ireland's GDP. This, plus the cost of a terrible recession in which unemployment rose to 15%, was far more than the country could afford. In November 2010, Ireland was forced to accept a sovereign bailout from the IMF and European Union, the price for which was extensive tax rises, spending cuts and 'structural reforms' to repair the government's wrecked finances. The final bank bailout was undertaken under the terms of the sovereign bailout.

But recapitalising the banks was not by itself enough to restore them. They also had to be stripped of their bad assets. So the Irish government created a government-owned 'bad bank,' the National Asset Management Agency (NAMA).

Through a special purpose vehicle, NAMA exchanged toxic assets on bank balance sheets for newly issued debt securities guaranteed by the Irish government. The banks could then pledge the securities at the ECB to obtain funding. Approximately €74bn of toxic assets were exchanged at a discount of over 50% to book value: to fund their acquisition, NAMA issued €32bn of debt securities.

Nearly 10 years later, NAMA has now repaid its debt and made an estimated profit for the Irish government of €3.5bn, but it is still trying to dispose of a hard core of difficult-to-sell assets, some of which are the subject of ongoing lawsuits.

And what of the banks? Anglo Irish Bank and INBS no longer exist. In 2011, they were forcibly merged by court order to create the Irish Bank Resolution Corporation. This was itself forced into special liquidation in February 2013 and its remaining debts of €27bn were replaced with government bonds.

However, the other banks, cleaned up and recapitalised, are now lending again, supported by a buoyant Irish property market. AIB, which is still 71% owned by the Irish state, reported mortgage loan growth of 9% in the first quarter of 2019. Of course, property prices are not (yet) back to where they were in 2007, and lending criteria are much tighter than they were before the bank solvency crisis. So this time will be different. Won't it?

STEPHEN KINSELLA

Banking Culture

Trust is a vital component in all successful human endeavours. Banks, which hold funds, quite literally in trust, have often let their customers, and wider society, down by failing to live up to the high standards imposed upon them. Since the financial crisis, banks globally are estimated to have incurred fines and penalties of more than $320 billion.

Why does this happen? Culture consists of group norms of behaviour and the transmission of the underlying shared values that help keep those norms in place. Recent research has shown that employees of a large, international bank behave, on average, honestly when treated as individuals. However, when their professional identity as bank employees is rendered an important element of their makeup, a significant proportion of them become actively dishonest. This pinpoints culture within banks themselves as the key determinant of poor behaviour. We know group identity can affect unethical behaviour, especially in highly competitive situations. If unethical behaviour is mainly driven by an unconditional desire to win, and large personal financial incentives exist when you win by extending credit to riskier borrowers, or by creating financial products laden with hidden risks, banking culture is in some sense to blame.

A major report into banking culture in Ireland by the Central Bank of Ireland found banking culture, even in 2019, displayed many of the problems of over optimism with respect to risks, top-down management styles, a poorly empowered senior management team, and of course, a series of continuing scandals around lending practices. This behaviour has consequences. In 2018, the Edelman Trust Barometer looked at 28 markets, and perhaps not surprisingly found Ireland was the least trusting of its financial services sector.

Domestic banking in Ireland was traditionally a very stable business. From 1969 to 1991, domestic credit as a percentage of total credit averaged 40%. It then grew steadily across the 'Celtic Tiger' period of the 1990s, effectively doubling the supply of credit into the economy, but surged dramatically again in the 2000s, with the crash after 2008 bringing it back to the levels of the early 1990s. Bank assets grew – and then collapsed – even more dramatically, driven by a surge in foreign borrowing by banks. Each of these increases in credit supply was caused by changes in external financing conditions, reactions to changes in regulation, increases in banking competition, and increased laxity in banking culture. Three official reports into Ireland's financial crisis highlighted inappropriate risk-taking as a key part of banking culture.

Roughly around three-quarters of the total lending by Irish banks – €420bn or about two and a half times the size of the economy's size in 2008 – was lent for property, construction and land speculation. Construction as a sector swelled to more than a fifth of economic output. These unsustainable processes were brought about because of increased credit, supplied by banks unable to stop themselves from lending out such large sums.

There is no known remedy for inappropriate banking culture beyond tighter regulation, altering individual incentives, and increasing transparency. Ireland's banks, as evidenced by the Eurobarometer survey, have a long way to go before applying this remedy to themselves and thereby regaining the trust of the population.

EOGHAN SMITH

Banville, John

John Banville's writing from 1970 to the mid-1990s can be read as a kind of artistic revolt against Ireland. This primary attitude did not change during the new social and economic dispensation of the Celtic Tiger years: 'To me, first of all,' he said in 2004, 'an artist must be against everything' and that good art 'is by its nature agnostic, is against received ideas, against the reigning pieties.' The reigning pieties, if they can be called such, of the Celtic Tiger years were peace in Northern Ireland, neoliberal globalisation, social liberalisation, and European political and monetary union. In Banville, this new cosmopolitan Ireland is barely registered in his writing. In 2005, at the peak of the boom, he stated of his work that 'one has nothing to say about the world, or society, or morals or politics or anything else'. In the 1990s and 2000s, however, many other prominent Irish writers were less interested in exploring the present than in excavating the architectures of de Valeran Ireland, and the Celtic Tiger offered them a vantage point from which to do so. Banville's work also turned back towards the past, sometimes exploring it from a personal point of view, sometimes from a political perspective. Works such as *The Untouchable* (1997), *Eclipse* (2000), *Shroud* (2002), *The Sea* (2005), *The Infinities* (2009), and *Ancient Light* (2012) all deal to varying degrees with historical legacies and personal secrets, of things previously unutterable, of the stirrings and effects of memory on the present.

In this sense, Banville's work in the Celtic Tiger moved somewhat closer to the mainstream of Irish writing, albeit retaining its celebrated experimental, philosophical and stylistic edges. His work is dominated by an overall feeling of crisis, disorientation and alienation, of the hauntings of the past, and how to live authentically in a world beyond human comprehension. Generally, his narrators are aging, solitary males who are looking at their self-created worlds receding in the rear-view mirror; in their nostalgic self-pity, they anticipate the gradual weakening of the patriarchal order that has privileged them and their kind. At the same time, their creator's imaginative energies far from weakened as Banville moved into a new phase of artistic output towards the end of the Celtic Tiger years. His greatest recognition to date came in 2005, when he won the Booker Prize for *The Sea*, the plot of which oscillates between the past and present. In 2007, he began producing the Quirke crime novels, under the Benjamin Black *nom de plume*, signalling not so much a reinvention as a reinterpretation of himself. This new direction did not diminish his output as 'John Banville'; remarkably, he has continued to publish Banville novels with the same frequency as the Black novels. As with many other works of Irish literature in this period, the Quirke novels are set in the much-maligned 1950s, a favoured decade of the contemporary Irish imaginary, presumably because of its monolithic symbolic status as the bleakest and most repressive of all.

In this sense, it is tempting to read Banville's work as retreating from the contemporary world and failing to spot the radical, transformative moment that was the Celtic Tiger. Yet, in spite of this obsessiveness with past, the landscape of Banville's in this period oeuvre is global: Ireland, Europe and occasionally America, and Banville's international reputation as an Irish writer, however much he may have disputed the validity of the adjective, played its own part in the Hibernian cultural assault on the world during the Celtic Tiger. And there is also in his Celtic Tiger fiction a deep – and indeed deepening – suspicion of the con-man, the actor, and the swindler; novels about ideological and political fraudsters such as Victor Maskell in *The Untouchable* and Axel Vander in *Shroud* can be read as contemporary warnings about the ruinous mistruths we tell ourselves.

CHARLES LARKIN

Barrett, Sean

Sean Barrett was born on February 19, 1944, in Cork. He grew up in Sutton, North County Dublin, is married to Maeve, and has one daughter, Melissa. He is a graduate of University College Dublin (BA, PhD) and McMaster University, Canada (MA). He has been a member of the faculty of the Department of Economics, Trinity College Dublin since 1977. While at Trinity College Dublin, he was the Junior Dean and Registrar of Chambers, responsible for student discipline and the allocation of accommodation.

Barrett became a Trinity Fellow in 1986. Barrett was well known for his support of open competition and deregulation in transport markets, most notably in creating competition in the taxi, bus transport and aviation transport markets. He was a critical influence on government policy related to air transport that allowed for the deregulation of the Irish aviation market in the mid-1980s which facilitated the growth of a small aviation firm called Ryanair, now the largest airline by passenger numbers in Europe.

Barrett's Transport Economics class was a favourite of students, and produced many illustrious alumni, including Ryanair CEO Michael O'Leary. He was elected to Seanad Éireann as an independent for the University of Dublin (Trinity College Dublin) constituency in 2011 for one term, finishing in June 2016. He was a member of the Joint Oireachtas Banking Inquiry and proposed several items of legislation:

1. Copyright and Related Rights (Innovation) (Amendment) Bill 2015;
2. National Mortgage and Housing Corporation Bill 2015;
3. Universities (Development & Innovation) (Amendment) Bill 2015;
4. Higher Education and Research (Consolidation & Improvement) Bill 2014;
5. Financial Stability & Reform Bill 2013;
6. Mortgage Credit (Loans & Bonds) Bill 2012;
7. Fiscal Responsibility Bill 2011.

SEAMUS COFFEY

Black Economy

Two of the most common forms of public deception are transfer fraud and tax evasion, both of which are related to the so-called black economy, which is also referred to as the shadow, informal, cash, or underground economy. Total economic activity comprises all production of goods and services whether sold in markets or not. The formal economy is that portion of total economic activity that appears in official estimates of national income in the national accounts.

The black economy comprises that part of total economic activity that is excluded from the official measurement process. These items should be recorded as part of national income, but are excluded from official estimates because they remain hidden from the authorities. Despite some conceptual differences, it seems likely that the level of black economy income is closely connected with tax-evaded income.

The scale of the black economy calls into question the reliability of official statistics, making national income look 'too low', and unemployment 'too high'. Taxation policy is based on redistribution. However, if it has to rely on inaccurate official data, it is left operating in the dark, perhaps helping those who are not badly placed, to the exclusion of more deserving others.

There is also the question of the 'missing' taxation. If a given volume of tax revenue has to be raised to meet expenditure commitments, evasion by some raises the tax rate faced by others. Given that people may have different opportunities to indulge in untaxed income sources, the tax system may end up receiving a disproportionate amount of its finance from easy sources.

There are a number of ways of trying the estimate the size of the black economy including surveys of households, using tax default data from the Revenue Commissioners figures or using aggregate data from the national accounts. A fourth approach is the monetary approach. The basic tenet here is that, in order to conceal black economy income, currency is the main transaction medium (the cash economy). By deriving estimates of excess currency holdings in the economy, and tracking this variable over time, it is possible to estimate trends in black economic activity.

This is based on the quantity theory of money. Multiplying the average velocity of circulation (this is the average number of times a unit of currency is used each year), by the volume of currency and bank deposits, yields the value of total transactions. Then this predicted nominal national income can be compared with that in the actual national accounts to give a measure of the black economy.

This approach was followed by Fagan (1994, 1997) to estimate Ireland's black economy and updated estimates are provided here using data to 2017. The approach involves the estimation of an econometric estimation of an equation for currency holdings which expresses this variable as a function of several common determinants (income, interest rates, a time trend) and in addition, a measure of the tax burden, which is considered to be the main driving force behind the black economy. The approach is not without its difficulties, but it does give useful baseline estimates.

The chart below gives estimates of the size of Ireland's Black Economy relative to official estimates of Ireland's national income for the 40 years from 1978 to 2017. GNP is used up to 1994 with GNI used since 1995.

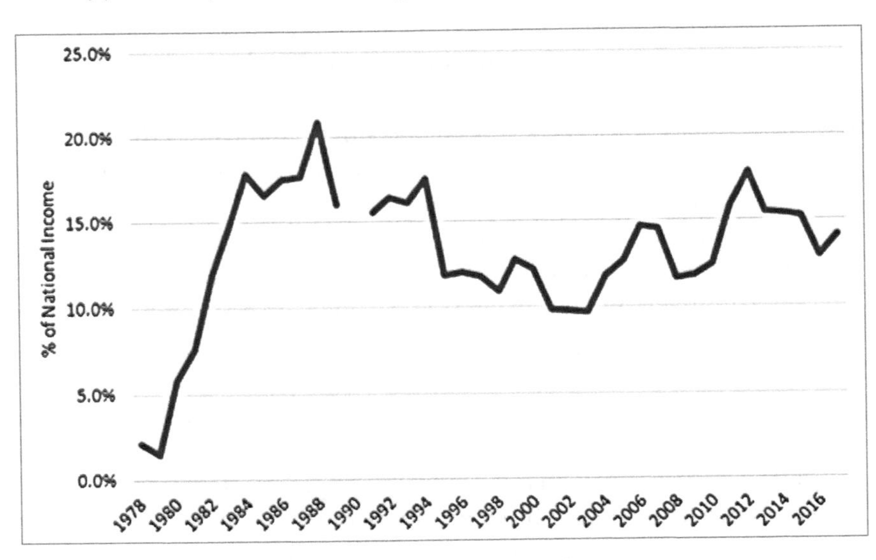

Figure 2: Estimates of Ireland's Black Economy

It can be seen that the approach suggests that excess currency holdings, and by assumption the size of the black economy, increased in the 1980s, as tax rates increased. This was reversed during the 1990s as formal employment and income growth reduced the need or incentive to engage in tax evasion. By the early 2000s, it is estimated that the income of the black economy had fallen to a level that was just under 10% of the official level of national income.

However, it is notable that estimates of the size of the black economy increased during the credit-fuelled growth period from 2004 to 2007 reaching 15% of national income. It is possible that this increase is linked to increased activity in the construction sector, and the associated levels of self-employment, as it can be seen that the estimates fall in line with the construction crash from 2008.

In line with the experience of the 1980s, the estimates of the black economy rose during the austerity years of 2009 to 2012 when income taxes were raised. And again, the expansion in formal employment and income growth since then has seen a reduction in the estimated size of the black economy. The 2017 estimate would put the size of the black economy at somewhere around €25 billion with a loss of tax revenue for the government likely to be in the range of €6–8 billion.

BRIAN LUCEY

Bondholders

A phrase that resonates with many from the banking crisis is 'burn the bondholders'. It conveys images of top-hatted capitalists being tied to stakes in town squares while mobs pile up gilded certificates around them prior to ignition. But what are these bondholders, and how would we have burned them?

Banks are corporate bodies like any other. They have assets, mainly in the form of loans. To match that they also have liabilities, which traditionally are in the form of deposits. So far so simple. Where things got complex was when banks began to expand their loan books, backed not just with deposits, but also with other liabilities. To reiterate, banks are like any other company and can take on debt to expand. These are the infamous bonds. Bonds are debt obligations owed to creditors. Some of these bonds were what are called 'senior' bonds – these are structured in such a way as to be essentially deposits. So a Dutch pension fund could loan money to an Irish bank (or an Irish fund to a Dutch bank) in two ways. It could put the money on deposit or it could loan it to the bank via a senior bond. Other bonds were what are called 'junior' or 'subordinated' bonds. The terminology here reflects a legal hierarchy: the theory was that in the event of a company getting into distress, these bonds would only be paid off *after* the senior bonds. They were subordinate to them.

The problem in the Irish context arose when the bank guarantee was put in place. This, quite controversially, not just guaranteed the deposits and the senior bonds, but also the junior bonds. Theoretically, the higher return that junior bonds provide is a reflection of the higher risk they take. The bank guarantee removed much of that risk. The then Taoiseach Brian Cowen was adamant that no 'burning' or partial payment of the senior bondholders would be possible without also treating the deposit holders the same way. Interestingly, the then Attorney General, Paul Gallagher, suggested the opposite. The incoming Fine Gael-Labour government, presumably acting on the same legal advice, was in favour of the senior bondholders of Anglo Irish and Irish Nationwide sharing losses, but this was torpedoed at the very last minute in the face of warnings from the then ECB president Jean Claude Trichet. This would have saved the state upwards of €6b.

Junior bondholders in the two most affected banks, Anglo and Irish Nationwide, were eventually faced with losses – a 20% of face value offer was made by the Irish state in 2010, in effect burning the bondholders there. However, this was an offer that was not accepted by all, and in 2018 these holdouts were in fact paid in full.

A related issue, one that is in effect unanswerable, is who exactly were these bondholders, senior and junior. It is unanswerable as bonds are tradable – I may be the original owner but there is no central register of who owns what in debt, unlike in shares. Even if we did find out the owners, it is a certainty that many would be shell companies, or fund managers holding the assets in trust for anonymous others. At the time of the bank guarantee in 2008 we know, from internal Department of Finance communications, some of the Anglo Irish Senior Bondholders. These included Finnish, Swiss and Dutch pension funds, German insurance companies and international fund managers. For the junior bondholders we know some at the time of the 20% offer, one of whom was Roman Abramovich. We also know that the Irish League of Credit Unions had some €600m in bank bonds, but the nature of these was unspecified.

The Irish experience of how to deal with bondholders, its good and bad elements, was a learning curve for not just domestic but also international policy makers. Rarely does an entire banking system in a modern developed country teeter on the brink of total collapse. The lessons learned on how to impose burden sharing beyond the taxpayer were later deployed in Cyprus, where, in what was crucially different to Ireland's situation, deposit holders and senior bondholders were forced to accept 'burning'. It is doubtful in the extreme if such would have been politically or socially accepted in the case of Anglo and Nationwide, given the widespread domestic deposit base.

In the end, bondholders, some of them, were burned. Perhaps not enough to satisfy popular demands, but that is a different story. The myth had taken hold that if only we could 'burn' sufficient bondholders we would be spared the austerity years. The reality is that the great majority of the increase in national debt and the consequent reining in of state spending arose not from the banking crisis costs per se but from the ballooning state deficit. This was the fruit of a skewed tax base and (despite what people may think) an unwillingness to impose deep cuts on current spending.

CHARLES LARKIN

Bord Snip Nua

Bord Snip Nua was the media term applied to the Colm McCarthy report of the Special Group on Public Service Numbers and Expenditure Programmes, published on July 16, 2009, outlining proposals for consolidating the fiscal position of the Irish State following the collapse of the property bubble in 2008.

Retired UCD economist Colm McCarthy was originally employed in 1987 to perform a similar piece of work as part of the late 1980s consolidation of the Irish fiscal position, which was called 'Bord Snip' by the Irish media at the time. 'Nua', being the Irish term for 'new', resulted in this second report by McCarthy being titled 'Bord Snip Nua'. The 1980s consolidation gave rise to a mythos of the 'expansionary fiscal contraction', a phenomenon for which limited empirical evidence has been found, but which became a popular explanation for the rapid economic expansion of Ireland in the early 1990s.

The cuts proposed constituted €5.3bn in savings with the loss of 17,500 public service positions. The application of the recommendations was incomplete on the part of the government of the time, with around €1.7bn in overall cuts imposed. The cycles of Financial Emergency Measures in the Public Interest and the Employment Control Framework progressed much of the consolidation in the public and civil service, with staff pay reductions and staff number reductions (by retirement and natural wastage as far as practicable). As of 2019 nominal pay restoration up to 2008 levels has yet to be achieved across the entirety of the civil and public service.

EUGENE O'BRIEN

Browne, Vincent

As the Celtic Tiger's proposed soft landing suddenly became a crash landing, and people began to realise that unemployment, crushing debt and homelessness were no longer abstract concepts, but instead staples of a new reality, the question as to how all of this had happened so quickly was one that few could answer. To paraphrase Bertie Ahern, we had moved from boomier to gloomier in an instant.

It was towards the start of the looming economic crisis that TV3 launched a new current affairs programme, and on September 4, 2007 *Tonight with Vincent Browne* was first broadcast. It ran from Monday to Thursday at 11:05 p.m. and lasted an hour. The programme would run until July 27, 2017, and in the process would succeed in informing the Irish television audience in an unambiguous manner about the causes of the boom and bust. Despite airing on what is usually considered a graveyard slot, the show was highly successful, drawing an average 166,000 viewers.

Browne had been a central and somewhat polemical figure in Irish journalism for a number of years, working for the *Irish Press* and the *Irish Independent*. He launched *Magill* magazine in September 1977, and it remained in print until 1990, being relaunched for 13 issues in 1997. In October 2004, he launched a current affairs magazine, *Village*, of which he was editor and which ceased publication in August 2008.

Tonight with Vincent Browne consisted of a discussion chaired by Browne with a panel of academics, politicians, spokespeople for different groups and people with information on the issues at hand. Government ministers were regularly grilled, and for a time, Fianna Fáil were reluctant to send spokespeople on the show. Regular contributors included Eoghan Corry, Eamon Delaney, Constantin Gurdgiev, Justine McCarthy, Eoin Ó Murchú, Kathy Sheridan, Noel Whelan, Sarah Carey, Sarah McInerney, Brian Lucey, Mick Wallace, Peter Mathews and Marie-Louise O'Donnell. Issues about the bank bailout, HSE overspending, the EU's role in managing Ireland's debts, the Troika were all aired, as were important social issues. The programme was critical in informing the Irish public about the case of Savita Halappanavar as the news of her death was breaking. The ramifications associated with the crash of the Celtic Tiger provided an ideal forum for the show's host to voice the nation's disquiet in relation to what was happening in Ireland at that time.

The style of the programme was unique in Irish media circles, as questions were posed in a manner that was far more robust and probing than was the norm in the more sedate surroundings of RTÉ. Browne would repeatedly ask the same question if he felt that he was not getting an adequate answer and his sighs, groans and snorts were semiotic signals of disgust which were very effective in letting an audience know how he felt. It made for riveting television, and many of the audience were educated on the finer points of banking, bonds and debt by Browne, Mathews, Lucey and Gurdgiev in particular. All the media training in the world could not protect politicians from Browne's insistent questioning.

Joan Burton asked Browne if he was 'asking me a question or just trying to harangue me', while when Conor Lenihan refused to resign over the Brian Cowen leadership vote, on being quizzed by Browne, Lenihan stood up angrily, glared, pointed his finger at Browne and shouted: 'It's easy for you to be cynical about people who go into public life and I really do resent the sneering insinuation that you're trying to put to me'. Browne's response was: 'Conor, you're not going to shout me down and you can take me full-on on this if you like', which is exactly what happened. Lenihan lost his seat dramatically in the general election the following February.

Browne's exasperation with some of the pabulum-like non-answers that some politicians gave was instructive and highly entertaining. After an interview with Fianna Fáil politicians Charlie O'Connor and Darragh O'Brien, following the vote of confidence in Brian Cowen, Browne said to camera: 'God, it would do your head in, wouldn't it?'. SIPTU president Jack O'Connor famously walked out of an interview on the programme, and, discussing the vexed issue of Irish Water and the putative water tax, on hearing that 'the fella who made a real cock-up' (former Environment Minister Phil Hogan) had been promoted to the European Commission, Browne's response was 'fucking amazing'. Browne attempted to qualify this remark by saying: 'I'm sorry, I've been off for a few weeks'. The Media hailed it as a moment of 'Classic Vincent!'

Browne was also known as the person who challenged Bertie Ahern publicly on his personal finances at a time when the Taoiseach still enjoyed considerable popularity. He also called the Troika to account for the austerity measures they were enforcing on Ireland. Fearless, dogged, uncompromising, pompous, Browne was the contrarian voice of the post-Celtic Tiger era.

KARL DEETER

Buy-to-lets

In the Celtic Tiger, everybody seemed to have a buy-to-let, even the taxi drivers who would pick up the young, drunk version of me at the time, and they would tell you all about their gaffs in far-fetched places like Cape Verde and Bulgaria. In Celtic Tiger vernacular, this was the Irish version of 'Joe Kennedy's shoe shine boy' moment, which relates back to the moment when JFK's dad got a stock tip from a shoe shine boy one morning. He said 'you know it's time to sell when shoe-shine boys give you stock tips, the bull market is over'. The buy-to-let sector is a vital part of any housing market; in Ireland, it tended to be primarily owned and operated by non-professional landlords who owned two or fewer homes.

They were also very unprepared, in the same way as 'accidental landlords', for a crash which would see their equity evaporate, while the rents that supported their repayments rapidly fell. The investors tended to do their best to hold out, a subject that was empirically analysed by Brian Lucey, Marie Hunt and Karl Deeter in their 2013 paper, 'Why do investors not sell underwater buy-to-let property?' This was for several reasons: in many cases, the loans were manageable because they were financed with trackers on an 'interest only basis', which meant that the loans were sustainable. As an example, if you had a loan for €500,000 on interest only, with a rate of 2%, your repayments would be only €10,000 a year, which works out at €833 per month.

Sometimes the way the loan was financed did not allow people to liquidate, because a common financial bit of engineering was to secure the loan on a debt-free primary home at the best rate on the market (often tracker mortgages with margins as low as 0.75%), and then use the cash to buy the buy-to-let with cash. This meant that loan clearance was not on the home the person was living in and it complicated matters when it came to landlord decisions on how to deal with the financial crisis. That arrears were higher in investment properties is logical, as people will not fight as hard to make payments on a house in which they do not live; in other cases, they would sequester the rent and use it to ensure that the main family home was being paid for.

This was further complicated with different court rulings when banks tried to take the properties back. What became more common was that the banks would appoint receivers, and by doing this they may not have been able to obtain possession, but they would certainly start to access any rental payments. There is a current debate (2019) about whether or not landlords are fleeing the market. The evidence shows that more people than ever are renting, so it cannot be said that stock is lower, but perhaps the make-up of the sector is changing as it professionalises.

Many people have called for professionalisation of the landlord business, and many firms have entered the space by buying large blocks of apartments, loan books, or by building in the 'build to rent' market where one owner brings a development to the market on a renting only basis. This does lead to greater specialisation, but it has also been the first time that Irish renters dealt with investors who on a large scale operated spreadsheets to maximise their return and who really knew the rulebook so that they could do so in a compliant manner. The rents charged showed up in headline rents as the rules that prevented inter-tenancy rent increases beyond 4% did not apply to new homes that had been brought to market for the first time during that period. Buy-to-let still remains an important creator of wealth in Ireland, in particular for large swathes of people who have used homes as a proxy for funding a pension.

CHARLES LARKIN

Cardiff, Kevin

Kevin Cardiff was born in Dublin in 1961, and was a civil servant. He was educated at the University of Washington, in Seattle (BA), and at University College Dublin (Master of Business Studies). He is a non-executive director of KBC Bank Ireland, and is the Chairperson of the Board of Audit of the European Stability Mechanism. Cardiff completed a six-year term of office beginning in 2012, as a member of the European Court of Auditors at the end of February 2018.

Previously, Cardiff was Second Secretary (second in command), in the Department of Finance of Ireland during the bailout period of 2006–10, and was appointed as Secretary General (lead position) of the Department of Finance in February 2010. He began his civil service career in 1984 after he returned from the University of Washington.

Cardiff's testimony and supporting documents to the Joint Oireachtas Inquiry into the Banking Crisis was extremely detailed, running to over 420 pages of text. It formed an important basis for the analysis of the Committee and the underlying understanding of what actually took place on the night of the Banking Guarantee of September 29/30, 2008.

CHARLES LARKIN

Chopra, Ajai

Born in India, Chopra attended the University of Bombay for his BA and then completed his PhD at the University of Virginia. His career was as an IMF Official from 1984 to 2014. He was most notable for the Irish Bailout as Deputy Director of the Europe Department prior to his retirement in 2014. Chopra previously managed the South Korean bailout programme in 1997. During his visits to Ireland for programme monitoring he became a well-received public figure. He engaged with the academic economics community, attending the Dublin Economics Workshop conference in Kenmare, Co. Kerry, in October 2011.

In testimony given to the Oireachtas Banking Inquiry, Chopra highlighted many of the deficiencies in the design and execution of the Troika Bailout brought about by policy mandates and inexperience on the part of the ECB and European Commission. Chopra highlighted the negative impact of ECB President Trichet's ultimatums on the Bailout and maintained that the ECB had gone beyond its mandate and had conducted its business in a fashion that was not in keeping with a member state organisation.

RUTH BARTON

Cinema and the Celtic Tiger

The Celtic Tiger years witnessed radical changes in Irish cinema. Not all of these can be ascribed to the new financial climate and there's a danger of categorising all cultural production under one heading where multiple factors are at play. 'Celtic Tiger cinema' is thus more a soubriquet than a watertight classification. Filmmaking in this period responded to a number of influences, including the Peace Process and with it the waning of the National Question as a narrative driver, and the loss of influence of the Catholic Church, neither of which can be seen to be contingent on the new economic order. Digital technologies, meanwhile, paved the way for cheaper, faster shooting and editing. When considering film production, it is also important to remember that a lengthy period can lapse between a film's conception and its release, so that the earlier films that appeared in the Celtic Tiger years (Neil Jordan's *The Butcher Boy* of 1997, for instance), responded more to concerns around rurality, national identity, and the weight of history than did the films of the early 2000s that originated in the Celtic Tiger period. I am thus focusing here on films of the early 2000s onwards.

The first films that appeared after the turn of the century responded very directly to a new metropolitan culture. *About Adam* (Gerard Stembridge, 2001) and *Goldfish Memory* (Elizabeth Gill, 2003) are contemporary urban romantic comedies that gleefully threw off the shackles of Catholic morality. In their place came guilt-free sex and queer relationships played out in the gleaming new cafés and clubs of a capital city dedicated to the leisure requirements of its young professional inhabitants. It was to the city that the Celtic Tiger filmmakers looked to set their stories, with the countryside relegated to a weekender playground (the location for instance for John Butler's *The Stag* of 2013).

These city films, however, soon took a darker turn. In 2004, an unknown director, Lenny Abrahamson, in tandem with an equally unknown screenwriter, Mark O'Halloran, released *Adam & Paul*, a story of two heroin addicts criss-crossing Dublin in search of a fix. With references to *Ulysses* and *Waiting for Godot*, and an aesthetic that recalled the pratfall comedies of early cinema, Abrahamson's film announced the arrival of a new auteur, one who would eventually find himself in the Hollywood limelight with his award-winning *Room* of 2015.

Abrahamson's refusal to celebrate the nation's new wealth found its echo in a slew of crime and gangster films, such as *Intermission* (John Crowley, 2003) and *Man About Dog* (Paddy Breathnach, 2004). Where Abrahamson's work remains distinctive is in its refusal to embrace the globally recognisable structures of genre filmmaking. It was this turn to genre cinema that became another distinguisher of Celtic Tiger filmmaking. Romantic comedies, thrillers, caper films, and horror all flourished in the new era of globalised film production. The Dublin musical claimed its place with the Oscar-winning *Once* (John Carney, 2007), a celebration of a new multi-cultural city, where differences melted away in the shared spaces of bohemian music making.

The rise of commercialised genre filmmaking caused no little concern in certain quarters. Co-productions might be a practical way of raising more money than one small filmmaking culture could achieve on its own, but to the critics of these films their globally recognisable storylines were a betrayal of local storytelling traditions. Certain of the horror films even seemed to be going out of their way to foreground settings that were literally unrecognisable – literally because co-production arrangements dictated that they be shot in Wales, for instance, or in other cases Luxembourg. The fact that the Irish Film Board (now Screen Ireland) actively supported co-productions reinforced a creeping disquiet that the neoliberal drivers of the new economy reached far into cultural outputs.

These remain legitimate concerns. Yet one of the most successful films, both critically and at the box office, in the Celtic Tiger years was Ken Loach's *The Wind That Shakes the Barley* (2006), a film that would not have been made without multiple financing sources. The same could be said of the Oscar-nominated *The Secret of Kells* (Tomm Moore, Nora Twomey, 2007) – the most local of films produced by Ireland's most globalised audio-visual sector, animation. The Celtic Tiger guaranteed money in the coffers for Irish filmmakers; it offered a new set of narratives around inclusion and exclusion to fuel many of their productions, and it confirmed, if that were needed, that to be a filmmaking country is to be part of a mobile economy of production deals, location shoots, and tax transfers. How to negotiate that, and still tell local stories is a challenge that is not going to go away.

BRIAN MURPHY

Coffee Culture

Much of the human experience revolves around our personal engagement with the nourishment we consume. And just like food, the beverages we drink can often act as key signifiers in social exchanges. Coffee is one drink that has the potential to convey a message about who we are or how we might like to be seen, and Ireland's relationship with coffee culture is a relatively new one. In a pre-Celtic Tiger era, our coffee often came from a jar, or sometimes from a filter pot during the rare visit to a local hotel or restaurant. The main bastion of Ireland's drink culture, the pub, was focused on the sale of alcohol rather than coffee. Words like 'cappuccino' and 'macchiato' were not yet considered part of common parlance.

Things changed quite dramatically in the early 2000s, and we can now point to a number of identifiable phases in Ireland's coffee culture. The first coffee phase began in the early Celtic Tiger years when domestic coffee chains began making their first forays into the Irish market. Companies like Insomnia, which opened its first store in 1997, and Cafe Sol, which was formed in 1998, joined existing market players like O'Brien's, and began to capitalise on an emerging culture that was associating coffee drinking with affluence. Ireland's demographic landscape also changed as a returning emigrant class brought home with them a taste for drinks other than those of their youth. Increased travel opportunities through newly formed budget airlines exposed people to the European coffee cultures of countries like Italy, Spain and France.

As the economy boomed and evidence of ostentation appeared in many areas of Irish life, coffee certainly fitted the bill, and the streets became filled with busy professionals who couldn't possibly greet the day without a tall skinny latte in hand. For quite a number of years, the Irish chains continued to dominate, but coffee is a high-margin product, and it was inevitable that international chains would turn their gaze on Ireland. 2005 was to herald the second phase of Ireland's coffee story. Both Costa and Starbucks entered the market around this time, and embarked on developments that would see their stores rapidly expand over a relatively short period of time. We are all familiar with the progress they have made since, and 2018 figures from *Hospitality Ireland* suggest they now have 102 stores and 79 stores respectively, making them the second and third largest players in the country after Insomnia.

The collapse of the Celtic Tiger economy would lead to another more unexpected third phase in Irish coffee culture. The recession brought hardship and many coffee lovers were no longer willing or able to spend 3 euro on a daily caffeine fix, and yet were not prepared to forego their high-end coffee experience either. The arrival of the Nespresso concept neatly fitted demands for high quality barista-style coffee that could be consumed at home. It chimed well with a nation, which still wanted indulgence, even in a period of decline and uncertainty. Brema Drohan, managing director of Nespresso in Ireland, recognised this at the launch of their flagship store in Dublin when she said: 'Then those things stopped. But people still needed treats and there is still discernment and an interest in quality. And people wanted these treats, so they brought them home'.

There is little doubt that the Celtic Tiger period changed our relationship with coffee. Ireland now has a proliferation of coffee chains to choose from, home coffee solutions are everywhere and barista coffee courses and competitions abound. In 2016, Ireland hosted the prestigious World Barista Championship. Thankfully, the Celtic Tiger period has also influenced one final phase in the Irish coffee story. While recent figures from *Hospitality Ireland* suggest that Ireland's top four coffee chains – Insomnia, Costa, Starbucks and O' Brien's – have almost 400 stores between them, we have also seen the emergence of the independent coffee house, sometimes unfairly dismissed as part of a mere hipster trend. These authentic coffee shops provide a welcome antidote to the branded approach of the larger chains. Coffee houses like 3FE have led the way in a market that is increasingly seeking out the local and the unique. Their proliferation around our cities, towns and villages is testament to the fact that, as a nation, we have embraced a modern, more European approach to coffee. Our coffee shops provide us with new and alternative opportunities for social engagement in places other than our traditional locales. Both through its rise and its demise, the Celtic Tiger economy is in large part responsible for that provision and has helped give birth to new Irish coffee culture that is here to stay.

LORCAN SIRR

Commission on the Private Rented Sector

In June 1999, mid-Celtic Tiger, at a time of rapidly rising rents and turbulence in the sector, a Commission was established by the then Minister for Housing and Urban Renewal to review the regulation of the sector, including:

1. Security of tenure;
2. Rent certainty;
3. Landlord and Tenant Code that balanced rights and responsibilities of Landlords and Tenants;
4. Investment in the private residential sector.

Following the Commission's findings and report, the Residential Tenancies Act 2004 provided for a modern system of residential landlord and tenant legislation. This included the establishment of the Private Rented Tenancies Board (PRTB) with responsibility for tenancy registration, dispute resolution and research, information and policy advice. The Commission was chaired by Thomas A. Dunne of Dublin Institute of Technology. The PRTB was established on foot of the Commission's report to register tenancies and also to act as a dispute resolution body between landlords and tenants. The Private Residential Tenancies Board became the Residential Tenancies Board (RTB) in 2016.

The Residential Tenancies Act 2004 was a watershed in the private rented sector in Ireland. Rapidly increasing house prices since the beginning of the Celtic Tiger, coupled with immigration of much-needed workers, had seen the purchase of housing pushed out of the reach of many households and a consequent reliance on the private rented sector. The Act was a substantial response to what was becoming obvious as a sector of greater significance for more people and for longer periods of time. Indeed, the size of the private rented sector doubled between 2006 and 2011, from 9% to 18%. The Act provided for reform of residential landlord and tenant law, based mainly on the recommendations of the Commission on the Private Rented Residential Sector. The Act outlined obligations for both tenants and landlords whether or not there was a written lease or agreement. Neither landlords nor tenants could contract their way out of these obligations, although additional ones could be included. The Act:

1. formalised rent setting and notice periods for rent reviews;
2. introduced new security of tenure provisions based on a four-year cycle (known as Part 4, and subsequently increased to six years);
3. brought in new periods of notice for the termination of a tenancy;
4. introduced mandatory registration of tenancies;
5. established the Private Residential Tenancies Board (see: Residential Tenancies Board);
6. put in place a dispute resolutions system for landlords and tenants via the Private Residential Tenancies Board.

One of the unappreciated legacies of the Celtic Tiger, both during its heyday and subsequently, has been the growth, development, regulation and reliance on the private rented sector by both the public and private sectors. The level of growth in the Irish economy meant that housebuilding could not keep up with demand, and prices could not keep in line with affordability. This thrust the private rented sector into a new, longer-term role for which it was arguably not prepared. The Celtic Tiger, especially that part of it in the twenty-first century, was the tipping point when the private rented sector changed from being a place to live temporarily while waiting to buy a house, to becoming a form of semi-permanent home.

BRIAN O'NEILL

Communications

The Celtic Tiger coincided with extraordinary changes in both the economy and technology of Irish media. The extent to which these can be attributed to the prevailing economic circumstances or would have come about anyway as a result of an evolving media scene is open to debate. Media were so much part of the *Zeitgeist* of the Celtic Tiger era that more than a decade later, it can be difficult to separate those aspects that are simply artefacts of Ireland's overheated economy as opposed to a more fundamental process of technological change. Regardless, it is the case that Ireland's media, both legacy and new, emerged from this period in a greatly transformed and much less certain state.

To position Irish media during the Celtic Tiger, it is important to consider the wider contours shaping the media landscape through this critical period. As observed by Horgan and Flynn in their updated edition of *Irish Media, A Critical History* (2017), the Celtic Tiger was particularly kind to Irish media. The buoyant economy contributed unprecedented advertising revenues to media organisations. Despite the collapse of the *Irish Press* in 1995, and the onset of online publishing, both regional and national press experienced increased circulation and new titles. Independent commercial radio, formally launched with the Broadcasting Act of 1990, had consolidated and established an evenly balanced share of the audience between local, commercial and national public radio. TV3, Ireland's first commercial channel, was established in 1998, placing further pressure on RTÉ, the public broadcaster, which found itself struggling not just for market share but also political support.

Thus, the familiar characteristics of a liberalised media environment were already well in evidence by the year 2000. All Irish media organisations, including RTÉ, enjoyed increased profits and expansion, introducing a pattern of acquisitions, mergers and takeovers that were a familiar feature of convergence in European and international communications. Irish media notably attracted interest from UK media conglomerates, eager to take advantage of the expanding media market.

Liberalisation in the telecommunications sector was also well established by this period. The 1994 Bangemann report on Europe in the global information society set out a policy template to accelerate the opening up of the communications sector to competition, laying the foundations for the single European audiovisual/digital services market and – replicating similar political responses in North America and elsewhere – to minimise or entirely remove any regulatory hurdles towards innovation in the development of Internet services.

Irish media, perhaps cushioned by its healthy finances, were slow to adapt to this changing technological revolution. The Celtic Tiger, for instance, coincided with profound changes not just in the technology of distribution, such as the switchover to digital broadcasting, but also with the ultimately profoundly disruptive emergence of online services and social media platforms. Newspapers in Ireland as elsewhere adopted a wait and see approach, publishing some content online but hesitating in terms of developing a sustainable business model for online to counteract what would later prove to be devastating decline in paid readership. Analogue switch off for television was similarly delayed, leaving the market open to exploitation to satellite television so that when Saorview was eventually launched, it had a much reduced audience base to cater to. Digital radio broadcasting arguably never really took off because commercial radio simply wasn't interested in it, and therefore the DAB (Digital Audio Broadcasting) platform could only ever offer simulcasts of existing RTÉ content, failing to develop long-promised new radio services.

The aftermath of the Celtic Tiger's collapse has thus left Irish media particularly exposed. Local radio and regional press, mimicking the property sector, carried huge debts incurred through borrowings based on inflated valuations, and were ill-prepared to respond to the rapid shift to online advertising and the sudden decline in their own revenue. Circulation figures for national newspaper titles declined rapidly after 2008 both for economic reasons and due to the shift in readership demographics. The loss of advertising revenue to television was particularly devastating, forcing RTÉ to engage in selling off properties and job losses.

Meanwhile, the inexorable rise of mobile and personal media devices has seen Irish audiences migrate to online services for news and entertainment in line with similar trends in other countries. Had Irish media organisations been more focused during the Celtic Tiger on this fundamental threat to their existence – instead of filling property supplements – they might be better prepared to navigate what will continue to be an extremely challenging environment for quality media content.

SHAEN CORBET

Contracts for Difference (CFD)

Contracts for Difference (CFDs) are structured towards those investors seeking additional levels of higher risk investments in their portfolios. Due to the leveraged nature of CFDs, market movements amplify the investors' gains and losses in multiples of the provided level of margin. In Ireland, CFDs are usually structured to allow an investor to obtain a 10% margin, while borrowing the remaining 90% of the investment from their CFD broker. This enables the investor to enhance their buying power tenfold.

When CFDs are used to invest, a price increase of 10% results in 100% profits, whereas a 10% fall in price leaves the investor at a total loss. When the investor is in this position, they must meet margin calls to maintain the position. Failure to do so results in the position being immediately closed. CFDs therefore act as an extremely cheap, non-selective source of investment finance due to the relative ease of account establishment. CFDs by their very nature thrive in periods of short term extreme volatility, such as that experienced during the collapse of the Celtic Tiger, as investors increase their use of leverage to maximise the amount of a particular equity that they can afford. Financial crises therefore generate a thriving environment in which CFDs can trade.

Longer horizon investors would refrain from using CFDs due to the commissions and overnight interest charges that must be paid for the use of margin to create leverage. In Ireland, CFD licences fall under betting and gambling legislation; therefore, all profits are tax free. These tax exemptions stemmed from the Charles Haughey era, as the Irish government attempted to enhance and develop the bloodstock industry. This tax free characteristic was particularly attractive to investors, who otherwise would have to pay capital gains tax on fully margined equity investments. In 2011, The Central Bank of Ireland raised particular concerns about the Irish CFD industry. They specifically pointed out that there was a serious deficiency in transparency, and a lack of information gathered by CFD brokers. Risk disclosures supplied by CFD brokers were often found to be inadequate and, in some cases, misleading.

There have been numerous instances of trading irregularities associated with CFD investment. In Germany, a report by the European Security Markets Expert Group (ESME) in 2009, found that a large unwinding by Porsche of options related to CFDs in Volkswagen (VW), combined with takeover rumours, had triggered and fuelled a 500% increase in share price in less than seven days in late October 2008. At the same time, CFDs were made famous in Ireland through their use by Mr Sean Quinn in his substantial investment made in the now collapsed Anglo Irish Bank. Through the use of the leveraged product, Mr Quinn was able to build up a position in excess of 20% of the total size of the bank. It was further contended that the bank had lent in excess of €2 billion to Mr Quinn to mitigate oncoming margin calls in the CFD position in itself. The diminishing ability of Mr Quinn to meet margin calls as the share price of Anglo fell further, led to an exceptionally complex repurchase agreement in advance of the bank's sharp demise with a group called the 'Maple 10' or 'Golden Circle' (a group of wealthy developers and persons with deep financial ties to the bank who were allegedly given hundreds of millions in loans by Anglo Irish Bank to reinvest in the bank's shares).

The legalities surrounding this arrangement proceeded to tested by the Irish legal system for the following decade leading to multiple prosecutions. In 2018, the European Securities and Markets Authority (ESMA) has imposed strict restrictions on the use of leverage in CFDs on the back of concerns that retail investors across Europe were suffering 'significant losses' due to the complexity of the products. The Central Bank of Ireland also echoed these concerns, adding that they had further issue with binary options (a financial exotic option in which the payoff is either some fixed monetary amount or nothing at all). However, investors continue to be attracted to such products, given the promise of high returns, easy-to-trade platforms and low interest rates, but appear to have failed to understand the inherent complexity of the products and their excessive leverage.

SUSAN BOYLE

Craft Beer

To reap, you first must sow and the seeds of Ireland's craft brewing renaissance were planted in the late 1990s while the Celtic Tiger was just a cub. Due to consolidation of breweries and domination of the Irish beer market by global multinational breweries, by the early 1990s there were only a handful of breweries remaining in Ireland. This is in contrast to more than 200 breweries dotted across the country at the beginning of the nineteenth century.

As a reaction to the homogenisation of the beer industry, and taking inspiration from other countries with established craft beer scenes, Ireland's craft breweries and brew pubs poured their first pints in the 1990s. This new wave of Irish craft brewing included The Carlow Brewing Company, established in 1996, Porterhouse brew-pub, Temple bar, 1996 and Franciscan Well in Cork, 1998.

For the next 10 years, Ireland craft brewing remained in a more or less latent state. During this time, the country's future craft brewers were traveling, drinking craft beer in other places and learning to home brew. Many of them worked in the IT sector or in jobs connected with the booming building industry. Meanwhile, the national road infrastructure was undergoing major improvements: essential to a successful brewery is ensuring a way of transporting beer to where it will be consumed. Moreover, industrial estates were popping up at sites close to these transport arteries. Units in these industrial estates would become excellent locations for breweries and since Ireland had developed strong trade links with other European countries during the Celtic Tiger, this opened up new export markets for Irish micro-brewed beers.

In 2002 Ireland was producing 8.7m hectolitres of beer per year. During the Celtic Tiger, our thirst for beer increased and we were drinking more of the beer brewed on these shores. While the overall production of beer did not increase enormously, there was a noticeable drop in the volume of

Irish beer exported, from 3.5m hectolitres in 1998, to 2.4m hectolitres in 2002. The first decade of the new millennium heralded the second wave of craft breweries in Ireland, which included breweries such as Trouble Brewing (Co. Kildare, 2009), Beoir Chorca Dhuibhne (Co. Kerry, 2008), White Gypsy (Co. Tipperary, 2009), Galway Hooker (2006) and Galway Bay Brewery (2009). The foundation of many of these breweries coincided with the last days of the Celtic Tiger. The Irish beer drinker could now find tasty Irish craft beers but the real renaissance for Irish craft brewing was to come as the as the economic climate changed and Ireland's Celtic Tiger gave its last roar. In 2012 the number of microbreweries in operation in Ireland had increased to 15, but in the following five years the number of breweries would increase by more than 500%. A number of factors influenced this unprecedented growth. In 2015, the Budget increased the volume of beer a microbrewery could produce and still avail of a 50% tax rebate to 30,000hl. This allowed breweries to produce more beer and made microbrewing more commercially attractive. Ireland had many well-travelled young people, who, having acquired a thirst for craft beer elsewhere, set up their own breweries. Due to the downturn in the economy, many traditional career paths were hampered, but this climate favoured entrepreneurial brewers who could avail of cheaper rent, incentivised rural development schemes funded by the EU and an increase in government-funded brewing education courses. More significantly, post-Celtic Tiger, these would-be brewers, had nothing to lose and few alternative employment options.

During the Celtic Tiger, who would have guessed that shiny glass-fronted car show rooms, with their reinforced floors, would make the perfect craft breweries once the economic bubble had burst?

STEPHEN KINSELLA

Credit Crunch

Like adding fuel to a fire, unwarranted credit expansions by banks fuel increases in economic activity. Consider a loan advanced by a bank to build a housing estate. This loan causes employment to rise, and in a tight labour market, wages to rise, and rent of plant and machinery to rise. In the case of the Irish banks in the height of the asset boom much of this money was borrowed from abroad and lent domestically.

Loans allow economic actors to secure scarce resources at higher prices, which in turn spurs increases in the prices of other goods and services, which help others repay other loans, and so the cycle continues. This is an unsustainable cycle, however, because the supply of credit is finite. Eventually, credit levels reach too high a point, and a rapid contraction in prices of assets takes place. Each credit boom contains the seeds of its own collapse, a so-called Minsky cycle.

Almost immediately, credit becomes unavailable for almost any purpose. Banks, rapidly replacing yesterday's greed with today's fear, become wary of any further credit extension, even for worthy projects undertaken by low risk borrowers. This is a credit crunch situation. The economy contracts more than it should, and loses potential output, as would-be successes are never funded. Losses in one market are then amplified into large dislocations and turmoil in other, usually financial, markets.

Credit crunches are comparable to episodes of starvation: they can have long-lasting effects on the economy, but can themselves be quite short-lived.

Credit crunches are really shortages of equity capital, which limits banks' ability to make loans. The credit crunch is really, often, a capital crunch.

The only known remedy for a credit (or capital) crunch in the private markets is an expansion of credit by the public sector. This injection helps restore the balance sheets of firms and banks at the same time, and provides the credit the economy needs to continue functioning. One example of a credit expansion scheme like this is the longer-term refinancing operations (LTRO) of the European Central Bank. This was a very large provision of central bank liquidity to banks affected by the 2007/8 financial crisis and the credit crunch it created. The LTRO had a positive impact on banks' credit supply to firms. For every €1 billion borrowed from the LRTO by banks from 2012 to 2013, an extra €186 million was injected by those banks into the real economy.

Credit crunches are an inevitable part of the credit cycle. They are, to use the well-known phrase, a feature, not a bug. Only effective prudential policies to stop unsustainable credit buildups can lessen their impact on the real economy.

STEPHEN KINSELLA

Credit Default Swaps

A credit default swap (CDS) is a contract which operates very much like an insurance policy. CDS contracts are extremely complicated. They are opaque to most market participants, and that creates a problem. CDS's exist for a wide variety of entities – government and corporate.

Say a government issues a bond. Many entities, for example companies and pension funds, purchase the government's bond, thereby lending the government money. But if the government has a history of sovereign defaults – say, for example, Argentina – the entities want to make sure they don't get burned if the government defaults. They buy a credit default swap from a third party. This third party agrees to pay the outstanding amount of the bond. The third party is often an insurance company, bank, or hedge fund. The swap seller collects premiums, just like a simple insurance company, for providing the swap. The buyer of the CDS enjoys protection from the loss caused by a default event, in return for paying the issuer of the CDS. Because a CDS itself has value until the term of the contract ends, it can also be traded. There are no exchanges for these trades, and it makes measuring the true value of the CDS market difficult, but not impossible.

CDS were unregulated until 2009. The market for CDS expanded rapidly during the 1990s. It then increased tenfold from 2000 to 2008, and after the global financial crisis, shrank. The market has seen a continuous decline after peaking at roughly $61.2 trillion at the end of 2007 to less than $9.2 trillion today.

The reason for this is increased regulation, combined with glaring examples of defaults – often called credit events – that never paid out. A credit event occurs when there is a substantial, identifiable loss. Credit events applicable to governments, banks, and companies are failures to pay out on outstanding debt or restructuring of their debt. When Spanish bank Banco Popular and Portugal's Novo Banco got into trouble, their supervisory authorities and national governments ensured there was no 'event of default' trigger that would lead to large CDS payouts. The CDS contract was therefore not worth the paper it was printed on. There have also been manufactured defaults, where a company holding a CDS engineered its own default to trigger a CDS payout. These have naturally increased distrust in the CDS as a product.

CDS are not just tools for bankers to make money for themselves. Their establishment allows for the backing out from their price a market perception of the likelihood of default. As the Celtic Tiger period ended, they were used to help price Ireland's sovereign debt. For Ireland, the rising CDS market price was used as an indicator it should enter an IMF bailout in 2010. Because buyers of a CDS were paying for insurance against a credit event on the underlying government debt, they were extremely interested in whether countries like Ireland, Greece, Spain, and Italy would default. CDS spreads – the difference between prices could buy and sell the contracts at – widened in response to news about the dire state of some of the economies. The resulting negative news needlessly worsened the outlook for Ireland and other peripheral countries.

The CDS is a perfect example of a financial innovation that was not, in fact, an innovation. They are damaging products that produce little or no value for society, except for the bankers who produce and market them.

SHAEN CORBET

Credit Rating Agencies

One of the most controversial issues that arose during the beginning of the collapse of the Celtic Tiger was based firmly on the role of the major international credit rating agencies. Quite simply, it was considered a fair question to ask what exactly they were thinking when offering advice about the widespread threats that faced Ireland both domestically and abroad.

Rating agencies had been stuck in quite a dilemma. Their key duty is to identify the main issues associated with the financial company or country under observation, offering a realistic view of their short-term viability, given the accumulation or absence of viable threats. The rating agency, should they have uncovered a detrimental result, must then decide whether to release such news, which could then trigger market panic, or they could choose to issue a negative outlook and proceed to monitor the situation for another short period of time. On an international level, this is what occurred, as some rating agencies issued vague warnings and expressed concerns relating to the rapidly increasing levels of credit being tied up in subprime markets, along with threats to exporting nations due to sharp movements in both currency and commodity markets.

However, there was very little warning presented with regard to Irish markets. This lack of warning was generally observed as a signal by investors that there existed little threat to continued growth. But what about those in the private sector whose role it was to monitor associated risk? We have repeatedly observed that financial markets themselves have the capacity to significantly misprice bubbles. There appeared to be a widespread belief that the markets were self-regulating. Credit rating agencies received significant negative attention in the aftermath of the international financial crises. It is considered that their actions possessed significant reverberations throughout financial markets.

The deterioration in Anglo Irish Bank was widely evident, supported by the sharp collapse in asset value from mid-2007 to late 2008, but all three major credit agencies (Standard and Poor, Moodys and Fitch) continued to denote Anglo as possessing investment grade status, up to very shortly before the point of nationalisation. Taking on board that significant negative international commentary did exist in credit rating reports in 2008, it was not until January 2009, the point of the nationalisation of Anglo, that the first significant downgrade of Anglo's credit rating occurred. This also acts as evidence that even large credit rating agencies were not in a position to correctly analyse Anglo's effective risk, particularly because of the tactics that were used to withdraw evidence of strife from Anglo's public accounts. Moody's downgraded Anglo to 'junk' status, and were the quickly followed by Fitch and then SP. By March 2009, Moody's and Fitch's ratings considered Anglo to be in default. SP during this time did not choose to downgrade Anglo to this category.

On a sovereign level, Ireland continued to be downgraded sharply throughout the period 2009 through 2012, further leading to increased borrowing costs, not to mention the associated negativity surrounding such news. The key risks were found to be a pronounced weakness in the economic activity, which translated into a severe deterioration of Ireland's public finances, with the country facing a considerably higher debt burden for the foreseeable future. The particularly negative outlook was primarily based on the view that Ireland would necessitate more financing before it could return to the private market, with an ever-growing possibility that even more liquidity would be needed following the end of the current EU/IMF support programme at year-end 2013.

In light of this, the role played by credit rating agencies, not just in Ireland, but across the world, had greatly diminished with far less attention paid to their views in the years after the collapse of the Celtic Tiger. Taking into consideration that market participants allow fair scope for error from the agency's selected methodologies, the credit agencies for the most part completely missed both the depth of the international subprime crisis and the scale and severity of the collapse of the Celtic Tiger. Trust in such views may never be fully restored in the future.

SARAH KELLEHER

Cross, Dorothy

For three weeks during February 1999, in the waters off the coast of Dun Laoghaire, a spectral vision appeared, glowing green against the night sky. The *Ghost Ship* was a gigantic temporary artwork by Dorothy Cross, one of Ireland's most fêted contemporary artists. Every evening the *Albatross*, a decommissioned light ship coated in phosphorescent paint, was exposed to UV light and then left to glow and fade over the course of three hours. The *Ghost Ship*, based on Cross's childhood memories of the sea, was her most public project and its reception the most broad-based and enthusiastic. The *Ghost Ship* stands as one of the most ambitious and impactful artworks of the 1990s in terms of scale, and, as the recipient of the Nissan Art Project fund awarded jointly by IMMA, one of the most generously sponsored. As such, *Ghost Ship* speaks to the burgeoning confidence in and ambition for contemporary Irish art practice. It is also lastingly significant as a marker of the changing nature of an Irish engagement with the sea.

By 1999, Cross was firmly established as one of Ireland's most important artists. Her sculptures used unconventional materials such as cows' udders to skewer cultural stereotypes relating to both gender and reductive readings of Irish national experience and were collected by institutions such as Tate Britain. Cross's career epitomises a moment when contemporary Irish art arrived on the international stage; in its focus on gender and post-colonial identity, Irish practice was in step with international norms, as critique of identities in previously marginalised societies like Ireland became central to contemporary cultural debates around the globe. However, the trajectory of Cross' career also speaks to a pronounced change in ambition palpable during the decade in terms of positioning Irish visual culture internationally. In 1993 for example, Cross, along with Willie Doherty from Derry, represented Ireland at the Venice Biennale, the world's preeminent stage for contemporary art, the first time that Ireland had supported a delegation of artists in 30 years.

Equally, by the 1990s, public art had become a regular feature of the Irish landscape thanks largely to the National Lottery and the '% for Art' levy imposed on all major building projects in the Republic. The Nissan Art Project initiated by the Executive Chairman of Nissan Ireland, Gerard O'Toole, and supported by IMMA, was designed to assist artists to make temporary, site-specific artworks outside the confines of the art gallery. The Nissan initiative also exemplifies a period of increased corporate sponsorship of the arts, building from AIB's drive to acquisition and investment in their art collection which started in 1980, and developing into culture-fuelled corporate promotion in events such as the Glen Dimplex Prize, held annually in IMMA from 1994 to 2001. Such sponsorship events reached a high-water mark with the Nissan Art Project for the Millennium, when the company pledged £100,000 for an open competition, ultimately won by Dan Shipsides' *Bamboo Support*, a temporary bamboo scaffolding attached to the Carlton Cinema Building on Dublin's O'Connell Street.

Despite its scale and dramatic impact, however, *Ghost Ship* was designed by Cross as an elegy rather than as a *son et lumière* spectacle. The *Ghost Ship*, she wrote in her submission, 'refers to the memory of the lightships whose role and presence were held dear around the Irish coast'. The vessel in question, the *Albatross*, was a relic of a period of Irish navigation history. Lightships had been located around the Irish coast to mark dangerous reefs that were too deep to allow for lighthouses. During the 1970s, most of the lightships were decommissioned and replaced by satellite buoys. However, *Ghost Ship* was less a memorial to an outmoded technology than it was a marker of the changing reality of the Irish experience of, or relationship to, nature and to the sea. As art historian Fionna Barber points out, the decade's numerous changes included a shift away from ideas of the land and the sea as dominating a sense of Irish identity and towards an increasing concern with the urban and the modern. The changing economic realities of the 1990s and 2000s hastened what had been a gradual population shift from the countryside to suburban and city living, and from the coast inwards towards the cities. As Cross argued in her artist's statement, 'The Irish coastline is being neutralised, atomised, Europeanised'. Indeed, the artist's antipathy to the increasing globalisation of Irish life registers a distinct current of anxiety surrounding a sense of displacement, one that finds echo in Séan Hillen's *Irelantis* satires. It is also tempting to extend the *Ghost Ship* metaphorical capacity still further, the glowing and fading phantasm functioning as both mirage and a warning of the brief and ultimately transitory phenomenon of the Celtic Tiger.

EOIN FLANNERY

Debt

Indebtedness is a form of future-capture; it often draws upon past economic or financial performance as a means of access to credit, but once such access has been granted, it hijacks the future of those who are indebted. In Ireland during the Celtic Tiger, such indebtedness commonly took the form of property purchases at premium prices.

Home ownership was not viewed as in a way punitive; rather, investment in the future was encouraged. The latter idea here of 'investment in the future' is the primary watchword of the debt economy, as consumers are solicited to burden themselves with mortgages. Yet 'investment in the future' is a little more than a metaphor, and its very figurative qualities were, and are, employed to soften, even shroud, the material precarity of substantial indebtedness.

Of course, flouting of regulations by mortgage lenders and an abdication of regulatory oversight permitted a critical intensification of debt creation, a point highlighted by Peter Nyberg in his subsequent report on the Irish banking crisis. In this report, Nyberg underscored the high-risk latitude given to property investors across the market as one of the primary causes of the financial crash experienced in Ireland. In sum, lending was more important than any sense of adherence to sectoral regulations.

A report produced by the Economic and Social Research Institute (ESRI) accepted that there was consented to view that: '(1) Personal debt in Ireland is very high relative to historic experience and (2) the pace of borrowing has persistently surprised on the upside and (3) there are few signs of an early turnaround in this trend'.

As global wholesale money markets became more accessible to financial institutions in Ireland from the late 1990s onwards, the supply of credit, and hence the capacity for individuals to assume mortgage and non-mortgage indebtedness, increased. In fact, in his analysis of borrowing outside the property sector in Ireland, the economist Seamus Coffey has illustrated that there were staggering increases in the levels of borrowing. Coffey notes that, 'loans to Irish residents rose from €83 billion in January 2003 to €195 billion by the end of 2008. This is still a rapid rise but is an increase of 135% rather than the 220% increase seen for all loans [including property and construction]. As a percentage of GDP loans outside of investment in the property sector rose from 66% of GDP in 2003 to 108% of GDP in 2008'. The rapidity with which indebtedness became, and remains, a staple of everyday economic activity, and subsistence, in Ireland during the Celtic Tiger is of primary concern when one reflects upon the differential cultural responses to this period of crisis.

While the Irish State's public indebtedness also reached unsustainable heights, at a personal level debt became a way of life, an experience of everyday living and an informing factor of individual performances of identity in Ireland during the short-lived, but now recrudescent, economic 'boom' of the Celtic Tiger era. The new gilded forms of Irish identity, together with the re-branding of Ireland as an entrepreneurial global citadel of consumerism during the Celtic Tiger period, cannot be disentangled from the country's implication in the global debt economy of the new era of financialisation. The displays and manifestations of economic and cultural assertiveness in the present are little more than economic fetters that persist into the future, beyond the fugacious plenty of the present moment.

JOHN O'CONNOR

Design and the Celtic Tiger

We have always had a tenuous relationship with the visual in Ireland. Words we understand and even respect: for example, we delight in the wit of Swift and Wilde, the bold modernism of Joyce and Beckett, the poetry of Yeats and Heaney, the drama of Friel. The Irish are rightly renowned for the unique contribution they have made to the English language. Clearly, visual culture does not enjoy anything like the same popularity or standing as literature in Ireland. And then, at the bottom of the visual heap, we have design. Variously referred to as decorative art or commercial art, the concept of design as a process never gained any real traction in Ireland until recently. Even haute couture fashion designers like Sybil Connolly were celebrated for their fame and connections and revered as having harnessed the mysterious and elusive power of creativity rather than accepted as serious entrepreneurs and business people.

Marketing practice was professionalised in the latter half of the twentieth century and its role has been accepted by the Irish business community since then, but the central role of design in strategic development was not accorded the same regard. Since the demise of the state-sponsored Kilkenny Design Workshops in 1988, major national brands viewed design as a subset of advertising. When they bothered with design at all, the major Dublin advertising agencies enjoyed the jaunt across the pond to retain London-based design consultancies. Significant brand development projects, such as the design of the AIB logotype in 1990 by Wolff Olins, were commissioned in London much to the dismay of Irish design firms. Nevertheless, a vibrant and professional design sector had emerged by the time the Celtic Tiger came into its own and new representative organisations such as Design Business Ireland along with the state-supported promotional body Design Ireland came into being. By the time Telecom Éireann was privatised as Eircom in 1999 the branding project was won by Irish design company, The Identity Business.

During the Tiger years, the design sector began to move from the margins, from simply being a business-to-business activity. Design was now adopted by the successful elite not solely for its contribution to profitability but because it supported the manifestation of their good taste. The increasing availability of significant disposable income accompanied by the desire to parade success explicitly led to a developing focus on design in the consumer sector. Home interior design, fashion, retail outlet design and other consumer facing activities began to recognise the opportunity and the design sector responded. This also coincided with, and was fed by, an increasing awareness among global corporations of the importance of design thinking as a mechanism for releasing innovative and disruptive approaches in product and service development. The lack of understanding in Ireland regarding what was truly innovative about companies, like Apple and Google as they developed entirely new ecosystems around their services as a result of being design-led, resulted in a fascination with the outputs and products of design. This is not to say that Apple and its global competitors were above confusing consumers by aligning good design with the luxury brand approach. However, in Celtic Tiger Ireland the emphasis was largely on the luxury product as a demonstration of consumer power coupled with an almost desperate attempt to claim innate good taste.

The national hangover suffered across the county following the Celtic Tiger excesses decimated the design sector, with many companies going to the wall. The real value placed on design by Irish industry was revealed: it was the first service to be cut. Since then design has changed irrevocably in Ireland. The growth of UX (user-focused) design and the recognition of the importance of a strategic design-focus by the global service sector has led to significant employment opportunities that did not previously exist. The state celebrated design by designating 2015 as the Year of Irish Design which culminated in the formation of the government-led National Design Forum. So, in a very real sense, the demise of the Celtic Tiger may be said to have triggered a national response that may prove to be every bit as innovative and farseeing as that of the launch of the national design service in 1963.

MÁIRTÍN MAC CON IOMAIRE

Dining Out

Dining out during the 1980s in Ireland could be summarised gastronomically by prawn cocktails, Chicken Maryland, Black Forest gateau and bottles of Blue Nun or Mateus Rosé. All this changed with the Celtic Tiger when the Irish public was introduced to Caesar salad, tomato and fennel bread, tapenade and Chardonnay. From 1989 to 1993, Restaurant Patrick Guilbaud was like a lone beacon of consistency in the Irish edition of the Michelin Guide. However, in 1994, five Michelin stars were awarded on the island of Ireland. Change was afoot. Many young Irish chefs and waiters emigrated during the 1980s although some, such as Kevin Thornton, Michael Clifford, Ross Lewis, Robbie Millar and Paul Rankin, returned during the late 1980s and early 1990s with knowledge of *nouvelle cuisine* and fusion cuisine gained in the leading restaurants of London, Paris, New York, California and Canada. They brought a new energy and confidence to the Irish restaurant industry on their return. Both Rankin and Clifford trained with the Roux Brothers in London, and Thornton with Paul Bocuse in Lyon. In 1988, Clifford left White's on the Green in Dublin to open his own restaurant in Cork.

The late 1980s and early 1990s saw the opening of exciting new restaurants in Dublin such as The Wine Epergne (Kevin Thornton) and Clarets (Alan O'Reilly), both of which produced fine dining in difficult economic conditions. They were joined by Ernie Evans of Towers Hotel in Glenbeigh, who opened 'Ernie's' in Donnybrook. During the Celtic Tiger years, clusters of award-winning restaurants appeared in Dublin, Cork, Kerry and Belfast, with individual restaurants emerging in a number of other counties around Ireland. A vegetarian restaurant, 'Café Paradiso', opened by Denis Cotter in Cork, was considered to be among the country's finest dining establishments. Restaurants run by a chef/proprietor were becoming the norm, though not all were financially successful. The demise of Colin O'Daly's The Park in

Blackrock opened an opportunity for him in Roly's Bistro, which became a mecca for Irish diners during the economic boom years.

One factor which led to the growing popularity of dining out in Irish restaurants, and the rising status of Irish chefs, was the growth in food writing in the national press from the 1980s. Restaurant reviewers such as Helen Lucy Burke in the *Sunday Tribune* became influential in the industry. New publications such as *Food and Wine Magazine* also profiled Irish chefs, reviewed restaurants and presided over annual award ceremonies, which helped transform chefs from unseen labourers into minor celebrities.

John McKenna, writing in *The Irish Times*, reported in 1996 that Ireland had the most dynamic cuisine of any European country. Factors influencing this new vitality included the rising wealth of Irish citizens, which made dining in restaurants a regular pastime rather than an occasional treat, and also the changing tastes of a public who were more widely travelled than any previous Irish generation. In 1996, the year Michelin awarded two stars to Restaurant Patrick Guilbaud, Thornton's Restaurant in Portobello received its first star. In 1998, another Michelin star was awarded to Conrad Gallagher's Peacock Alley in Dublin. Gallagher's brash self-confidence and his use of the media, is emblematic of the Celtic Tiger era. His meteoric rise to fame and fortune was matched by his equally well-publicised fall from grace. In 1999, the chief executive of the Restaurant Association of Ireland (RAI) declared 'we have a dining culture now, which we never did before'.

In 2001, Kevin Thornton became the first Irish chef to be awarded two Michelin stars. In the first years of the new millennium, Michelin stars were awarded in Dublin to L'Écrivain (Derry Clarke) and to Chapter One (Ross Lewis), which had both held Red 'M's from the mid-1990s. Two new Michelin stars were awarded in 2008 to Bon Appétit (Oliver Dunne) in Malahide, and to Mint (Dylan McGrath) in Ranelagh. Both Dunne and McGrath trained in Ireland's best restaurants, as well as in London with Gordon Ramsay, Tom Aikens and John Burton Race. The food of these award-winning Irish chefs is often described as 'new Irish cooking' in that it champions local, seasonal, often artisan ingredients or food, and presents them with their own individual flair. McGrath's Mint restaurant became the first high-profile closure of the recession. However, many believe that the recession was a positive development for Irish food culture and restaurants, in that it pushed Irish chefs to be more creative and to do more with less. Dining out in Ireland actually continued to rise during the recession. In January 2011, *Le Guide du Routard*, the travel bible for the French-speaking world, praised Ireland's restaurants for being unmatched the world over for the combination of quality of food, value and service. The Celtic Tiger played a large role in this transformation of dining in Ireland.

FINOLA KENNEDY

Divorce: 'Till Debt Do Us Part'

To begin with, some good news about the Celtic Tiger: between 1994 and 2006, National Debt fell by €1 billion from €37 billion to €36 billion. Then between 2006 and 2009 national debt more than doubled, a feat previously matched by Garret FitzGerald's government in the difficult 1980s. Since 2009, national debt has increased fourfold and now stands at in excess of €200 billion. The ratio of debt to GDP may fall as a result of economic growth but this does not alter the fact that interest on the debt represents over €3,000 in tax revenue per year for each worker.

When a couple decides to get married their debt focus is much more likely to be on mortgage debt than on national debt. In the Celtic Tiger years mortgages could be obtained with minimal deposits. One of the consequences was a surge in borrowing and a subsequent wave of repossessions following the crash. Household debt which was 51% of GDP in 2002 soared to 118% of GDP in 2009. It now (2019) stands at 74%. In absolute terms, total household debt is now close to €160 billion or in excess of €34,000 for every person living in Ireland.

Over the longer term marriage tends to move with economic growth. More people marry when times are good. It is interesting to observe that as debt levels rose so too did the age at marriage. Marriage is at least being delayed. In 1994 the average age for a man at marriage was just under 30 years and for a woman just under 28 years. By the end of the Celtic Tiger these ages had risen to 33.4 and 31.3 years respectively. By 2014 they had risen further to 35 and 33 years. Thus over the 20-year period from the start of the Celtic Tiger in 1994, the average age at marriage rose by 5 years for both men and women.

There are many reasons to postpone marriage or to choose not to marry apart from any questions related to debt or financial insecurity. Many more people choose to cohabit and many more births take place outside marriage, some to cohabiting couples and some to single mothers. In 1994, one in five births was outside marriage. This had risen to one in three in 2014. In Limerick City one in two births is outside marriage.

Since 1996 it is possible to obtain a divorce when a marriage breaks down. The number of divorces grew steadily during the Celtic Tiger years, peaking at 3,684 in 2007. The rate is low compared to other EU countries. A factor often cited in divorce cases is financial pressure. Remarriage following divorce has increased and is partly reflected in the marked rise in the share of civil marriages over the Celtic Tiger years. By 2013, just 30% of marriages were civil marriages.

Social patterns are changing. Since the advent of the Celtic Tiger the number of one-earner households has fallen while the number of dual earner households has increased. More mothers are in the work force whether by choice or economic necessity to service the mortgage and pay the bills. Probably relatively few households could manage a mortgage on one income. On the other hand the number of one-person households rose throughout the Celtic Tiger years. Among the younger age cohort this may have reflected an earlier move from the family home perhaps into rented property or undertaking, what proved for many, a high-risk mortgage. At the other end of the age spectrum, one in four persons over 65 now lives alone, reflecting longer life expectancy.

The coming generation is faced with a serious debt legacy, not only in terms of household debt but also their share in the tax burden due to servicing the national debt. There is little capacity or incentive to save. Debt makes its own demands. Household debt appears to be more under control but national debt continues to increase. Debt has not gone away and needs to be addressed by policy makers.

MEGAN GREENE

ECB

The European Central Bank conducts monetary policy for the Eurozone with a mandate of maintaining price stability, or inflation close to, but just below, 2%. Its capital stock is held by the national central banks of member states and the ECB is governed by a governing council comprised of national central bank governors from all the member states and six executive board members.

The ECB is somewhat different from other central banks in that it is not a clear lender of last resort to the banks; lending in the Eurozone is decentralised, with loans coming from the national central banks. If the loan is defaulted on and collateral does not cover the loss, then the losses are shared by the entire Eurosystem. When banks have used up all their eligible collateral to obtain funds from the ECB but still need to borrow more, they can give non-eligible collateral to their national central bank in exchange for Emergency Liquidity Assistance (ELA).

ELA is one extraordinary monetary policy measure that the ECB employed during the euro crisis, and Irish banks were one of the biggest recipients. Other extraordinary measures included the Securities Markets Programme (SMP) and finally in 2014 quantitative easing (QE). The ECB was often the swiftest institution to act in the euro crisis because of its independence. That being said, the ECB still arguably had political facets.

Ireland was exposed to some of these political tendencies during the crisis on at least two occasions. In late 2011, Irish banks were kept on life support by billions in ELA from the ECB. In a letter to then Irish Finance Minister Brian Lenihan, on November 19, 2010, ECB President Jean-Claude Trichet said that the central bank could not continue to extend ELA assistance to Irish banks that seemed insolvent unless the country entered a bailout programme. Ireland requested a bailout two days later.

In 2011, the ECB also weighed in on the Irish government guarantee of Irish bank debt. The Irish government had provided a guarantee of all Irish bank debt in 2008 in order to shore up investor confidence in the banks. The guarantee expired in 2010 and there was a debate about whether to impose losses on some of the senior bondholders in Anglo Irish Bank. Mr Trichet told the new Irish coalition government in 2011 that an 'economic bomb would go off in Dublin' if Anglo Irish bondholders were burned, and consequently senior bondholders were not forced to accept any losses.

The ECB's failure to operate as a clear and comprehensive lender of last resort most likely made the euro crisis deeper and longer. There has been an attempt to address this by creating a banking union with a common set of regulations, a single supervisory body, a common source of funding for bank resolution and a common deposit insurance scheme across the Eurozone. So far, the first two items have been established but the other factors remain elusive.

MEGAN GREENE

Economists

Ireland was truly unique in the Eurozone for the level of sophistication of understanding the population had for political and economic analysis during the economic crisis. From passport control agents to makeup specialists to taxi drivers, seemingly everyone could deliver a cogent rant about Irish government bond yields in 2010–11. There is even an economics comedy festival, Kilkenomics, held in Kilkenny every autumn where mainly Irish laymen travel to attend panels of economists (moderated by comedians to ensure that minimal jargon is used).

This cultural underpinning allowed a group of 'celebrity economists' (a term coined by Garret FitzGerald in 2011) to emerge in Ireland leading up to and during the financial crisis. One definition identifies celebrity economists as economists more often cited in the media and social media, than by fellow economists in academic papers.

Celebrity economists during the global financial crisis were certainly not unique to Ireland – the United States, for example, had the likes of Nouriel Roubini, Paul Krugman and Jaimie Galbraith. However, Ireland racked up a list of celebrity economists longer than that of any other country. At the top of virtually every list in Ireland was David McWilliams, who at the height of the crisis was not only providing policy advice to the government, but also appeared on bus stop ads for cider clad in a leather jacket.

The main criticism of celebrity economists in Ireland was that they were not well placed to offer policy advice to decision makers in the throes of one of the country's greatest ever crises. This is undoubtedly at least partly correct. David McWilliams, for example, gave then Finance Minister, Brian Lenihan, the idea of the fateful bank guarantee in 2008 (and then retroactively offered scathing criticism on how the government implemented it).

However, there was some overlap between celebrity and academic economists in Ireland during the crisis. Morgan Kelly, for example, is a Professor of Economics at University College Dublin. He fell squarely in the academic economist genre until he wrote a series of columns for *The Irish Times* correctly predicting both the Irish property crash and the swiftness with which it would decimate Ireland's banks. This arguably earned Mr Kelly celebrity economist status in Ireland even as he shunned the limelight. Phillip Lane, an employee at the Central Bank of Ireland, also appeared in some Irish celebrity economists rankings but now is not only the governor of the Central Bank of Ireland, but is also the Chief Economist at the ECB – both highly academic institutions.

Even when a clear delineation between celebrity and academic economists can be drawn, it does not necessarily hold that academic economists can provide better policy advice than those who appear more in the media. Much of the theoretical underpinnings of academic economic literature has very little bearing to the real world. Celebrity economists were at the forefront of highlighting during the crisis that the relationship between the economic theory and practice of the crisis did not always add up. This has become even more the case in the aftermath of the crisis as the developed world has sustained a long, sluggish recovery.

JOHN MCDONAGH

Electric Gates in the Celtic Tiger

In March 2017, a lavish, 10,000 square foot property, Gorse Hill, on Vico Road in Howth, was placed on the market at an eye-watering €8.5 million. The O'Donnell family had resisted one of the highest profile evictions in the state since the onset of the crash in 2008, fighting Bank of Ireland all the way to the Supreme Court before being forced to leave and sell their home over unpaid debts of over €70 million. In 2006, the house was valued at over €21 million and much of the debt was raised against the seemingly inexorable rising value of the property, a common occurrence in the overheated market of the Celtic Tiger era.

In the latter stages of the long-running and high-profile media saga, the O'Donnells found unlikely allies in the New Land League, a latter-day version of Michael Davitt's nineteenth-century anti-eviction resistance movement. Nightly news reports featured its founder, Jerry Beades, disappearing behind the large imposing timber electric gates of Gorse Hill, pursued by journalists and TV cameras, all desperate for a glimpse of this icon of the boom. The repossession of Gorse Hill appeared to embody the attempt to make someone pay for all the excesses of the banking crisis, a trophy house of a family whose 1 billion property empire exemplified the worst extravagances of the era.

The assembled media, therefore, were confronted on a daily basis by the impressive 8ft tall electric gate, its opening heralded by a flashing orange light and electric buzzer. The privacy and security afforded by this gate was undeniable, and for a time, on the nightly news, the gate all but insulated a one-time property billionaire and poster-boy of the Celtic Tiger from the prying eyes of a society desperate to find those culpable for the banking implosion of late 2008. Perhaps O'Donnell was something of a visionary after all.

Between 1998 and 2000, according to the CSO, house prices in Ireland rose by 29.8%, 17.9% and 21.3% respectively. Small rural towns within commuting distance of the more expensive urban centres began to witness the emergence of mini-suburbs, new estates of tens to hundreds of houses, projects often funded by generous government tax breaks that were very often disproportionate to the needs of the local population. The necessity to maintain this unsustainable level of building, despite clear signs of overheating in the market, led to a spectacular collapse in house prices after the crash in 2008. At its height, in 2010, it was estimated that there were over 600 ghost estates in Ireland, with nearly 30,000 empty and often derelict houses. These unsustainable developments were supplemented by the building of large, detached houses, with sweeping stone driveways and imposing entrances.

These trophy houses, out of character with their modest Bungalow Bliss-inspired 1960s and 1970s predecessors, mimicked their classic Georgian and Edwardian counterparts, with half-moon collonaded entrances leading to sweeping serpentine driveways. However, it was the now ubiquitous electric gate, complete with neon-blue intercom and keypad, that became the ultimate symbol of the property-addicted Celtic Tiger *arrivistes*. Like a contemporary version of the *Star Trek* swooshing doors, the electric gate embodied the pretentiousness of required privacy as well as technological savvy, bequeathing the owner with an aura of social importance and monetary wealth. Indeed, the electric gates clearly indicated that there was something valuable behind it that necessitated their installation. This electric portcullis was an integral part of the optics of the Celtic Tiger, built as they were on an illusion of wealth, despite the fact that their very proliferation eventually diluted the initial effect.

These self-closing gates kept people out and clearly signaled to the casual observer that the era of the open door, of dropping in unannounced to your neighbours, was over. The gates symbolised the increased individualisation of the Celtic Tiger era, and were yet another manifestation of the extent to which the physical landscape of the country was changed by the arrival of cheap and easily borrowed money. Alongside the outdoor hot-tub and the gadget-laden SUV, the electric gate represented a tangible sign of prosperity that any would-be visitor was likely to notice. In *The Pope's Children* (2005), David Mc Williams's referred to what he termed the 'decklanders', a Celtic Tiger manifestation of wealth that noted the proliferation of new outdoor wooden decking visible in the gardens of Ireland in the 1990s, and the electric gate is an equally if not more readily associated icon of the Celtic Tiger *Zeitgeist*.

In Percy Shelley's 1818 poem 'Ozymandias', a traveller recalls a visit to a desert where he saw the ruins of a once impressive statue. Two huge legs of stone are all that remain, as well as 'on the sand / Half sunk a shattered visage lies'. The mutability of wealth and the transience of power are the dominant themes of Shelley's prescient sonnet, and it can certainly be argued that the electric gate embodies a manifestation of the words of warning engraved on the plinth of this decaying monument: 'Look on my works, ye mighty, and despair'. The self-importance and ultimate ephemerality of power and wealth, manifested in atrophying objects, is just one of the many legacies of the Celtic Tiger era, and the electric-gated, ghost-estate stands as a tangible representation of Ireland's 'colossal wreck'.

MEGAN GREENE

Emergency Liquidity Assistance (ELA)

When euro area banks have come under strain, they have borrowed from the ECB via refinancing operations by stumping up collateral in exchange for the loans. When put under severe strain, some of these banks have run out of collateral, and have had to use non-eligible collateral with large haircuts in order to receive loans from the Eurosystem in the form of Emergency Liquidity Assistance (ELA).

Even though a number of ELA programmes existed in the Eurozone at the beginning of the crisis, the ECB did not offer an official description of how they worked until late 2013. ELA programmes are not actually ECB programmes – they are unilaterally issued by a national central bank to banks deemed to be solvent and the ECB is informed within two days of the operation being carried out. The ECB's governing council can then decide with a two-thirds majority vote to reject the ELA programme for interfering with the objectives of the Eurosystem. If losses are incurred because of ELA programmes, they fall on the national central bank rather than the Eurosystem as a whole.

Irish, Greek and Cypriot banks were the largest recipients of ELA during the euro crisis. Even after its nationalisation in early 2009, Anglo Irish Bank suffered from severe deposit outflows, and so the Central Bank of Ireland decided to shore Anglo Irish up with €11.5 billion in ELA in March 2009. Over the course of the following 18 months, all six Irish banks came under pressure from deposit outflows and applied for ELA. By November 2010, total Eurosystem funding for Irish banks amounted to roughly 85% of Irish GDP, and a quarter of total Eurosystem lending. Ireland's ELA programme only ended in February 2013, when Anglo Irish's successor organisation, the Irish Bank Resolution Corporation, was put into liquidation.

Ireland's ELA programme played a role in the Irish bailout. On November 19, 2010, ECB president Jean-Claude Juncker sent a letter to

Brian Lenihan saying that the ECB could no longer support insolvent institutions and threatening to cut Irish banks off from the ELA programme if Ireland did not request a bailout. The Irish government requested a bailout two days later.

The provision of ELA programmes is problematic in that the ECB claims not to be in charge of them but then has the power to shut them off. ELA programmes were developed when national central banks supervised banks and so it made sense that those banks that got into trouble were the responsibility of national central banks and so the risks associated with lending to them should be borne at the national level. Now there is a European-level supervisor, the Single Supervisory Mechanism (SSM), ECB and all Eurozone banks are forced to undergo European-level asset quality reviews and stress tests. Addressing this could reduce the opportunity for the ECB to intervene to influence political outcomes in the Eurozone.

CONSTANTIN GURDGIEV

Entrepreneurship

Entrepreneurship is defined as 'the capacity and willingness to develop, organise and manage a business venture along with any of its risks in order to make a profit. The most obvious example of entrepreneurship is the starting of new businesses'.

When it comes to the Celtic Tiger, this traditional definition has to be expanded to also include rent-seeking (pursuit of subsidies, state contracts, and supports), and rampantly speculative real estate development. Modern Irish entrepreneurs can thus be divided into several, sometimes-overlapping categories. On the one hand, there is a large number of genuinely creative and value-additive entrepreneurs who built successful, sustainable financially and economically (although not always socially or environmentally) companies like Ryanair, Cooley Distillery, Superquinn, Jordan Grand Prix, Stripe, Altech, and others. On the other, there is an equally formidable army of Irish entrepreneurs who have gone from being rich to becoming bankrupt, and making and losing fortunes in real estate development and speculation. The third, and perhaps more Celtic Tiger-proximate tribe of Irish entrepreneurs, are the rent-seeking, state-connected leaders of businesses that built their wealth on exploiting Irish governments' penchant for financial and tax engineering, and in some instances cronyism and corruption that permeate Irish society.

The power of the first group of entrepreneurs drove both the original Celtic Tiger and the real, tangible economic progress over the last two and a half decades. In contrast, speculative and state-reliant entrepreneurs and real estate developers have been responsible for asset bubble inflation and subsequent crises linked to the dot.com blowout, the Global Financial Crisis fallout in Ireland, and the subsequent Sovereign Debt crisis and the Great Recession.

DARRAGH FLANNERY

ESRI

The Economic and Social Research Institute (ESRI) was founded in 1960 by a group of civil servants led by TK Whitaker, the then Secretary of the Department of Finance. It has a commitment to independent research, free from government or political influence; however, it does receive around 25% of its funding from the government. While the institute conducts research across a range of topics such as health, education and the labour market, one of the most prominent areas of focus is the macro-economic modelling of the Irish economy.

Using the HERMES macro model, this helps forecast, among other things, the future economic growth, unemployment rate and debt to GDP ratio of the Irish economy, and forms the basis for publications such as the Medium Term Review and Quarterly Economic Commentary. With the onset of the banking and public expenditure crisis in 2008–9, these reports came into greater focus. In its Medium Term Review No. 10 published in 2005, the ESRI noted that 'The Irish economy is now exceptionally dependent on the building industry for growth and employment', while also drawing attention to the broader economic implications for a downturn in the construction sector and suggested some government policies that may alleviate such a decline.

While this may be seen as a clear warning to policy makers of the eventual collapse of the sector later that decade, the same report also outlined that 'in spite of the dangers that exist, the Irish economy is basically robust and can look forward to an average growth rate in GNP per head of around 2% a year out to the end of the next decade'. The report also made no mention of exposure of the Irish banking system to such a collapse. This was also true of their Medium Term Review No. 11 published in the summer of 2008. While this report did again acknowledge some of the potential dangers facing the Irish economy at the time, it also outlined that 'the essential message of this Review is that the economy will eventually rebound, and return to its medium-term growth path'. A similar theme is evidenced in the institute's Quarterly Economic Commentary of summer 2008. It is noteworthy that the institute's summer 2007 Quarterly Economic Commentary contained a special article by UCD economist Professor Morgan Kelly outlining the likely extent of falls in Irish house prices as well as the causes and consequences of such a fall.

Some useful insight into the ESRI across this period was gained by the appearance of Professor John FitzGerald at the Oireachtas Banking Inquiry in 2015. Professor FitzGerald worked at the ESRI for 30 years and was heavily involved in the macroeconomic forecasting side of the institute. At the inquiry, he noted that the ESRI did highlight risks such as stimulatory fiscal policy, over-reliance on the construction sector and house price inflation in various reports from 2001 to 2008 but did not undertake any assessment of the banking sector on a formal basis (Banking Inquiry, 2016). Professor FitzGerald also spoke of seeking a meeting with the financial regulator in 2007 to raise concerns about the quality of stress tests faced by Irish banks at the time but never had such a meeting. He also suggested that he brought concerns about the potential overleveraged positions of Irish banks to the Central Bank but was not received positively. Perhaps most importantly, Professor FitzGerald stated that ESRI could have better alerted the government to the looming economic crisis.

DAVID BEGG

Euro

The flagship project of European integration was Economic and Monetary Union (EMU). While first advanced via the Werner Report in 1969, the project languished until after the Single European Act was passed in 1987. It was taken off the shelf, dusted down and represented in a different format by Commission President, Jacques Delors, in 1989. What really breathed life into it though was the prospect of German reunification consequent upon the fall of the Berlin Wall in 1990. Apprehensive at the prospect of a reunited Germany, and all that implied in a historical context, France promoted the idea of creating a 'European Germany', as distinct from the feared 'German Europe'.

The instrument by which EMU was ushered in was the Maastricht Treaty, which was signed on February 7, 1992 and came into force on November 1, 1993. The currencies of the member states of the Eurozone, including Ireland, were locked on January 1, 1999 and the euro came into being as the single currency in 2002. The period between the signing of the Maastricht Treaty and realisation of the single currency was a turbulent one. Major speculation in financial markets forced the British pound and the Italian Lira out of the Exchange Rate Mechanism (ERM), and the Irish Punt was devalued by 10% in 1993. This devaluation gave a major impetus to the emergence of the Celtic Tiger.

The European Central Bank (ECB) was set up in 1998. It is the most important institution of the European Union. It is a central bank without a fiscal counterpart. To soothe German fears that it would go too easy on inflation, it was modelled on the Bundesbank and based in Frankfurt. It was given the single objective of price stability, leaving growth and employment to be determined by market forces.

Clearly, Britain's decision to stay out of the single currency was a blow to Ireland. A large proportion of the domestically owned small business sector was critically dependent on the British market, as indeed it still is. While the latter consideration features largely in current public policy discourse about Brexit, it made much less of an impact in the considerations which led Ireland to participate in EMU.

An analysis of Dáil Éireann debates at the time reveals that the most common argument advanced was that the economic policy embedded in the Maastricht Treaty represented good economic governance, to which there was no sensible alternative. The consensus was broadly based across the political spectrum. It was, and continues to be, articulated as a non-negotiable external constraint.

The essential flaw of the single currency was elementary. In giving up their national currencies, Eurozone members lost important policy levers. This was to prove to be a major problem during the years of the Celtic Tiger. When interest rates converge, the rate may be too low for some countries, and such countries would experience rapid, credit-fuelled growth along with high inflation and a loss of international competitiveness. This is what happened to Ireland. The Irish economy constitutes only 1% of European GDP and interest rates set to suit countries like Germany are never likely to be appropriate for us. Irish policy makers could not use higher interest rates to cool an overheating economy, and especially the property markets, during the Celtic Tiger period.

Moreover, when the crash came in 2008, we could not devalue the currency as we had done in 1993. The burden of adjustment came instead through labour markets and public spending cuts: in a word – austerity. Unfortunately, the embedded ideology of EMU fails to accept the basic economic reality that fiscal austerity prolongs economic distress. There was an asymmetry to the ECB's policy. It was prepared to act to preserve price stability only if inflation went up, but not when it went down. In the end, Mario Draghi did realise that concerns over inflation were unfounded and in 2015 introduced quantitative easing (QE) to stave off deflation. Had that been done earlier, it would have avoided some pain.

But, as the former senior IMF official, Ashoka Mody, points out in his book *Euro Tragedy: A Drama in Nine Acts*, the original conundrum remains. A single monetary policy for diverse countries cannot operate effectively without a mechanism to share risks in crisis conditions. Eurozone leaders have not yet been able to agree to a risk-sharing mechanism based on a democratically legitimate political contract. Under pressure during the crisis years, they agreed on technical arrangements to share risk, no more than this. Such is the enduring vulnerability of the flagship project of European integration.

STEPHEN KINSELLA

Euro: Cause and Consequences

The Celtic Tiger proper lasted, roughly, from 1996 to 2002. The Euro was introduced towards the end of this period, and many argue that it created the conditions for the asset boom and bust which followed the Celtic Tiger, booming from 2003 to 2007, and then busting from 2008 to 2013.

The Euro was created to increase the degree of economic integration between member area countries of the EU. It followed the wave of increased economic integration the European Union had taken from the 1950s onward. The monetary union envisaged by the introduction of the Euro was not accompanied by the fiscal union required to recycle capital flows and to bailout systems more or less automatically.

The Irish decision to join the Euro was as much a political one as an economic one. Authors Patrick Honohan and Gavin Murphy have noted the tradeoff, 'While financial issues were to the fore in the discussions, the final decision to join was based on a strategic vision that Ireland's economic and political future lay with Europe, rather than the former colonial power'.

As of 2019, the common currency is shared by 19 of the EU 28 member states, and is used by well over 340 million people. The Euro, introduced in 2002, encouraged cross-border trade but did not reduce the dispersion of prices for products between states. Prices had in fact converged during the 1990s following the establishment of the EU's Single Market. The Euro did spur the increase of cross-border money flows between the banking systems of Europe, which resulted in the sometimes severe imbalances between member states receiving funds – those in deficit such as Ireland, Spain, Greece, Italy, and Portugal, and member states remitting funds – those in surplus, such as Germany, France, and Finland.

The introduction of the Euro coincided with a fall in the cost of funds across Europe, and this, combined with the availability of more funds in peripheral economies, led to credit booms, asset price bubbles, and the eventual reversal of the boom. Asset price bubbles coincide with unrealistic expectations about both the rate of growth of housing prices, and the future availability of credit. The existence of increased opportunities for funding is a necessary but not sufficient condition for an asset price bubble. The key change is poorly regulated financial intermediaries, with a banking culture incentivised to increase rates of debt issuance to income levels far beyond historical averages. At the Celtic Tiger came to an end, Irish household debt to income ratio was 110%. By 2006, the ratio was 212%. A clear failure of prudential regulation of banking behaviour, combined with a large inflow of loanable funds from Euro-area banks, created the bubble, which would cost the Irish taxpayer almost €40 billion by the end of 2008, the 4th largest banking system bailout in history.

The Euro did not create the Celtic Tiger; the Single Market did. The Euro hastened the Celtic Tiger's demise.

EUGENE O'BRIEN

Fianna Fáil

'When I have it, I spend it', said former Fianna Fáil Finance Minister Charlie McCreevey in 2001, and the 'boom times are getting even more boomier', said former Taoiseach Bertie Ahern in 2006. These two soundbites, as much as anything else, have come to symbolise the role of Fianna Fáil in taking the country from being a very underperforming economy, to becoming a mirror image of the Tiger economies of Southeast Asia. A further soundbite, from Ministers Dermot Ahern and Noel Dempsey, denying that there would be any International Monetary Fund bailout of Ireland on November 13, 2010: 'We have not applied, there are no negotiations going on'. The bailout and ensuing austerity measures took place eight days later, on November 21.

The Celtic Tiger is indelibly associated with Fianna Fáil. Through very light-touch regulation, which meant that businesses were not restricted in terms of development or financially advantageous dealings; a protracted and structured regime of social partnership, which resulted in very few strikes or disputes from a compliant workforce; the financial services centre in Dublin, which became a hub for all sorts of financial deals, including the developing Internet sector; and a low corporate taxation regime, Ireland was an ideal nursery for economic development.

Most of these schemes had been created under the auspices of Fianna Fáil, who had been in power from 1987 to 1994 (firstly with the Progressive Democrats and then with Labour), and from 1997 to 2011 (with the Progressive Democrats, the Green Party and various independents). Taoisigh Albert Reynolds, Bertie Ahern and Brian Cowen were seen as pro-business and tailored laws and practices to benefit business. Social partnership and investment in education brought about an educated and motivated workforce, while the IDA targeted foreign investment with a low corporation tax regime, while EU inward investment also provided much-needed infrastructure, which aided communications and attracted investment. Nine of the world's top 10 pharmaceutical companies and 12 of the world's top 15 medical products companies have substantial operations in Ireland serving global markets.

Construction, development and house building became central pillars of the Celtic Tiger, and Fianna Fáil was traditionally associated with developers and took much of the credit for the new prosperity. Bertie Ahern was especially seen as someone who was oiling the wheels of business. In the end, a series of allegations investigating allegations of corruption in the planning process resulted in the Mahon Tribunal.

This was set up to investigate alleged payments from developer Owen O'Callaghan, something that Ahern denied. The tribunal damaged Ahern, and in the 2007 general election, the party was saved from a very poor early campaign by Brian Cowen in a series of strong television performances which defended the then Taoiseach. When the tribunal reopened in March, Ahern's former secretary, Gráinne Carruth, was forced, on evidence presented to her by the tribunal, to accept as a matter of probability that a lodgement of 15,000 pounds she had made into an account on Ahern's behalf had been in sterling. This directly contradicted Ahern's previous assertion that the money was from his salary. On April 2, Ahern announced his intention to resign from the position of Taoiseach, effective from May 6, 2008. Cowen was elected leader of Fianna Fáil and Taoiseach.

As a former Finance Minister, Cowen was widely seen as a safe pair of hands, and one of the core Fianna Fáil election planks was that they could be trusted to continue the boom. However, in 2008, world events dictated a recession and Ireland was ill-prepared for this. Our light touch regulation had been criticised by *The New York Times* in 2005 as the 'Wild West of European finance', and there had been an over-dependence on the construction and development sector, which represented nearly 12% of GDP and was a significant factor in the nearly full employment figures. Fianna Fáil and Progressive Democrat taxation policies were seen as responsible for a doubling in house prices between 2000 and 2006. Entering recession officially in 2008, Fianna Fáil also faced what seemed at first to be a bank liquidity problem, but this quickly turned out to be a solvency problem, which meant that there was a real danger of the big banks collapsing with the amount of money involved being approximately twice Ireland's GDP. On a fateful night, after an incorporeal cabinet meeting, Brian Cowen and Finance Minister Brian Lenihan, agreed on a bank bailout, which eventually resulted in the socialisation of some €64 billion of private debt by the Irish people.

The major defaulting bank was Anglo Irish, an institution with which Fianna Fáil was seen to have close ties, and which was intrinsically connected to developers and the construction industry. As a result of this bailout, and as measures to cut public expenditure were enforced, GDP collapsed, unemployment soared and the notion of the public being made responsible for private debt made Fianna Fáil hugely unpopular. The 2010 budget imposed pay cuts of 5% to 10% on public sector workers, and unemployment rose dramatically. Austerity measures were deemed necessary to bring the economy back to some level of normality, but they were not seen as sufficient, and on November 21, 2010, Ireland entered a bailout programme where fiscal oversight was surrendered to the 'troika' of the European Union (EU), the International Monetary Fund (IMF) and European Central Bank (ECB) funders.

Ireland's economic sovereignty was thus given over to outside agencies. The Croke Park Agreement guaranteed no job losses in the public service and no more pay cuts, with the unions allowing redeployment and an Employment Control Framework dealing with replacing people who retired. Some 7,000 jobs were shed through such non-replacement of retired workers. Unpopular at the time, in retrospect it can be seen to have provided stability in a period of increasing chaos.

The Cowen government survived two votes of confidence, on June 9, 2009 and on June 15, 2010. On foot of details about a meeting between Cowen and the former CEO of Anglo Irish Bank, Sean Fitzpatrick, a third motion of confidence was mooted in the Dáil. Pressure within his own party saw the resignation and sacking of a number of ministers, and Cowen opted to resign as leader of the party on January 22, 2011, while remaining Taoiseach until the next election.

This election, precipitated by the Greens withdrawing from government, was a disaster for Fianna Fáil, with the loss of 51 seats, and dropping from 41.6% support to 17.4%. The new Leader, Micheál Martin, was elected on the second ballot on January 26, 2011, and vowed to gradually rebuild the party over the post-Celtic Tiger years. At the moment, in late 2019, their popularity has risen to 30% and they have the largest representation in terms of local government seats across the country, which suggests that they are no longer held completely responsible for the crash of the Celtic Tiger.

MAURA ADSHEAD

Fianna Fáil and Social Partnership: The Boom

Developed in response to the deep economic crisis experienced in the late 1980s, social partnership was feted as representing 'a unique set of institutional innovations for creative, dynamic, and self-reflexive governance for social and economic development', and credited with providing the economic stability that underpinned the Celtic Tiger. It was also, certainly, a political arrangement intimately associated with Fianna Fáil.

The story of An Taoiseach, Charles Haughey, calling together representatives from business and trades unions in an attempt to solve the economic crisis is recalled by participants on all sides. Though popularly portrayed as the genius stroke from a charismatic Taoiseach and his cunning Secretary General, Pádraig Ó hUiginn, in fact the journey to this 'historic compromise' was less direct and involved the interplay of a much broader range of interests, within the Fianna Fáil party, the government, and the economy.

During the 1987 election campaign, the idea of 'creating an industrial consensus' with the 'Social Partners' was promoted by Charles Haughey in the Fianna Fáil Programme for National Recovery. Though the exact balance of credit for the initiative is open to interpretation, certainly this was a development that would likely only occur within a Fianna Fáil government. Fine Gael were on record at the time as being against 'capitulating to interest groups', and the rift that had grown between the Labour party and the trades unions during their period in office is already documented. Moreover, since the General Secretary of the influential LGPSU (Local Government and Public Services Union), Phil Flynn, was also a member of Sinn Féin, it was perhaps inevitable that only 'the Republican Party' would feel comfortable in negotiations. Six months into government, responsibility for the emerging partnership was placed in the Office of the Taoiseach, under the stewardship of Pádraig Ó hUiginn, signalling the full support of the Taoiseach's office, Ó hUiginn's chairing of the NESC ensured that he had close personal relationships with the Social Partners as well as a ready understanding of the terms necessary for them to agree to a national agreement. As Minister for Finance, Ray MacSharry's reputation for competence amongst the business community was complemented by the then Minister for Labour, Bertie Ahern's extensive informal networks within the trades unions. Albert Reynolds involvement as Minister for Industry and Commerce confirmed the government's commitment to securing a deal.

Despite heading up a minority government, Charles Haughey enjoyed a reputation for strong leadership, which was augmented by 'a strong Minister for Finance who was evidently committed to restoring fiscal balance', plus 'a Minister for Labour who had all of the creative powers to keep the people at the table'. Any differences that did exist between these key departments 'were differences about tactics rather than fundamentals'.

Table 1: Social Pacts and Governments in Office 1987–2005

Programme	Government
Programme for National Recovery (1987–90)	Fianna Fáil minority government Fianna Fáil/Progressive Democrat coalition (formed July 1989)
Programme for Economic and Social Progress (1991–3)	Fianna Fáil/Progressive Democrat coalition Fianna Fáil/Labour coalition (formed January 1993)
Programme for Competitiveness and Work (1994–6)	Fianna Fáil/Labour coalition Fine Gael/Labour/Democratic Left coalition (formed December 1994)
Partnership 2000 (1997–2000)	Fine Gael/Labour/Democratic Left coalition Fianna Fáil/Progressive Democrat coalition (formed June 1997)
Programme for Prosperity and Fairness (2000–2)	Fianna Fáil/Progressive Democrat coalition (re-elected 2002)
Programme for Sustaining Progress (2003–5)	Fianna Fáil/Progressive Democrat coalition
Towards 2016 (T16) (2006–16) *Towards 2016: Review and Transitional Agreement 2008–9*	Fianna Fáil/Progressive Democrat coalition Fianna Fáil/Progressive Democrats/Green Party coalition (elected 2007)

Over the following two decades, as the economy recovered and the so-called Celtic Tiger emerged, explaining the Celtic Tiger became a central a central concern to many social scientists in Ireland and abroad. So much so that the 'recipe' for Irish success is now quite well rehearsed: notably, the post hoc rationalisation for the Irish economy's remarkable growth was always to include a reference to Social Partnership. A happy coincidence of good luck (making the most of its position mid-way 'between Boston and Berlin' and experiencing a parallel growth trend with the US economy during the 1990s), and good judgement (developing multi-annual strategic planning in a relatively stable macro-economic framework supported by European Monetary Union as well as a consensual approach to the management of the economy, spearheaded by Social Partnership), combined during a period when the Irish economy was also fortunate to benefit from significant investment (in terms of the EU Structural Funds and Cohesion Funds) and an unusually elastic labour supply (in the form of returning emigrants and new immigrants as well as demographic and structural changes to the labour force).

Though some commentators have sought to identify or prioritise a single explanation, the more considered view tends to be that the Irish boom was a long time coming and in many ways reflected no overnight miracle, but the eventual and delayed structural transformation of a traditional agriculturally based economy into a more modern and productive one. Throughout this period, the impact and influence of Fianna Fáil acting as the 'guardians of Social Partnership' should not be underestimated. In the words of one senior political leader: 'from March 1987 to the end of 1994, without a break, it was Haughey, Reynolds, MacSharry and Ahern [...] keeping social partnership going, keeping very tight'.

MAURA ADSHEAD

Fianna Fáil and Social Partnership: The Bust

The vicissitudes of Irish Social Partnership, and its eventual demise are well documented. For some critics, removing key economic negotiations and decisions into the system of Social Partnership shifted economic management into a technocratic arena and undermined parliamentary democracy by effectively presenting law-makers with *faits accomplis*. TDs and Senators had little influence over the deals that were struck and if they tried to rescind some part of the arrangements, they ran the risk of unravelling the whole.

By the time of the negotiations for the sixth programme, *Sustaining Progress (2003–5)*, there was a sense that the process 'had evolved to the point of over-reaching itself in terms of detail and structure'. Social partnership was now charged with 'creating a governance mire'. There was a long delay in starting formal talks on the negotiation of a successor pact to *Sustaining Progress* and when talks began, they proved difficult and protracted. Irish Trades Unions were increasingly concerned that the opening of the Irish labour market after EU enlargement was facilitating both the exploitation of migrant workers and an undermining of existing employment rights and standards. Their concerns were epitomised by the high-profile Irish Ferries dispute in 2006, when ICTU refused to join partnership negotiations until the dispute had been satisfactorily resolved. These circumstances, combined with Ireland's above euro zone inflation, economic slow-down and a severe deterioration in public finances created the most difficult conditions for negotiation since 1987. Talks began in Spring 2008 and broke down in August. An interim agreement entitled *Towards 2016: Review and Transitional Agreement 2008/09* was reached in September 2008 but the collapse of Lehman Brothers and the Irish economy shortly afterwards rendered the pact redundant.

Undoubtedly, the Taoiseach who was best able to manage this task was Bertie Ahern, who was not only uniquely experienced (having been involved with social partnership from the very start, first as Minister for Labour and later as Minister for Finance) but also seemed to have a natural flair for political bargaining. With the exception of the negotiations for *Partnership 2000*, Ahern was part of the negotiating team for five social partnership agreements and implemented six. For Ahern, involvement in social partnership provided an extensive political resource, both formally within government and informally, outside of it.

Formally, governmental responsibility for social partnership enabled him to boost the influence of the Taoiseach's Department in pursuit of special initiatives that were part of social partnership and, just as importantly, vis-à-vis the Department of Finance. Though some senior civil servants and ministers were sceptical of having their departmental initiatives included in the social partnership negotiations and agreements (because there was a sense that they lost ownership of policy as a consequence), such initiatives arguably stood a much better chance of being actioned when pressed in a national agreement with the backing of the Taoiseach's office. In this way, some initiatives that might never have been approved by the Department of Finance were allowed to happen.

Informally, the myriad of connections created by his central involvement in social partnership gave Ahern access to a range of political opinions and developments at first hand, providing him with the most up to date information and keeping him 'politically sharp'. This certainly allowed him to develop his reputation as 'a man you could do business with' who was willing to develop policy on a pragmatic, consensual and collegial basis.

Other Taoisigh found their involvement in social partnership to be less symbiotic. Reynolds was supportive but happy to stay out of it – with Bertie Ahern continuing to play a central role in the negotiation of partnership as Minister for Labour and later Finance, Reynolds could devote his leadership to settling the Good Friday Agreement in Northern Ireland. Bruton is alleged to have held an antipathy towards Social Partnership, though he was also constrained by the need to hold together a coalition not of his choosing in an unusual change of government. Although there is no doubt that the international recession and economic crisis contributed to the difficulties in delivering the seventh agreement, some credit for partnership's demise must also go to the incoming Taoiseach, Brian Cowen, who – even before the crisis – was regarded as not having the same emotional attachment to partnership bargaining and negotiation. Widely perceived as being no admirer of trades unions, he also had the disadvantage of entering the frame just as many of the older partnership personnel were changing. And arguably, when the global consequences of the Lehman brothers collapse began to unravel, this was a shock that Brian Cowen could not manage.

EUGENE O'BRIEN

Fine Gael–Labour Government 2011–2016

The general election of 2011 saw a sea change in Irish politics. In the wake of the financial crash and the bailout, and amid austerity measures that were biting across the whole country, Fianna Fáil went from 77 seats to 20 and were clearly no longer in a position to form a government. The major beneficiaries of the election were Fine Gael, who went from 51 to 76 sears, Labour, who went from 20 to 37 seats, and Sinn Féin, who went from five to 14 seats (though there was surprise that a party of protest did not do better in the midst of swingeing austerity). A series of negotiations took place between the parties, which were generally seen as amicable.

Enda Kenny was set to be Taoiseach, something that seemed unlikely in 2010 when he was the subject of a challenge from Richard Bruton, after a poll had seen the Labour party as the most popular in Ireland. Nine of the Fine Gael Front Bench felt that Kenny would not be vibrant enough to lead them into government. However, with the aid of Phil Hogan, later to become an EU Commissioner, Alan Shatter and Michael Noonan, who had hitherto been languishing on the backbenches, Kenny prevailed and now had triumphed in an election.

As a result, on March 9, 2011, a new government was sworn in, with Enda Kenny as Taoiseach, Eamon Gilmore as Tánaiste and Michael Noonan as Minister for Finance, a key portfolio in a time when austerity was being enforced and when Ireland's budgets were being previewed in the *Bundestag* before being announced in Ireland. The Troika (EU/IMF/ECB) had been in charge since November 27, 2010, and the position of the government, both politically and financially, was compromised. The response by the government was to appoint a Minister for Public Expenditure and Reform (Labour's Brendan Howlin) who would be part of a finance team with Noonan, and who would attempt to deliver on the targets imposed by the Troika.

This was further underscored by the Economic Management Council, a group formed to respond to the Troika, and to ensure that the dealings with that body would be coherent. It was comprised of Enda Kenny, Eamon Gilmore, Michael Noonan and Brendan Howlin. Politically this was an astute move, as there were two Labour and two Fine Gael members, which meant that both parties had equal representation and there was less chance of political upsets. The secrecy and power of the group was criticised, but what could not be criticised was that it operated smoothly, under difficult circumstances, and the government managed to alter some of the conditions imposed by the Troika, which was one of the first measures of independence achieved under the bailout regime.

Kenny's leadership was very much that of a chairperson as opposed to a visionary figure, but given the constraints within which he worked, this may, in hindsight, have been an advantage. The internecine struggles that had been part of a lot of Irish coalition governments were not a factor in this one, as Kenny and Gilmore had quite a strong relationship, as had Noonan and Howlin. The Taoiseach managed to steer the austerity programme carefully, and one of his first actions was to reduce his own salary and that of ministers, as an exemplary gesture. He also made changes to the ministerial cars arrangements, something that had been problematic for the previous government who had been seen going to a meeting in Farmleigh to discuss austerity in a fleet of black Mercedes.

Ironically enough, Ireland was part of a further bailout given to Greece, and during the discussions negotiated that, in the event of not reaching targets at the end of the bailout, it would not have to go directly back to the markets. Some controversy arose when a plan to fund job creation measures by taxing pension funds was mooted in May 2011. In July 2011, Kenny announced that an agreement had been reached by Eurozone leaders to reduce Ireland's interest rate by 2% and extend the repayment period, which was seen as a win by the Irish public. An unpopular decision was the payment of €700 million to Anglo Irish bondholders, in November 2011, and the introduction of a property tax in 2013 was also contentious, but was seen as unavoidable under the circumstances. Despite a lot of pressure, the government held firm in Ireland's quite low corporation tax rate of 12.5%, refusing to raise it, as it was seen as crucial to reinvigorating the economy. In February 2013, a deal was negotiated on the promissory notes that was used to bail out Anglo Irish Bank, which resulted in a €20 billion reduction in borrowing by the NTMA.

On the social front, one of the most ringing assertions made by this government was in response to the Cloyne Reports on child abuse. Kenny, on July 20, 2011, set out a separation of Church and State for possibly the first time in the Oireachtas:

> This is the *Republic* of Ireland 2011. A republic of laws, of rights and responsibilities; of proper civic order; where the delinquency and arrogance of a particular version, of a particular kind of 'morality', will no longer be tolerated or ignored.

On February 19, 2013, Kenny officially apologised to the survivors of the Magdalene laundries on behalf of the state. At a time when our financial independence was problematic, the voicing of such a secularist position was a popular one, and possibly indicative of an increasing sense of confidence on behalf of the government. Ireland left the bailout on December 16, 2013.

In 2015, a series of issues relating to the Gardaí resulted in the resignations of the Garda Commissioner, Martin Callinan, and the Minister for Justice, Alan Shatter. The Dáil was dissolved, and a general election was held on February 16, 2016.

Overall, the Fine Gael–Labour government could be seen as a success: in very difficult circumstances, this government left Ireland a better place than it found it.

STEPHEN KINSELLA

Free Market

The free market is an idealised place where buyers and sellers come together to transact for goods and services with little or no regulation. The forces of supply and demand are therefore able to find the 'true' price for the goods and services, because there are no price ceilings or price floors. Each exchange between buyer and seller happens as a voluntary agreement. Each party to the agreement expects to benefit. The free market with many buyers and sellers is also the condition economists have found theoretically makes the wealthiest people better off. It is usually the textbook example in introductory microeconomics.

The free market is also a political shibboleth, used by pro-business or right-wing politicians to discuss ways in which regulation is reducing innovation or creating conditions where resources like labour and capital are poorly allocated. Left-wing politicians will also use the free market as a pejorative, particularly after the 2007/8 crisis, and point to its extreme tendencies and its socially damaging consequences. It leads to absent regulation, they claim, the market booms and busts, it creates much, and destroys much, and therefore should be regulated heavily.

The reality is that a true free market as taught by the textbooks has never existed. All markets contain rights, like the right to property, social norms, safety regulations, and codes of conduct, and all markets contain people who are either regulated by a third entity, like a government, or who self-regulate by means of a guild- or union-type structure. In 1890, economist Alfred Marshall gave the example of a fish market, where buyers and sellers come together to find the best price for a highly perishable good – different types of fish. In a situation where the fish could not be frozen, their prices were found to stabilise over time. In 2006, 116 years after Marshall, economist Kathryn Graddy looked at the classic fish market example with a modern slant. Graddy found a highly regulated and complex international business, with little in the way of stable prices. The market participants had changed. There were now buyers who purchased on behalf of retail fish stores and markets, wholesalers or dealers at the market, and the suppliers who caught the fish in the first place, and a host of other actors within one New York fish market. Thousands of regulations governed the market.

The free market was embraced as an ideology in Ireland by the Progressive Democrat party. Historically Ireland had been socially conservative and fiscally populist, in encouraging increases in transfer payments like pensions and social welfare rather than investing in services and market creation. In the late 1980s and early 1990s, the Progressive Democrats introduced 'free market' ideas of deregulation, privatisation, and lower taxes. In coalition, the Progressive Democrats achieved many of these aims, and one outcome of their policies was the Celtic Tiger itself. Ireland now has a socially liberal and fiscally liberal political and economic structure, but no free markets.

JOHN MULCAHY

Gastro-tourism

Some commentators would assert that the Irish were so busy travelling to other parts of the world two and three times a year (remember New York for weekend shopping, visiting Santa Claus in Finland, Leaving Cert holidays to Magaluf, or skiing anywhere in Europe?), there was no time, or appetite, to indulge in gastro-tourism at home. And what is 'gastro-tourism' anyway? I would suggest that it involves travelling somewhere to experience a specific gastronomic treat. That treat might be, for example, a destination restaurant (usually Michelin-starred or maybe one of the top 50 in the world), a particular product like beer in Prague or pizza in Naples, a gastronomic destination like Lima (Peru), Lyon (France), or Barcelona (Spain), or simply just a desire to indulge in an ethnic cuisine nearby. In this context, I'd be reasonably certain that very few of the 4 or 5 million visitors, on average, that travelled annually to Ireland during the Celtic Tiger did so for a gastronomic treat. But all those visitors did have to eat a few times a day, which usually translates into 30–35% of visitor spend averaging out at about €2 billion annually.

So, I would argue that gastronomic activity depended on tourism activity. It's not generally acknowledged that the number of visitors to Ireland tripled during the Celtic Tiger, from just under 2 million in 1986 to over 7.5 million in 2007. With more visitors came increased demand, but changes in where the visitor came from determined how that demand was met. In the late 1980s visitors from Britain made up almost 60% of Ireland's overseas markets – remember that their food preferences were very similar to ours, so not much effort was required from our kitchens. But by 2007, their share had dropped below 50% (it is now in the mid-1930s). During the same period, Europe's share of the market grew from 25% to over 30% (France & Germany), alongside that of Poland and other East European countries, caused largely by the influx of other nationalities anxious to ride on the Tiger. These market changes had obvious implications for the range of gastronomy options in Ireland. As one would expect, they all brought their own food influences.

At the Celtic Tiger peak in 2007, nearly 30% of visitors to Ireland were classified as VFR ('visiting friends and relatives') tourists. The difference was that the traffic was both ways, and more frequent. Similarly, domestic tourism (Irish people holidaying at home) grew by over 30% from 2000 to 2005, and holiday spending (domestic and abroad) grew at around 20% annually between 2000 and 2007. By that stage, just under 8 million domestic trips created revenue of €1.5 billion in 2007. Whether international visitors or domestic tourists, they brought with them new attitudes, tastes and knowledge about eating – a mixed grill, or meat, piled high with two potatoes and two veg, accompanied by a cup of tea, bread and butter, could no longer be the only option. Although, strangely, there was some semblance of that, as plates still had to be full-sized portions – no *nouvelle cuisine* yet for Ireland, thank you!

So, once they got here, where did they tourists go? It turns out that the travel behaviours of overseas and Irish tourists were quite different, and this is likely to have influenced how the Irish dining out market reacted. Ireland found itself with a two-phased gastronomy. Among overseas travellers, the preference was for the cosmopolitan Dublin region as well as the east in general. In 2006, of the 5.7 million overseas visitors to Ireland, almost 76% visited Dublin. As a result, the Dublin region's share of overseas tourism revenues went from 22% in 1990 to 36% in 2006. In contrast, more than 94% of domestic trips and 97% of holiday nights were outside of the Dublin region, concentrated as one would expect, on Kerry/Cork (30% of domestic expenditure), along with the south-east and west. Hence it should be no surprise that gastronomic experiences mirrored the complementary roles played by overseas and domestic tourism in different parts of Ireland.

So, in Ireland, there was much greater demand to eat out, and if it offered the opportunity to demonstrate new tastes and knowledge, so much the better. It wasn't exactly gastro-tourism; rather, it was the further development of the Irish palate. In fact, it was the development of the idea that a meal was more than just 'grub' or 'dinner'. In many ways, the Celtic Tiger was the prelude to the emergence of a new vibrant Irish gastronomy that continued to thrive after the crash.

ROB KITCHIN

Ghost Estates

The term 'ghost estate' was first used by the economist David McWilliams in 2006 to describe empty or unfinished housing developments in Ireland. As the Celtic Tiger period ended and the crisis deepened, the term became part of the common lexicon of Ireland and a symbolic icon of the crash.

The National Institute for Regional and Spatial Analysis (NIRSA) calculated that there were 620 such estates in Ireland at the end of 2009, where a 'ghost estate' was defined as a development of 10 or more houses in which 50% of the properties are either vacant or under construction. A Department of the Environment and Local Government survey in May 2010 revealed that there were 2,846 'unfinished estates' in the country, a term employed to describe a housing estate of two or more housing units where development and services have not been completed and estates completed from 2007 onwards where 10% or more of units are vacant. The total number of units on these estates was 121,248, with planning permission for an additional 58,025. 78,195 units were occupied. 23,226 were complete and vacant, and 19,830 were under-construction. Only 429 estates had active construction at the time of the survey.

Ghost estates are universally referred to by the Irish State as 'unfinished estates'. Indeed, the word 'ghost' is a somewhat of a misnomer in that nearly every estate had people living on them. These residents had to endure a host of issues. The 2013 government survey reported that 47.9% of dwellings had incomplete roads, 18.7% incomplete footpaths, 21.9% incomplete lighting, 19.4% lacked potable water, 18.6% lacked fully operational storm water systems, and 19.4% lacked fully operational waste water systems. Households also found themselves dealing with anti-social behaviour and vandalism, an unsafe environment for children to play in, a diminished sense of place and community, and often poor access to services such as schools, crèches, medical centres, and public transport.

A number of factors explain the ghost estates phenomena, including a laissez faire and pro-growth planning system, over-lending by banks and a lack of due diligence on development loans, and generous tax incentives. These led to a situation in which housing supply was outstripping demand, despite a rapidly growing population. Between April 1991 and April 2006, the number of households in Ireland increased by 440,437 (43%). However, between January 1991 and December 2006, 762,631 housing units were built. This was despite the fact that the 2002 census had reported 177,254 vacant units (excluding holiday homes).

While house prices slowed quickly, then started to fall, housing construction took longer to tail off. 244,590 units were built between January 2006 and December 2009. The extent of the oversupply was clarified by the 2011 census, which reported that 230,056 units were vacant (excluding holiday homes). Allowing for a base vacancy rate of around 6% then oversupply was approximately 110,000 units. Given this over-construction, ghost estates were inevitable.

Addressing the ghost estates phenomena was slow and piecemeal. Severe cutbacks and austerity budgets meant a minimum-policy, minimum-cost approach. A policy of Site Resolution Plans (SRPs) was introduced in October 2011 with a budget of €5 million for tackling health and safety issues (e.g. knocking down unsafe structures, fencing off and tidying up areas). SRPs were to be created by a coalition of vested interests linked to individual estates (local authorities, developers, banks, residents) to deal with key issues. They were, however, voluntary, had no statutory basis, and had little finance beyond the government fund. Their effectiveness varied widely between local authorities and estates.

The last unfinished estates survey took place in 2017. It showed that the number had dropped to 276 estates. Of these, 97 (38%) developments are entirely vacant, consisting mainly of partially constructed units. 159 developments contained residents, but only 5% had some level of construction activity. While a shortage of housing now exists in the principal cities and commuting areas, unfinished estates are mostly located in more rural counties where household growth has been slow. As such, it will be a few more years until they are all completed and occupied.

EAMON MAHER

Golf Clubs

Golf clubs were traditionally associated with the wealthy and upwardly mobile classes in Ireland. Before and during the Celtic Tiger, many developments sprung up that incorporated golf courses, leisure centres, hotels, houses and apartments. The idea was to cater for what was considered to be an ever-expanding domestic and international market based around the leisure industry in general, and golf in particular. It helped that there were healthy tax incentives in place to encourage speculators to invest in these projects. Inspired by the success of Adare Manor near Limerick, Fota Island in Cork, the K Club in Kildare, which hosted the 2006 Ryder Cup, Mount Juliet in Kilkenny, The Old Head in Kinsale, others quickly followed. Carton House, Castlemartyr, Concra Wood, Glasson, Faithlegg House, Killeen Castle, Knightsbrook, Lough Erne, The Heritage, Mount Wolseley, Tulfarris, Moyvalley are but a random sample of the growing popularity of such developments dotted across Ireland. In addition to these, there were also the member-owned links clubs such as Ballybunion, Lahinch, Portmarnock and Royal Portrush (venue for the 2019 British Open) which were well known to golfing enthusiasts visiting Ireland.

Golf resorts became popular for those interested in combining business with pleasure. Within the complex, one could enjoy excellent leisure facilities, restaurants, health spas, hairstyling facilities – in brief, anything one would require when away on a weekend break or a business trip. Banks were very much to the fore when it came to organising corporate golf outings, but developers and other high-profile companies were also expected to invite their customers to such events on a regular basis. Anglo Irish Bank's charismatic Chairman, Sean Fitzpatrick, a keen golfer, was to the forefront of corporate golf hospitality, where participants usually got sponsored golf balls and umbrellas and competed for prizes like golfing trips to Spain or the Algarve. A long-time member of the former venue for the Irish Open,

Druids Glen, located near his home in Wicklow, Fitzpatrick often used his home course to host such outings. Politicians, famous sport personalities, TV and radio stars, entertainers and celebrities of all types made regular appearances on the 'corporate' circuit. At one point at the height of the Celtic Tiger, people could be playing in a couple of these events a week from April through to September, such was their popularity.

However, the economic crash had a catastrophic impact on golf clubs, as sponsorship dried up and the labour and running costs became unsustainable. Many went into receivership or were taken over by the banks or NAMA. The big developments, because of their strong links with construction, were vulnerable when the downturn took root, but in many cases, the banks had invested too heavily in them to allow them to fail. The number of golf courses in Ireland largely exceeded demand, and post-crash people were largely in a position to pick and choose where they wanted to be a member. The expensive signing-on levies are largely a thing of the past, as clubs are vying with each other to offer the most attractive deals to stay afloat. That said, the massive investment by J. P. MacManus in Adare and the announcement that it is to host the 2026 Ryder Cup, shows that people are once more in a position to pay big green fees to play on iconic golf courses. It helps also that there has been an increase in US visitors to Ireland in recent years, which has been a major boost for the highly regarded courses that are to be found in every corner of the country.

MARTINA FITZGERALD

Harney, Mary

Mary Harney left the political stage in early 2011, when Ireland was in economic and political turmoil. She had spent the previous 14 years in government – a time that coincided with the three stages of the Celtic Tiger – its beginning, taming and brutal demise.

As leader of the Progressive Democrats (PDs), Harney first formed a coalition government with Bertie Ahern's Fianna Fáil in 1997. She was appointed Tánaiste and Minister for Public Enterprise and Employment. Despite leading the smaller party in the coalition arrangement, Harney established a powerful alliance with her long-time friend and political ally, Finance Minister Charlie McCreevy. Together they championed a low-tax agenda to drive economic growth.

Giveaway budgets became the policy norm. The PDs were not slow in taking credit for driving income tax cuts, halving capital gains tax, increasing the state pension and reducing unemployment. Harney's party gained seats in the 2002 general election and willingly agreed to continue their coalition deal with Fianna Fáil. Despite promises to the contrary during the 2002 campaign, it emerged afterwards that spending cuts were being proposed by McCreevy to counter higher than expected public expenditure and a slow-down in tax revenue.

McCreevy eventually departed to become Ireland's EU Commissioner. At that time in 2004, Harney voluntarily became Minister for Health – a decision that moved the PDs away from their traditional association with economic matters. While Harney talked about reforming the health services, she was at the epicentre of a public backlash when the economic crisis first took hold.

In an emergency budget in October 2008, then Finance Minister Brian Lenihan announced the abolition of an automatic entitlement to a medical card for those aged over 70 years of age. Within days, 15,000 elderly people marched on Leinster House. The irate pensioners rattled an already troubled government. A dramatic climbdown quickly followed.

Harney faced calls to resign. She later admitted that she hadn't foreseen the medical card furore although she still justified the original decision. She also rejected the idea that the controversial proposal came from her party. In the book *Hell at the Gates* Harney said: 'The PD ideology would be people at the bottom should be given the support of the state. Those who are well off, people like me, if I was seventy, shouldn't have free medical cards. Why should I?'

Despite her seniority in government, Harney was not involved in the talks leading to the Bank Guarantee in 2008. She excused herself as, along with her husband, she held shares in Bank of Ireland. However, she told Lenihan she 'would support whatever decision yourself and the Taoiseach arrive at'.

As the banking crisis unfolded – and the scale of the difficulties in the main retail banks became clearer – Harney and the PDs were criticised for their long-time advocacy of light touch regulation in the banking sector. There was particular scrutiny, and considerable criticism, of the 2003 decision to establish the Irish Financial Services Regulatory Authority as the single regulator of all financial institutions. This flawed institutional arrangement was associated with the PD agenda in government.

Harney later said she had favoured this new regulatory regime on the back of numerous cases involving banks ripping off consumers. At the Oireachtas Banking Inquiry, however, she conceded that the Fianna Fáil–PD government should have been 'more proactive in ensuring that appropriate resources were devolved to the regulation of the financial institutions'.

Reflecting on the financial crash, Harney admitted the government had made mistakes by placing 'undue confidence' in the regulatory system, not foreseeing an enormous explosion of cheap credit, and allowing public spending to grow too quickly. She also expressed regret that cabinet ministers 'did not dig deeper and ask harder questions'. She admitted that: 'I, as a member of the Government, have to share responsibility and I deeply regret all of those mistakes'.

Harney stood down as PD leader in 2006. With her party losing six of its eight seats in the 2007 general election – including that of her successor Michael McDowell – Harney took the leadership again for a short period.

With the PDs in disarray – and eventually disbanding in late 2008 – Harney remained in government as an Independent Minister until 2011. By that time she had spent 34 years in national politics. She expressed pride in what the PDs – the party she helped establish in 1985 – had achieved in successive governments. Yet, it is difficult to escape the fact that the PDs faced a similar fate as the Celtic Tiger: extinction.

VIC MERRIMAN

Higgins, Michael D.

Desmond O'Malley, founder of the Progressive Democrats, notoriously claimed that 'Michael D Higgins would go mad in government', an apparent slur that has lingered in Irish political folklore. An alternative interpretation of O'Malley's remark would be that Higgins was seen as someone who would resist a Civil Service that was prone to thwarting the projects of reforming politicians. His point was that Higgins would find that intolerable. Whichever version of O'Malley's colourful prediction you opt for, the political upheavals which accompanied the Celtic Tiger's initial steps, were to test its veracity, beyond the realms of political cut-and-thrust.

During the 1980s, mainly through the disproportionate influence of O'Malley's Progressive Democrats on Fianna Fáil and Fine Gael alike, Irish public life deferred to fantasies of marketisation and managerialism as social panaceas with the status of religious dogma. Neoliberal political economy was articulated first in Charles Haughey's 1980 address to the nation, and consolidated as that to which there was 'no alternative', when Fine Gael adopted a complicit 'Tallaght Strategy' (1987). Globally, the shadow of Thatcherism, Reaganism, the social conservatism of Karol Wojtyla, the future Pope, and the implosion of the Soviet communist monolith, unleashed unfettered capitalism. In what was travestied as 'Ireland Inc.', in a post-Delors European Community, the received wisdom of policy-makers and opinion-forming pundits alike, placed egalitarianism, and social democracy beyond the pale. It seemed inevitable that Ruairí Quinn's sardonic codicil to Brendan Corish's 1965 slogan, 'The Seventies Will Be Socialist' – 'the socialists will be seventy' – had come to fruition, in an 'end of history' moment.

Then came the election of Mary Robinson as Ireland's first female president (1990), and popular support for Labour's egalitarian policies at the 1992 election. On January 10, 1993, a Special Delegate Conference of the Labour Party endorsed a *Draft Programme for Government* with Fianna Fáil, establishing – among other innovations – a full government department for Arts, Culture, and the Gaeltacht. Thus, the concerns of the incoming cabinet expanded to include vital areas of Irish life hitherto ignored, or addressed in an *ad hoc* manner. A seat at cabinet guarantees a dedicated budget line, and, in Michael D. Higgins, Arts, Culture and the Gaeltacht would be represented by an outstanding parliamentarian, thinker, and communicator. Confounding O'Malley's prophesy, he was to prove a formidable negotiator of the labyrinths of the 'official mind'; as astute in policy design and implementation as he had been in advocacy, since first appointed to Seanad Éireann (1973).

In office, Higgins negotiated conditions arising from the intensification of *laissez-faire* capitalism with an ethical compass set for egalitarianism and human betterment. Beginning with astute appointments, including Colm Ó Briain (Special Advisor), Kevin O'Driscoll (Programme Manager), Ciarán Benson (Chair of An Comhairle Ealaíon/The Arts Council), and Lelia Doolan (Chair of a promptly reconstituted Bord Scannán na h-Éireann/Irish Film Board), Higgins's department placed cultural work at the centre of Celtic Tiger Ireland's economic landscape. He established Téilifís na Gaeilge (1996; TG4, since 1999); deployed the Cultural Development Incentive Scheme with vision and imagination; renewed Ireland's waterways; and championed national cinema against the global monoculture of corporate entertainment. In 'Film and the Life of Culture', the Opening Address at *Irish Film: A Mirror up to Culture*, he acknowledged the allure of images and narratives emanating from Hollywood, but argued that 'as a Minister for Culture, I fail to see why all the images of the world should emanate from one place'.

An insistence on autonomy-in-diversity is a hallmark of Higgins's socialism, born, not of zealotry, but out of an unflinching – and constantly evolving – commitment to an ethical, polyvocal, cultural space. It is to be found in his published speeches and academic papers, and is a core dynamic in his poetry, since his first collection, *The Betrayal* (1990). If the political world of the Celtic Tiger is widely viewed through the lens of its traumatic demise, Higgins's achievements in public office, and his historic vote share in successive presidential elections in 2011 and 2018, testify to Ireland's commitment to creativity and social solidarity incubated during that period. His presidencies, embodying an enduring potential for collective visions of human flourishing, are best understood, not as being unique in an otherwise inhospitable political landscape, but among a series of collective events and achievements in a progressive trajectory: the election and presidency of Mary Robinson, the Good Friday Agreement (1998), and political and social reform by constitutional referendum (1998; 2015; 2018; 2019).

SARAH KELLEHER

Hillen, Sean

Séan Hillen's *Irelantis* series, 24 photomontages made between 1994 and 1997, summed up perhaps more effectively than any other imagery the frenetic pace of change during the Celtic Tiger years. The fractured and sutured surfaces of each collage register the tectonic shifts in Ireland's political and social landscape – the rapid transition from a Catholic monoculture to an increasingly secular society, the reshaping of the political and constitutional relations between the Republic, Northern Ireland and Britain, the dizzying fact that by 1995 Ireland had become Europe's fastest growing economy – a set of conditions, or indeed cumulative jolts to the national psyche, that found echo in his gleefully hallucinatory images.

Hillen's carefully constructed works follow in a long tradition of satirical photomontage, first exploited by the Berlin Dadaists in the wake of the First World War. Artists such as Hannah Höch and John Heartfield pieced together images cut from magazines and other sources to register something of the chaos of social instability following the war, but also to provoke the viewer to critically evaluate and challenge cultural norms. Hillen's fantastical, absurdist collages are deployed towards the same ends, skewering an Irish nostalgia for a lost rural utopia based on fantasy, as much as they work to parody the mass media euphoria surrounding the high-tech, multi-national, increasingly globalised Ireland of the 1990s. Each work from *Irelantis* concocts a fevered, jarring scene from familiar yet diverse sources: the technicolour nostalgia of John Hinde postcards, religious iconography, fragments of architecture, ancient and modern. Using lo-fi methods, Hillen pieced together tiny postcard sized panoramas that clashed the archaic with the hyper contemporary, presenting a vision of a fantastical Ireland of impossible contradiction.

The Oracle at O'Connell Bridge (1994–7) places the Oracle of Delphi on the banks of the Liffey, overlooked by a bank of skyscrapers beneath a lurid orange sky. In *Collecting Meteorites at Knowth* (1996), Hillen reworks Hinde's iconic image of the red-haired children filling the donkey's basket, not with turf but with sinister glowing rocks in front of a blood red sun. *The Queen of Heaven Appears at Newgrange* (1994–7) condenses religious belief in Ireland from the prehistoric to the present, the Stone Age, the New Age and the Virgin Mary rubbing shoulders in a shaft of honey coloured light.

Fintan O'Toole, a frequent commenter on Hillen's work, designated the artist as 'licensed visual punster for the Ireland of the Celtic Bubble'. The *Irelantis* works caught the *Zeitgeist* in a way that captured the popular imagination and Hillen's works were widely adopted as a visual shorthand for the Celtic Tiger era, seized on by both the corporate world and the cultural intelligentsia. On the one hand, Hillen was commissioned by Bank of Ireland to design ads which showed ATM machines embedded variously in the Blarney stone, a dolmen and a round tower. Guinness adopted his 'cyberspace' imagery for their website, 'the first website by a brewery, ' in 1996, exhorting early adopters to go horse racing in the ruins of Stephen's Green, or battle in the Colosseum in Cork. On the other hand, images from *Irelantis* were reproduced on book covers ranging from historian R. F. Foster's *The Irish Story* to Sheila Lindsey's *Time Travels of an Irish Psychic*, and on academic journals covering everything from ethnography to art criticism, from economics to utopian studies. In 2004, Hillen even achieved a kind of official sanction when his work was exhibited at the European Council headquarters in Brussels to mark the Irish presidency of the EU.

The *Irelantis* series' surreal juxtapositions were hugely successful in capturing the exhilaration of a country re-imaging itself, but Hillen consistently undercut the hilarity of the images with a dark, ominous tone which continues to resonate. Blatantly apocalyptic motifs appear throughout *Irelantis* – lowering skies, whirlpools, volcanoes and ruins, Trinity College perched on precipice of the Cliffs of Moher – that seem in retrospect to forecast the Celtic Tiger's spectacular implosion. In *Horse Racing in the Ruins of St. Stephen's Green* (1995) the shattered dome of the shopping centre is an uncanny double of Hiroshima's Genbaku Dome, while a snow-capped volcano threatens the oblivious gamblers beneath. Seamus Heaney perceptively noted that the anxiety in these works stems from the fact that they ask 'Who are we?' Hillen's acerbic mash-ups of John Hinde stereotypes and international landmarks parody both a misplaced nostalgia for an imaginary past and the fetishisation of a networked, globalised future. With *Irelantis* he forged a visual language that captured the incongruities thrown up by the seismic changes in Ireland's political, social, economic and cultural realities during the 1990s, their cataclysmic imagery registering in retrospect the precarity and unease of the decade.

MEGAN GREENE

Honohan, Patrick

Patrick Honohan served as the Governor of the Central Bank of Ireland, and as a member of the governing council of the ECB from 2009 to 2015. Before running Ireland's national Central Bank, Mr Honohan was a Professor of International Financial Economics and Development at Trinity College, Dublin, and has also worked as a senior advisor on financial sector policy at the World Bank and as a Research Professor with the Economic and Social Research Institute.

Mr Honohan was appointed governor of the Central Bank by then Finance Minister Brian Lenihan. This represented a break from tradition, as typically the most senior civil servant in the Department of Finance was promoted to the position. As Central Bank Governor, Mr Honohan developed a reputation for having academic rigour, being a straight-talker and ensuring his office's independence from government (which had not always previously been the case). The latter two qualities were in full display in November 2010, a time when government officials were vehemently denying that Ireland was in talks with the IMF, European Commission and ECB about a bailout programme. Mr Honohan called RTÉ's *Morning Ireland* programme to contradict the government on the record and reveal a bailout was in fact imminent.

One of Mr Honohan's legacies is the May 2010 Report on the Irish Banking Crisis, the so-called 'Honohan Report'. This report was an in-depth analysis of the regulatory and supervisory shortcomings that contributed to the Irish banking crisis. More specifically, the report sought to identify why the danger from the imbalances in the banking sector were not detected and addressed sooner and how officials could have contained the banking crisis more effectively.

The 'Honohan Report' argued that the Irish crisis was largely home-grown, with the government relying far too heavily on the construction sector and other transient sources for revenues. Mr Honohan placed the blame for the banking crisis primarily on the regulator, and on the directors and senior management of the banks that got into trouble. There was a significantly light-touch approach to regulation, with no more than two members of staff from the regulator directly involved in prudential supervision of each bank.

Mr Honohan concluded that there was a pervasive culture of deference to the managers of major banks, an issue that continues to plague Ireland today. According to his book published in July 2019, *Currency, Credit and Crisis: Central Banking in Ireland and Europe*, Mr Honohan believes there remains a culture of corporate entitlement among Irish banks. He argues this is evidenced by high margins on mortgage lending.

Mortgage deposit rules became a key issue for Mr Honohan in the final year of his term at the Central Bank of Ireland. He pushed for new rules that ensured tighter loan-to-income levels and required home buyers to produce a much larger deposit of up to 20%.

Since his retirement from the Central Bank of Ireland, Mr Honohan has focused primarily on the degree to which US multinational firms have distorted Ireland's national accounts, creating a huge wedge between real and nominal GDP.

EUGENE O'BRIEN

Howard, Paul

> Books, education, learning, these things have their place in the life of young men, of course. But not in yours. Because you are an élite ... A good number of you will meet a fellow at your new club who will get you a highly paid, yet unfulfilling, job that requires you to wear a suit – perhaps in a bank or some other such financial institution – where you'll open envelopes for fifty or sixty thousand pounds a year.

These words were spoken by Father Denis Fehily, a character in *The Miseducation Years* by Paul Howard, one of a series of books featuring the adventures of an upper-middle-class character called Ross O'Carroll-Kelly.

Ross is one of the Celtic Tiger's most famous cubs – a rugby-playing, hard-drinking, womanising trustifarian. Beginning with self-published books, which he delivered to bookshops in his own car, Ross' creator, Paul Howard, is now past the million copies mark in terms of sales. His list of characters are metonyms for the Celtic Tiger and all of its excesses, and he charts both the boom and the bust in a satirical and hilarious manner.

Very much in the satirical Irish literary tradition of Swift, Flann O'Brien (Myles na gCopaleen), George Bernard Shaw and Oscar Wilde, he paints a picture of an Ireland with which we can all identify. Ross's father is a property developer, financier and corrupt politician Charles O'Carroll Kelly and his solicitor sidekick Hennessy Coughlin-O'Hara (the hyphenated names and ostentatious wealth redolent of a certain type of south Dublin entitlement) aids and abets all his nefarious dealings. His mother, Fionnuala, is a 'lady who lunches', usually in Avoca Handweavers, and who has campaigned to move Funderland to the Northside.

The Miseducation of Ross O'Carroll-Kelly (2000) deals with Ross's schooldays in Castlerock College under the benign if slightly Nazi headmastership of Father Fehily, where he wins the Leinster Senior Cup while taking serious doses of steroids. *Roysh Here, Roysh Now ... The Teenage Dirtbag Years* (2001) covers his first year at UCD and his J1 in the USA – very much a Celtic

Tiger rite of passage. *The Orange Mocha-Chip Frappuccino Years* (2003) sees him become an estate agent, while in *PS, I Scored the Bridesmaids* (2005) he marries Sorcha while at the same time having sex with her bridesmaids. In *The Curious Incident of the Dog in the Nightdress* (2006) he discovers that he has a son, Ronan, living in a working-class area, and in *Should Have Got Off at Sydney Parade* (2007), Sorcha becomes pregnant and his daughter Honor is born. In *Mr S and the Secrets of Andorra's Box* (2008), he becomes a coach to the Lichtenstein rugby team, and finds out that Erika, a woman whom he had greatly desired for years, is actually his sister.

Things take a darker turn in the next four books as the boom moves towards the bust in the Celtic Tiger. In *Rhino What You Did Last Summer* (2009), we see the beginning of the end of the Celtic Tiger as Sorcha's boyfriend, Cillian, assumes a Cassandra-like role in prophesying the implosion of the American sub-prime mortgage structure, with the ensuing knock-on effects, while in *This Champagne Mojito Is the Last Thing I Own* (2008), his father is imprisoned and he is broke:

> all I can think to say is, 'Dude, what the fock am I going to do for, like, money?' and Hennessy's like, 'I'm sorry if this sounds a touch old-fashioned, but have you considered working?' I sink back into the seat and go, 'Fock, things really are that bad'.

The next three books serve as a Celtic Tiger trilogy, dealing with the bust: *The Oh My God Delusion* (2010); *NAMA Mia!* (2011) and *The Shelbourne Ultimatum* (2012). In a very symbolic gesture, he and his father open a mobile shredding business, which will allow for the shredding of any incriminating files which businesses and banks may wish to hide in the aftermath of the Celtic Tiger – the business is entitled 'Shred Focking Everything'. Perhaps the core of the books is that sense of a certain class of people being immune from the consequences of their actions. As Ross says in *The Oh My God Delusion*: 'They're saying even people like us are going to have to stort tightening our belts,' I go. 'I mean, a year ago, who would have seen Habitat being gone from Suffolk Street?'

The later books focus, again, on the personal. In *Downturn Abbey* (2013) Ross becomes a grandfather, while in *Keeping Up with the Kalashnikovs* (2014) Ross has to rescue a kidnapped Fionn and becomes the father of triplets, and as a direct result of this, in *Seedless in Seattle* (2015) Ross is pressured to have a vasectomy. In *Game of Throw-ins* (2016) Ross returns to the rugby field with Seapoint rugby team and in *Operation Trumpsformation* (2017) Charles sees Donald Trump as a role model. *Dancing with the Tsars* (2018) sees Ross and Honor enter a dance contest, and in *Schmidt Happens* (2019), Ross forms a strange telephonic connection with Irish head coach Joe Schmidt, who becomes something of a guru to him

Howard's work allows us to laugh at Ross, while at the same time coming to a clearer understanding of the attitudes and consequences of the rise and fall of the Celtic Tiger.

NA FU

Human Resource Management

During the 1990s, Ireland attracted significant foreign direct investment (FDI) which is evidenced by the amount of multinational companies who set up in Ireland. Given the emphasis on knowledge-based economy and service industries, people who embody knowledge and deliver services became the most important and valuable resource in organisations. Human Resource (HR) professionals emerged to help organisations to attract, select, develop, and retain people in order to accomplish business objectives, and as such, were a central factor in the creation of the Celtic Tiger.

Human resource management (HRM) has shifted from the traditional personnel management, that is, mainly administrators, to the strategic HRM where appropriate people management strategy is designed to align with business strategy; varied HRM practices are designed to achieve the people strategy. Despite inconsistency in the definition of HRM, a number of HRM practices are commonly used by organisations, including selective recruitment, training and development, compensation, performance and rewards management.

As the strategic emphasis within organisations has increasingly shifted to focus on people as key resources and competency development as a core activity, the role of the HRM function has taken on an ever more decisive importance. Along with such demands, universities and colleges list HRM as a core discipline area within Business Schools, and offer MScs or postgraduate diplomas in HRM. Chartered Institute of Personnel Management (CIPD) is the main professional body for HR and people development in Ireland. CIPD began in the UK more than 100 years ago and expanded into Ireland in 1937. CIPD is responsible for championing better work and working lives. CIPD helps the profession to set the gold standard in people management and development and influence policy and practice in the world of work. Both research and practice in HRM have attracted increasing attention.

HRM research during the 1990s and 2000s had mainly focused on employee relations, industrial relations, and trade unions. A number of Irish scholars made extraordinary contribution to this field both nationally and internationally. They are Professors John F. Geary (UCD), Michael J. Morley (UL), Patrick Gunnigle (UL), Paul Teague (QUB), Tony Dundon (UL), and William K. Roche (UCD). Later research on strategic human resource management, mainly conducted by Professor Patrick Flood (DCU) and his team, adopted a systemic perspective by proposed high performance work systems (HPWS) to strategically manage human resource in organisations. Other significant research on how to best manage people in organisations includes HRM in knowledge-intensive firms led by Professors Kathy Monks and Edel Conway (both at DCU) as well as in the public sector led by Professor Alma McCarthy (NUIG), which has advanced our understanding of the importance of people in organisations as well as the best practices in people management. HRM research supports the importance of each HR practice such as recruitment, selection, training, compensation, performance and rewards management. In addition, consistent findings reveal that high-quality frequent communication, consultation, and employee involvement, participation in decision making are critical for employee motivation and retention.

Overall, the strategic management of human resources has been recognised as a key component for enabling an organisation to achieve high performance and sustainable growth. It was true no matter what time period we live in, but was especially pertinent during the Celtic Tiger.

NEIL DUNNE

IAS 39

IAS 39 *Financial Instruments: Recognition and Measurement* was the International Accounting Standard most closely associated with the banking crisis. International Accounting Standards (and their contemporary variant, International Financial Reporting Standards), effectively comprise the rules that accountants of large EU companies must follow. Some accounting standards apply to virtually every company (e.g. IAS 7 *Statements of Cash Flows*), whilst others are more niche (like IAS 41 *Agriculture*, for example). These standards are issued by the International Accounting Standards Board (IASB), and reinforce the IASB's long-standing drive towards global uniformity of accounting.

So what made IAS 39 so culpable? Introduced in 2001, one of IAS 39's original intentions was to prevent entities from baselessly recognising potential future losses in their accounts, a practice often synonymous with profit-smoothing. Specifically, IAS 39 required banks to follow an 'incurred loss' model, which required objective evidence before a loan could be written down, and thus restricted the banks' ability to provide for future loan losses. Adherence to IAS 39 meant that, towards the end of the Celtic Tiger era, banks were carrying overstated financial assets in their accounts. This deviation from commercial reality severely limited the accounts' usefulness and predictive value. In addition, although accounting standards are complex at the best of times, IAS 39 was perceived to be overly complicated and laden with inconsistencies. Accordingly, when explaining themselves at the Committee of Inquiry into the Banking Crisis, the Big Four accounting firms took the opportunity to castigate IAS 39. PwC claimed, for instance, that 'IAS 39 is acknowledged by many as not fit for purpose'.

IAS 39 has now been replaced by IFRS 9 *Financial Instruments*, itself the outcome of a lengthy development process. Although IFRS 9's first iteration was issued in 2009, the final version, that is, the one that superseded IAS 39, was not issued until 2014, and did not became mandatory until accounting years beginning on or after January 1, 2018. To complicate proceedings for accountants (and accounting students), until IFRS 9's mandatory introduction, entities could apply either IAS 39 or IFRS 9.

A substantial feature of IFRS 9 is the 'expected loss' model, which, unlike IAS 39's 'incurred loss' model, recognises loan losses when they become expected, rather than requiring accountants to wait for the loan loss to become incurred. This requires banks, for example, to be mindful of future losses from the outset of the loan's inception. So, where IAS 39 was backwards-looking, IFRS 9 looks to the future. Unsurprisingly, for financial institutions carrying significant numbers of loan assets, this is not a trivial task.

As the IFRS 9 project developed, IAS 39 was progressively replaced, and has now joined counterparts such as IAS 4 *Depreciation Accounting* and IAS 6 *Accounting Responses to Changing Prices* in the home for retired accounting standards. It certainly made its mark, and, notwithstanding its original well-intentioned remit, is unlikely to be remembered fondly, either by the accountants that deployed it, the auditors that signed off on it, or the readers of accounting information that had to untangle its complex rules and inconsistencies.

SARAH KELLEHER

IMMA

The opening of Ireland's Museum of Modern Art in 1991 was a milestone for Irish art, reflective of both changing cultural priorities and a growing confidence and ambition regarding Ireland's position on the international stage. An institution that had been proposed in different forms for decades, IMMA was anticipated in major projects throughout the twentieth century, from the foundation of the Dublin Municipal Gallery (later the Hugh Lane) in 1908, to the organisation of the Rosc exhibitions from 1967. The museum that finally opened in 1991 was the culmination of years of concerted effort from important figures in the history of Irish art from critic Dorothy Walker to collector Gordon Lambert. Timed to coincide with a moment when Dublin was the focus of international attention as the European Capital of Culture, the opening of IMMA represents a reframing of Ireland's cultural production from a previous emphasis on literature, and an assertion of Ireland's visual arts on the world stage.

Dublin's designation as European Capital of Culture came when the country was still in the economic doldrums: however, it was a uniquely effective spur for state investment in culture. IMMA was just one facet of a programme of significant capital development projects, along with the Dublin Writer's Museum and, later that year, the inauguration of the Temple Bar Cultural Quarter redevelopment scheme. Perhaps inevitably, given the stakes involved, IMMA was attended by controversy from the outset. Originally two potential locations for the museum were considered: Royal Hospital Kilmainham and Stack A in Dublin's Docklands. The RHK, as it was colloquially known, is the oldest classical building in the country and was deemed inaccessible, too far from the city centre and too small to house major art works. In contrast, Stack A had a city-centre location and the chance to provide a large, state-of-the-art venue. Despite this, Charles Haughey's cultural adviser, Anthony Cronin, who was closely involved in the establishment of the museum, said there was no contest. IMMA would simply not have happened at Stack A, he said, it would have been too costly and ambitious a project and would have been put on the long finger. As a result, the Department of the Taoiseach decreed RHK as the location of Ireland's first museum of contemporary art and in 1990 it was announced that IMMA would open in January 1991. Despite the incredibly short timescale and with a very modest budget, within 12 months the museum's board of directors, chaired by Gillian Bowler, had appointed a director, organised renovations to the main building and was ready to open to the public by May 1991.

Declan McGonagle's appointment as IMMA's first director was vital to the institution's early success. McGonagle joined IMMA from the Orchard Gallery in Derry where he had been its director from its founding in 1978 until 1984 and then again from 1986 until late 1990. In Derry he had worked with the community to support local initiatives, commissioned and hosted ambitious shows, and had succeeded in bringing international artists to the city, effectively putting Derry on the international arts map during the height of the Troubles. In 1987 he was nominated for the Turner Prize for his curatorial work, something unique in the recent history of the award. McGonagle was therefore uniquely equipped to deal with the IMMA's potential weaknesses. He looked on the museum's would-be problematic aspects – its peripheral location, the fact it was a historic building, its relative poverty in terms of both its collection and its operating budget – as opportunities rather than limitations. McGonagle championed the RHK as 'a building that exudes its political and social identity', thereby positioning IMMA as a venue that could foreground a renegotiation of Irish cultural history and frameworks of identity. Similarly, he dismissed the problem of Kilaminham's distance from the then city centre, championing an innovative outreach programme and a close engagement with the local community.

IMMA was reliant on donations and loans for developing its early collections. Despite this, within a decade the institution captured international attention for its innovative approaches to access and collecting. It hosted major shows by an impressive and eclectic roll-call of international artists and was resourceful in generating links with corporate sponsors to develop opportunities for Irish artists. Some examples of this are the Glen Dimplex Artists Award, sponsored by the Irish-based company, which took place annually between 1994 and 2001, positioning contemporary Irish artists on a par with their international peers, while the Nissan Art Project allocated substantial funding for temporary off-site public artworks such as Dorothy Cross's *Ghostship*. IMMA continues to be enormously important in the Irish cultural fabric. Its founding, at a pre-Celtic Tiger moment, signalled a significant growth in both confidence and ambition, not least in raising the profile and standards of modern art in Ireland, but in raising the profile of contemporary Irish art internationally.

CHARLES LARKIN

Independent Politicians

The February 2011 general election resulted in an expansion of numbers of independent politicians elected to the Dáil and Seanad. While independent members of both houses existed in the past, this was a change from previous elections, in that they constituted a wider response to the political turmoil brought about by the collapse of the economy in 2008 and the subsequent December 2010 Troika Bailout.

The 32nd Dáil began with 14 independents and closed with 19 as members left their respective parties (out of 166 seats). The 33rd Dáil elected in March 2016 had 19 independents (out of 158 seats) at the start and has 22 as of July 2019. The 24th Seanad had 12 independents (out of 60 seats) and the 25th Seanad has 14 independent members (out of 60 seats).

Independents must form 'technical groups' in order to achieve speaking and legislative rights within both houses. The Dáil minimum is seven members to form a group. The Seanad minimum is five members. Independents in the Seanad typically congregated in the two university panels for the National University of Ireland (UCD, UCC, UCG/NUIG, Maynooth) and Dublin University (Trinity College Dublin) collectively making up six seats. In 2011 a break took place with many more members declaring to be independent, including some the 11 appointed by the Taoiseach.

The Dáil independents includes a more heterogeneous group, many were previously part of parties that they left, or from which they had resigned or were asked to resign due to external circumstances. These independents are termed 'gene pool' independents, and can be relied upon for votes if circumstances require, typically with the enticement of 'auction politics' where local 'pork barrel' projects are supported.

A separate group of independents represent localised interests (rural Ireland, rejecting a local hospital closure, local grandee/family dynasty) or extreme left of right positions that would otherwise not find a home within the largely centrist policies of that dominate the Fianna Fáil – Fine Gael political spectrum, which have historically constituted the main political parties in Ireland and enabled Ireland to be described informally as a 2.5 party system, with Labour making up the 0.5. Administratively, independents are treated as their own 'micro-parties', and are afforded a leader's allowance and supports in recognition of their lack of a party headquarters back office to provide them with administrative support.

DAVID BEGG

International Context

As Ireland contemplates a future in Europe without Britain, thoughts are turning to the possibility of new alliances. Recent efforts to establish a 'New Hanseatic League' is a case in point. This would see Ireland making common cause with a group of small open Northern European countries including Finland, Denmark and the Netherlands. In this context, it is of interest to explore the policy approaches of these countries between 1993 and 2008, the period associated with the Celtic Tiger, and how they adjusted to the subsequent global financial crisis.

The 1990s was the era of 'employment miracles'. In Denmark, this was achieved through a combination of active labour market policies (ALMPs), combined with 'flexicurity' (guaranteed high welfare payments conditional on willingness to accept retraining), and public investment to stimulate the economy. In the Netherlands, employment restructuring involved increased female labour force participation and large numbers of part-time jobs in services. These jobs were properly regulated through collective bargaining agreements between employers and unions. In Ireland's case, 450,000 new jobs were created in the most sustained period of economic expansion the country has ever known. A major factor was the stimulus given to the economy by foreign direct investment (FDI) attracted by the opportunities for access to European markets made possible by the 1986 Single European Act. However, 80% of those jobs were not related to exports per se, but to domestic demand. Finland was an outlier during this period. It suffered a double blow in the loss of markets following the collapse of the Soviet Union and the implosion of its banking system. It had to re-orientate its entire economy towards the West but it successfully achieved this in the second part of the decade.

A core strength of the Northern countries was that they had high long-term productivity – growth rates based on extensive investment in research and development. That said, there are risks to putting all your eggs in one basket as Finland later found out. In 2012, the country's flagship technology company, Nokia, fell on hard times propelling the country into a long recession. But Finland made a strong recovery from this setback and the Finnish economy's long-term prospects remain bright.

In some respects Ireland is the mirror image of the small open economies of Northern Europe. Whereas they invest heavily in research and development to develop indigenous industry, Ireland relies on attracting foreign direct investment with the incentives to persuade multinationals, principally pharmaceuticals, biotechnology and computer services, to locate in Ireland. The global demand for these products and services remained steady even during the crisis years. The crisis impacted most severely on the construction sector, which employed 286,000 people in the period between 2001 and 2007 when the economy moved away from the more sustainable model which had characterised the 1990s. Nevertheless, the multinationals provided Ireland with a vent for export growth, which helped counter the contractionary effect of austerity.

There were also positive exogenous factors which were of help to small open economies. The 1990s saw significant global, and particularly American, economic expansion. However, some factors were unique. Ireland, for example, devalued the Punt by 10% in 1993, which helped competitiveness. Finland devalued the Markka by 30%, which helped it recover quickly from the banking crisis of 1993/4. On the other hand Denmark and the Netherlands had pegged their currencies to the German DM in 1982 and the 1970s respectively.

Social democracy has deeply influenced the politics of the comparator countries, whereas it has never had more than a tenuous foothold in Ireland. The period between 2001 and 2008 saw some unwinding of the social policy achievements of centre left governments, but the basic framework remained intact. Unfortunately, the same period saw a movement away from the sound developmentalism of the 1990s in Ireland and towards a more speculative economy. In addition, the institutions which mediate societal tensions in Finland, Denmark and the Netherlands have deeper roots, and while all countries were affected by the 2008 crash, they were able to handle it better than we were. A stark example is social partnership. It is so deeply embedded in the other countries as to be the first recourse in a crisis, whereas in Ireland it was the first institutional casualty of the crash.

The resilience of the Northern small open economies is in marked contrast to the Southern countries. This economic divergence within the Eurozone has had political consequences. Through the course of the post-2008 crisis, the North has remained wary of having to finance the South. Political tensions between these respective groups of countries have grown. These tensions are not likely to ease anytime soon. In joining the New Hanseatic League, Ireland has consciously nailed its colours to the Northern mast.

CHARLES LARKIN

International Monetary Fund

This is an international financial institution created in July 1944. It is a multilateral treaty organisation that is made up of 189 members around the globe. The initial design of the IMF was to act as a credit union for countries with balance of payments difficulties, and to administer a global currency system that would prevent competitive devaluations and limit the possibilities of economically disruptive balance of payments crises.

The 'Bretton Woods System' was a structure that linked the US Dollar to gold at the convertible value of $35 per ounce, which then created a latticework of fixed exchange rates to the US Dollar that required IMF approval to modify, and that set up a structure of strict capital controls. This system remained in place until August 1971, when President Nixon ended this link to gold and created the current currency system based on floating exchange rates and free capital flows.

The IMF subsequently became heavily involved in providing 'bailouts' to developing and emerging market economies that had entered into balance of payments difficulties. Although bailouts are generally designed to be for 36 months, many have required extensions and some countries have had repeated IMF interventions. These policies have been criticised in the past for encouraging risky behaviour on the part of advanced-economy banks and underwriters in supporting lended and bond issues by developing and emerging market economies, as well as imposing external conditionality on bailout counties.

Conditionality is the IMF's method of ensuring repayment of these short-term loans and typically contain a suite of measures related to fiscal consolidation, tax changes and privatisation of state assets. Those policy options are sometimes referred to as the 'Washington Consensus'. Such policies have been critiqued in Latin America, South East Asia and most recently in Greece, but also Portugal and Ireland. Despite its global role, the

IMF has limited resources, with only $1 trillion in lending capacity. This is small when compared to the current global foreign exchange reserves of $11.4 trillion.

The IMF's location in Washington, DC is a requirement of its foundation treaty, as the US is the largest funder of the IMF. This has caused many concerns about the IMF being a tool of economic diplomacy and at its 75th anniversary a core question was how best to prepare the IMF for an 'Asian pivot' as the economic role of China expands beyond rapid growth into the realm of economic diplomacy.

CATHERINE MAIGNANT

Internet

In 2019, the Industrial Development Agency (IDA) could rightly claim that, 'Ireland is fast becoming the Internet capital of Europe', due in the main to its attractiveness to both 'established and new players from the world of Search, Social, Games, E-Commerce, Online Payments and Marketing'. Google, eBay and Yahoo established premises in Ireland in 2004; Facebook and LinkedIn opened their first offices in Dublin in 2008 and 2010 respectively; in 2011, Twitter set up its international headquarters in Dublin while Google was building its first data centre there, and Bioware was choosing Galway as its location for a major games hub. In 2015, Facebook, Google and Apple announced the creation of new data centres in the country, creating hundreds of jobs in the process. In 2016, Apple thus had a workforce of 6,000 in Cork, whereas Google had 6,000 and Facebook 1,000, both in Dublin. Siliconrepublic.com, the prominent Irish science and technology news service launched in 2002, recently announced that Amazon planned to buy energy for its web services cloud from a wind farm in Donegal. Meanwhile, the enforcement of the National Broadband Plan was necessary to allow remote working to develop. All sectors of life in Ireland have been (or will soon be) affected by the spectacular development of the Internet. Global Ireland is now the home of a multinational multilingual internationalised industrial sector, which naturally boosts indigenous initiatives and promotes the creation of Irish start-ups. The IDA rightly notes that 'Ireland has become an internationally recognised hot bed for tech talent'.

Nothing of the sort could have been expected in 1987, when the European Commission launched its Special Telecommunications Action for Regional Development programme (Star), to help 'less favoured regions' to catch up in the field of computer networking and demand for such services. Ireland was eventually to receive 50 million euros from Star, and made the best of these funds. It is sometimes estimated that this European programme led the way towards the development of the Internet in the 1990s. The emergence and growth of web services actually coincided with, and contributed to, Ireland's economic take-off and astounding success in that decade. The sector actually provides an excellent illustration of the strengths and weaknesses of the Celtic Tiger and of the boom to bust to projected boom cycle it experienced.

The very first Internet connection was established in Trinity College in 1991. It operated as part of a shared infrastructure with Ireland's first Internet Service Provider (ISP), a campus start-up company called IEunet whose goal was to sell Internet access to external customers in partnership with the Irish UNIX Users Group (IUUG), itself an offshoot of the European UNIX Network (EUnet), an informal international network launched in 1982. In 1992, Internet pioneers Barry Flanagan and Colm Grealy launched Ireland-On-Line from Flanagan's Galway home. It was the first consumer-oriented ISP. Even then, however, it was uncertain whether the Irish public would be interested. In an interview with the *Irish Independent* the two entrepreneurs recalled that one day when they felt in a particularly dejected mood, not knowing if they were going anywhere, they went to a Dun Laoghaire McDonald's where they heard a girl announce to her friends that she had got the Internet that day and that it was Ireland-On-Line! Success ensued. ISPs grew and multiplied: Netscape (1994), Indigo (1995) and Tinet (by Eircom, 1997) were launched among others. Some were sold, bought, sold again and bought again for astronomical sums. In 1997, Ireland-On-Line was purchased by Post-Gem for IR£2.5m, and Esat Telecom bought Post-Gem two years later for IR£11.5m.

Excessive speculation flourished in the global dot.com bubble where Ireland was now a real player. As a result, there was a crash between 2000 and 2002. When the dot.com bust hit Ireland, half of the 23 data centres that had opened in Dublin in 2000 (for IR£500 million) were closed. Large foreign companies that had been attracted to Ireland by its attractive tax incentives collapsed and caused a recession in Ireland. Baltimore Technologies, Ireland's digital security giant, had grown rapidly after 1996. In 2000, it announced annual revenues of $110m. In 2001, it reported net losses of $138m across the world and it started shedding staff. By 2003, it had completed a divestment programme. Several companies of the same type suffered a similar fate: for instance, Dublin's Software and Systems Engineering, a part of Siemens and Danu Industries, connected to a Moscow company, which had to shut down. Viasec, a Donegal email encryption company with offices in several European and American cities, had a similar fate.

Continued tax incentives ensured that Ireland was able to seize new opportunities once the economy picked up. Hence, there was a new boom in the Internet sector when some giants arrived in the country. In 2016, the top 10 born on the Internet companies in the world had a base in Ireland, while nine out of the 10 international software firms operated in the country as well. In the meantime Ireland has changed. Nearly 90% of households and 100% of businesses have Internet connections. The regular use of the Internet has revolutionised daily life, access to information and consumption habits. It has also internationalised Ireland further. In spite of unpleasant side effects such as fake news or cybercriminality, there is no going back. The digital revolution is comparable to that of the printing press. And Ireland is playing a key role in the new world that has only started to emerge.

SEAMUS COFFEY

Irish Fiscal Advisory Council

The Irish Fiscal Advisory Council (IFAC) is an independent fiscal institution that was created in 2011 when Ireland was in an EU/IMF rescue programme, and it was put on a statutory footing with the passing of the Fiscal Responsibility Act in 2012. IFAC comprises a five-member council, and a secretariat with a staff of six. The annual budget is around €800,000.

The Council Members are appointed by the Minister for Finance, are drawn from academia, research institutions and public policy practitioners, both from Ireland and abroad, and can serve up to two consecutive four-year terms. The first chairperson of the Council was John McHale, Professor of Economics in the National University of Ireland Galway (NUIG).

Since IFAC's creation, it has become a requirement under EU regulation for all EU countries to have an independent fiscal institution (IFI), and by the end of 2018 all EU member states bar Poland had established an IFI, many of which are similar in scope and scale to IFAC.

In the context of IFAC's mandate, the word 'advisory' may be a bit of a misnomer. IFAC does not sit down with the Minister for Finance or officials in the Department of Finance to discuss the appropriate direction of fiscal policy. The formal mandate of IFAC is set out in the Fiscal Responsibility Act, 2012 (as amended), and is one that is more oversight than advisory. As of the end of 2018, the formal mandate of IFAC is made up of five elements:

1. to endorse, as considered appropriate, the macroeconomic forecasts prepared by the Department of Finance;
2. to assess the official forecasts, both budgetary and macroeconomic, produced by the Department of Finance and included by the government in the Stability Programme Update in the spring and the Draft Budgetary Plan in the autumn of each year;

3. to assess whether the fiscal stance of the government is conducive to prudent economic and budgetary management, with reference to the EU Stability and Growth Pact (SGP);
4. to monitor and assess compliance with the domestic budgetary rule as set out in the Fiscal Responsibility Act, which requires that the government's budget is in surplus or in balance, or is moving at a satisfactory pace towards that position;
5. to assess whether any non-compliance with the domestic budgetary rule is a result of 'exceptional circumstances' such as a severe economic downturn and/or an unusual event outside the control of government which may have a major impact on the budgetary position.

Up to the end of 2018, IFAC had undertaken 11 endorsement exercises with the macroeconomic forecasts produced by the Department of Finance, and published 15 bi-annual Fiscal Assessment Reports. In all of these, IFAC endorsed the macroeconomic forecasts produced by the Department of Finance and has yet to assess a significant deviation from the domestic budgetary rule, though there have been a number of occasions when the alignment of the government's fiscal stance with prudent economic and budgetary management has been questioned.

The impact of IFAC has been broader than its formal mandate and under the chairmanship of Professor McHale the new body, though small, quickly established a significant presence in the economic policy sphere in Ireland. As well as undertaking its formal tasks this was achieved through various broadcast media appearances, presentations at conferences and events, and attendances at Oireachtas Committees.

Assessing the impact of IFAC on the direction of fiscal policy is more difficult to establish, as we can never be certain of the counter-factual that would have occurred if IFAC was not existence. The reason we put burglar alarms on our houses is not so a siren goes off in the event of a break-in, it is to discourage the break-in in the first place.

One of the key roles of a fiscal council is to increase the costs of bad policy. This can be achieved by the mere presence of a fiscal council, but like a burglar alarm, it must actually work and sound an alarm if the event it is supposed to discourage actually occurs.

Fiscal councils must be able to undertake independent, reliable, and sound analysis to be able to assess what good policy would look like and be able to offer a credible counter-argument to bad policy. In its short history, IFAC has built up a reputation for good technical analysis.

Fiscal councils also have a broader audience than those directly involved in policy. The council's original chair frequently said that one reason for having a fiscal council in Ireland was to 'institutionalise the memory of the crisis', so that the consequences of bad policy are not forgotten.

Indeed, it may be that the Irish experience with bad fiscal policy in the 1980s and in the recent crisis has been part of the reason why IFAC was able to build up such a visible presence in a short period of time. Discussions within the EU network of IFIs (Irish Financial Institutions) frequently point to IFAC as a success story within the new group of IFIs established in the last few years. Other countries may be able to replicate the design and structure of IFAC within their own IFI but they cannot replicate the scars that bad fiscal policy has left on the Irish psyche. Hopefully with an effective fiscal council we can avoid adding to them.

AOIFE CARRIGY

The Irish Pub

In 2007, as the roar of the Celtic Tiger was starting to falter, a young Darran Cusack of Mulligan's of Poolbeg Street – the self-proclaimed 'home of the pint' – won a DIT Cocktail Challenge for his Jameson-based creation, 'Darran's Delight'. Open to Dublin Institute of Technology hospitality students working as bartenders, the competition was conceived 'in direct response to the growing demand for new cocktails and exciting new drinks'. Other establishments represented included the Russian-themed Pravda, one of the sprawling 'superpubs' that had come to dominate Dublin's pub scene in the preceding decade, owned by multi-venue groups and known for their vast capacity and affluent young clientele. Also represented was The Four Seasons Hotel, name-checked in Ross O'Carroll-Kelly's 2007 satirical Dublin travel guide for the 'uber-cool Ice Bar and its famous range of outrageously priced Mojitos'. Darran Cusack, however, represented the third generation of the publican family behind Mulligan's, proud bastion of what remains a diminishing breed of staunchly traditional pubs.

What had for decades been a standardised social drinking scene typified by traditional pubs predominantly selling beer and whiskey and, increasingly, other spirits like vodka had diversified during the previous decade of prosperity. The pervasive influence of US television show *Sex and the City* had ushered in the age of the Cosmopolitan and related cocktails. Irish drinkers were demanding new drinking experiences and new venues in which to experience them.

In the early 2000s, at the peak of a sharp rise in alcohol consumption of 48% over two decades, Mulligan's featured in RTÉ's television series *Bachelors Walk* as the central characters' local boozer. It was chosen as the antithesis to a dramatically transformed Dublin characterised by social spaces like The Globe: a new breed of café-pub-nightclub that, by day, served cappuccinos to Celtic Cubs starring in their own episodes of *Friends*; and, by night, trays of Baby Guinness shots to off-duty waiters from Dublin's thriving restaurant scene blowing that night's three-figure share of tips.

Even the most traditional Irish pubs weren't impervious to change, however. On March 27, 2004, then Minister for Health, Michael Martin, choose Mulligan's as a venue to publicise the game-changing smoking restriction that came into effect two days later. The smoking ban was one of several legislative changes widely recognised as having changed Irish pub culture during this mercurial period. Others included a progressive tightening of drink-driving laws, which hit rural pubs particularly hard, and changes to licensing laws – although an attempt to extend alcohol licences to cafes was blocked. Irish drinking habits shifted considerably during that pivotal decade as people visited pubs less often, choosing instead to drink at home or in restaurants.

By 2007, the word on the street was that once-beloved traditional pubs were a dying breed, closing at a rate of one per day. Between 1991 and 2016, some 3,000 pubs closed across the country, a reduction of over one quarter. Almost a third of those closures occurred in the five years of economic decline that began in 2007.

Most of the pubs that survived did so by evolving during that period of prosperity. Some appealed to niche markets, repackaging themselves as sports bars, music venues or gay bars. Many pubs diversified with cocktail menus or wine lists, or by adding food to their offer in a bid to gain from rather than lose to the significant rise in dining out.

Others appealed to a growing number of tourists who had experienced this aspect of Irish culture through an Irish pub in their own home country and who counted it high among their desired experiences during their Irish holiday. Many publicans expanded their premises, often refurbishing their tobacco-stained bar and domestic-style lounge. In the 1990s, the new aesthetic often mimicked the 'Irish pub' export model so successfully commodified by companies like Irish Pub Company and the Irish Pub Design & Development Company, while in the early Noughties, they embraced the more open, light-filled aesthetic of the contemporary urban superpubs.

Mulligan's survived the boom and bust intact and remarkably unchanged, positioning itself as one of the last remaining resolutely traditional pubs.

Author Frank McCourt's observation in his 2008 PBS-produced television documentary, *Historic Pubs of Dublin*, stands true today; Mulligan's remains 'a tabernacle to the serious drinker; no food served here'. They don't serve cappuccinos, cocktails or anything fancier than vodka and tomato juice, according to Darran, who says: 'It's just not that kind of pub. As the changing landscape transformed around it, this once-ordinary pub became something extraordinary.

BRIAN LUCEY

Kelly, Morgan

When somebody whose main area of expertise is the economic effects of disruptions to economic growth, begins to speak about your banking system as being in crisis, that should really set some alarm bells ringing.

For many commentators and policy makers, that realisation came about with the publication of a short but powerful piece by UCD economist Morgan Kelly, in summer 2007. Published in the *Quarterly Economic Commentary* of the Economic and Social Research Institute, it argued from a historical perspective that, yes, indeed, Irish house prices were significantly overvalued. More than that, it suggested, based on historical precedent, the extent of probable falls, and the depth and time of the crash that would endure in house prices. It was remarkably accurate, especially given that the quality of the data for the Irish property market was, bizarrely in retrospect, at that stage of lower quality than for other OECD countries. Kelly's paper had been circulating in draft format for some months prior to the formal publication, and his results had been replicated. Kelly had memorably appeared on *Prime Time*, the main evening news-analysis programme, on RTÉ in April in 2007, where he presented in a forceful manner the main points of his argument.

Although not a formal government publication, the *ESR Quarterly Bulletin* was generally seen as authoritative and at least semi-official. There had been warnings about overvaluation and the dangers both of a house price crash and its likely effects on the economy and government finances prior to the report – the 2003 IMF country report, 2004 Central Bank Financial Stability Report, a 2006 OECD report, as well as some academic commentary. However, this paper, although backed by analysis and econometrics, was nonetheless written in accessible, at times rather acerbic language, and captured the emergent sense that things were going very wrong. It certainly seemed to hit a nerve with the then Taoiseach, Bertie Ahern, who infamously noted, in what was seen by many to be a response to Kelly and others: 'Sitting on the sidelines, cribbing and moaning is a lost opportunity. I don't know how people who engage in that don't commit suicide because frankly the only thing that motivates me is being able to actively change something'.

Subsequent to this, as it became clear throughout the next 18 months that the wheels had indeed fallen off the wagon, Kelly would be a familiar fixture in the media, both broadcast and print. He argued very strongly in the opinion pages of national newspapers, and on rare but pungent TV interviews, that the housing market was indeed broken; that this would take the banks and the government finances down; and latterly suggested that the economic and social dislocations that the subsequent adjustment would entail would be such as to see the rise of rightwing politics in Ireland. While the last forecast has, to date, been avoided, due in large part to the protean nature of the main Irish political parties, and one can hope to the good sense of the Irish political system, the rest of his predictions were in all essential terms correct. A major element in the final prediction was the dislocated effects a wave of repossessions would cause. As we have seen elsewhere in this book, such a wave has not, for many reasons, happened.

Kelly has a BA in Economics from Trinity, and a PhD in Economics from Yale, and his academic work involves, mainly, detailed statistical and economic analysis of issues in economic history. His early work focused on modelling and understanding economic growth, and more recent work has been on analysis of innovation and how it impacts on economic growth. He has rarely, since 2010, engaged in media commentary on the crisis or its consequences.

STEPHEN KINSELLA

Liquidity Crisis

'How did you go bankrupt?' 'Two ways. Gradually, then suddenly'.
— ERNEST HEMINGWAY, *The Sun Also Rises*

A liquidity problem happens when a person, a firm, a bank, or a government cannot meet demands for payments. Most of the time, they just do not have the liquid cash on hand. A liquidity crisis happens when a large number of economic agents have the same problem, and this aggregate shortage of liquidity can render many of them insolvent, meaning the value of their assets are not sufficient to pay their debts. Liquidity crises happen because banks and other financial intermediaries borrow from each other constantly to fund their activities.

The failure of one or two banks can then lead to a cascade of failures, and a possible total meltdown of the system. This process is called financial contagion. Contagion happens because bank failures lead to a contraction in the common pool of liquidity. Banks recall, lend and borrow with each other in the short and medium term. Without lots of liquidity, credit and product markets seized, it is very hard to establish prices for goods and services, and the likelihood of defaults increase. This is a liquidity spiral: lower prices induce liquidations and business failures, which lowers prices further.

The correct policy response in a liquidity crisis is to ease credit conditions by providing what Walter Bagehot advised in the nineteenth century: lend without limit, to solvent firms, against good collateral, at 'high rates'.

In 2007, the Irish government assumed its banking system had a liquidity crisis, which could be solved by an injection of credit by the international markets. Why would international markets voluntarily lend to banks obviously in trouble? They would do so because the banks' assets and liabilities had been guaranteed by the government. The origins of the 2007 guarantee come from this fundamental misdiagnosis of the problem facing the banks – a liquidity crisis was assumed when a solvency crisis was in fact the true situation. The Irish bank assets were mostly loans – for second houses, credit card purchases and home equity releases – that conceivably might never be repaid, because they were far too risky. Their liabilities were what they owed to the rest of the world to fund their own loans, their deposits, and their shareholders' equity. The crisis wiped out shareholders' equity, saw a deposit outflow, and a movement of tens of billions of bad loans to a new bank, the National Asset Management Agency.

The difference between a liquidity crisis and a solvency crisis can be hard to assess in real time. A liquidity crisis can happen when firms and banks are financially solvent– their assets are greater than their liabilities – but they cannot get the cash to keep paying their bills in the short term, because of the liquidity contagion effect described above. A solvency crisis happens when the firm or bank will likely never pay what it owes. In a deep crisis, both look the same. Ireland's politicians, most of them not experts on finance and banking issues, deserve some leniency for finding it hard to tell the difference between liquidity and solvency crises. Ireland's financial regulators and financial policy makers should have known the difference, and perforce deserve none.

KATE SHANAHAN

Media and the Celtic Tiger: The Watchdog that Didn't Bark

In an interview with the *Sunday Independent*, writer and commentator David McWilliams proclaimed that the best economist, 'understands love and emotion, all the things that drive us ... feelings not figures drive the world'. Back in the heady days of the Celtic Tiger, McWilliams sounded some of the few cautionary notes on the boom. This was not a peculiarly Irish phenomenon. Writing in the *Telegraph* about that era, Edmund Conway (now Economics Editor at Sky news) admitted to a similar failure in the UK: 'It was the media's duty to make more noise, to scream rather than mutter our worries about the instabilities of the economy'.

Many factors have been cited about the failures of business media in particular during the Celtic Tiger era, everything from the fact that financial journalism is beholden to the titans of finance for access and interviews, to the poor understanding by journalists who did not have specialist training of the instruments they were analysing, to the fear of litigation when dealing with powerful interests. Dependence on experts who had 'skin in the game' has also been cited as to why the alarms were not sounded earlier. Broad sweep reporting does not allow for context or indeed the kind of drilling down which might unearth worrying trends. And the trends were there. That's if you wanted to see them. McWilliams' 'Jeremiah-like' pronouncements did not make him popular among his fellow economists. While working as McWilliams' Series Producer on *The Big Bite* TV programme on RTÉ 1 (2005/6), one disgruntled fellow economist hissed to me as he left the studio, 'I can't stand the guy, negative, negative, negative. You know no-one who's anyone agrees with him'.

One of my fellow team members on the *The Big Bite* was equally concerned as he watched a robust on-air discussion on over-dependence on the housing market. 'We won't bring down the economy will we?' he asked me. I reassured him, even though I was feeling concerned myself. The now much-derided 'soft-landing' scenario had gained so much traction among media (even today it is quoted as being the reason that journalists, despite mounting evidence that the economy was on the slide, did not sound the alarm), that even I wondered if a pip-squeak of rebellion from a small afternoon show could sound the death-knell of prosperity. The inhibition caused by 'not wanting to stop the party', as the Nyberg report into the banking crisis put it, did not just affect banks and regulators. As a financial journalist quoted in one academic study explained: 'It's hard to run against the tide when everyone is getting rich'.

So could it happen again? Much has been made of new regulatory frameworks, the increased scepticism of journalists towards banks and big business, the fact that ordinary people no longer have a blind trust in institutions, or media for that matter. But as the business model of journalism takes a hammering, who will pay for the kinds of investigations, the in-depth story-telling that makes economic analysis more than just a set of annual figures? Speaking at the Oireachtas enquiry into the crisis, Dr Harry Browne outlined the shift in power in newspapers which impacted on their coverage during the boom, namely the predominance of an unquestioning pro-business ideology, where the existence of entire sections of newspapers was dependent on, or linked to, their advertisers' agenda.

If over-reliance on property and other advertising caused a conflict of interest for newspapers in the Celtic Tiger era, what chance do they have when Facebook and Google are cannibalising current revenue streams? As news outlets close or amalgamate, how does an even greater concentration of media ownership impact on a newsroom's ability to report without fear or favour? One study of the BBC *Today* programme during the bank bail outs, for example, showed that critical commentators and the voices of civil society were muted in favour of those from The City.

The lack of diversity within newsrooms themselves is also now cited as a factor in the uncritical coverage of 'elites', from Washington to Berlin, and beyond. In the UK, media is in general seen as being a predominantly middle-class or upper-middle-class profession. In the US, newsroom diversity shrunk as the recession killed off jobs. The first ones let go were the last ones in, younger men and women from working-class and minority backgrounds. As analysts predict another recession in the near future, will newsrooms rise to the challenge? Reflecting on the lessons learnt from 2008, 10 years on, former *Economist* editor Bill Emmott was not too hopeful, saying that 'financial reporting is not back where it should be'.

The coverage of Brexit in the UK is a case in point. Have we really learnt the lessons of the past? In the broader media when people's stories are not being told, or are being framed in such a way that their agency is diminished, the tiny drumbeats that tell us that it is not just an economy, but also democracy which is at risk, are drowned out. As trust in media is undermined, or negated, extremist views can and will proliferate on other platforms. The *Lügenpresse* [lying press], 'fake news' trope and the rise in anti-journalist sentiment both suggest that if it's in 'mainstream media', it isn't true. If what Ed Sibley of the Central Bank predicts is true, that we are closer to the next down turn, strong independent journalism may be one of our few safeguards against the ensuing chaos.

MARTINA FITZGERALD

Merkel, Angela

Angela Merkel was named *Time* magazine's 'Person of the Year' in 2015 for her leadership of Europe's refugee and Greek debt crises. There were further accolades for the German Chancellor that same year, when she ranked in an international poll as the second most popular world leader, behind then US president, Barack Obama.

Merkel's standing, however, proved more divisive in Ireland. A Red C poll suggested a significant proportion of Irish people (45%), had an unfavourable opinion of the German leader. The pollsters attributed 'a sour taste in the nation's mouth' to the extensive spending cuts and tax increases imposed on Ireland under the 'Troika' bailout programme. For many Irish people, Merkel was an overzealous cheerleader for economic pain. Her stance on Ireland's corporation tax regime most likely also lessened any positive public sentiment.

When the global economic crisis hit in 2008, Merkel was in her third year as German Chancellor. She opposed the idea of a joint European Union fund to rescue troubled banks. She was also a severe critic of Ireland's 'Bank Guarantee' scheme. Her opposition mainly focused on the fact that the guarantee – introduced in September 2008 – covered deposits at Ireland's six major retail banks:

> 'The Irish way is not the right way,' Merkel said, 'protecting without coordination one's own banks, without including other international institutions that paid taxes in Ireland for years, and thereby of course hurting competition, is in my opinion unacceptable'.

Ironically, Merkel's coalition government did help to rescue a large German commercial-property lender – Hypo Real Estate. Moreover, in October 2008, she promised to guarantee all private savings account deposits. She later clarified that the pledge was a political move that would not be backed by legislation.

The German leader's stewardship of the European debt crisis drew sharp criticism from those worst affected. A clear example occurred in October 2010 just before Ireland formally applied to enter the Troika programme. Merkel – along with then French President Nicolas Sarkozy – delivered their infamous 'Deauville Statement' that private investors should be prepared to take losses in future bailouts. This intervention spooked the markets. Greek Prime Minister George Papandreou accused the two leaders of pushing up bond yields. 'This could create a self-fulfilling prophecy ... This could break backs. This could force economies towards bankruptcy,' Papandreou warned.

Then Taoiseach Brian Cowen told authors John Lee and Daniel McConnell in their book, *Hell at the Gates*, that the Deauville Statement 'had caused further market jitters and the damage was done and bond yields jumped further'. Cowen was left frustrated when it was later clarified that the debt restructuring provision would only apply to new debt after 2013. There were even stronger words from Green Party Minister Eamon Ryan, who later described the statement as 'a reckless mistake that immediately undermined an already weak Irish position'.

The Fine Gael-Labour coalition that came to power in early 2011 learnt a political lesson from Deauville. New Taoiseach Enda Kenny knew Merkel through their shared membership of the European People's Party. However, Kenny was left under no illusion about the depth of their friendship when he attended his first EU summit as Taoiseach.

The Fine Gael leader went to the Brussels summit seeking an interest rate reduction on Ireland's bailout loans, but he found himself ambushed by Merkel and Sarkozy. The two leaders offered interest rate cuts in exchange for a move on Ireland's corporation tax rate. 'Fucking blackmail' was how one Irish official was later quoted in Pat Leahy's *Price of Power* as describing the Franco-German offer. Ultimately, neither side blinked. There were no concessions on Ireland's corporation tax rate, and Kenny left the summit empty-handed.

Merkel had demonstrated a willingness to use tough tactics to wrestle concessions from 'friends' when they most needed help. This strategy most likely lessened the German Chancellor in the eyes of many Irish people, although during the Euro 2012 soccer finals Irish supporters had some fun at the her expense.

A group of Irish fans, who travelled to the co-hosted finals in Poland and Ukraine, hoisted high a flag which read: 'Angela Merkel thinks we're at work'. On social media the hashtag #donttellmerkel started trending in a country where the economic crisis had moved unemployment from 4.6% in 2007 to almost 15% by 2012.

Merkel described Ireland's exit from the bailout programme in December 2013 as a 'tremendous success story'. But, this 'best in class' compliment held little succour for many Irish households adversely affected by successive rounds of harsh budget cuts that were key conditions of the bailout programme.

EUGENE O'BRIEN

Mobile Technology

At the beginning of the Celtic Tiger, in the early 1990s, mobile technology was not really a factor in Irish life. Seeing car phones on television was quite exotic and watching characters on television or film holding what looked like large walkie-talkies was a glimpse into a different world. Like answering machines, coffee on the go and a sense of economic optimism, such phenomena were not the norm in the Ireland of the 1980s.

Now, as I write this entry, I have Google tabs open on my mobile phone so that I can research aspects of mobile technology and I am writing on a laptop in a train. Mobile technology enables me to work as efficiently from a train or a plane as from my office. The evolution of technology has been huge, and mobile technology was a significant part of the Celtic Tiger at all levels. On average, people check their phone 57 times a day and 44% of the population check it during the night, 40% within five minutes of waking up.

Eircell commenced operation in 1986 as the Mobile and Broadcast division of Telecom Éireann, and it handled the Irish mobile phone networks from 1984 until its transfer to Vodafone in 2001. Usage of the service remained low until it became a separate subsidiary, Eircell Limited, in 1997. In October 1997, Eircell introduced the analogue prepaid pay-as-you-go system under the 'Ready To Go brand', and turned mobile communications in Ireland into a mass-market product. From early 1997, Eircell faced competition from ESAT Digifone, then from a joint venture between Denis O'Brien's ESAT Telecom Group plc and Telenor of Norway. Other main players included Meteor in 2001, while 3 Ireland launched its service in 2005.

Mobile technology has added words to the language with 'mobi' becoming an affectionate name for the mobile phone, and 'google' becoming a very frequently used verb; not to mention tablet IPad, Wi-Fi, Bluetooth, 5G – the list goes on. Since 2012, there are far more mobile phones in Ireland than fixed lines: the ratio is now 5:1, with some 90% of the population having access to a smartphone – which is higher than the European average.

Mobile technology has transformed Irish people's access to the Internet: in 2018, smartphones and mobile PCs were used to access the Internet by 86% of individuals, with over 93% of individuals aged 16 to 44 years employing this method, versus just 56% of persons in the 60 to 74 years age group. In the Dublin region, 93% of individuals who accessed the Internet in the last three months used a mobile phone or smartphone to do so. Use of tablets for Internet access has increased 6% since 2016 – 43% in 2018, compared with 37% in 2016. Nearly one quarter (24%) of individuals who recently used the Internet (in the previous three months) used a desktop computer. Note that respondents may use multiple devices to access the Internet.

The social and business effects have been transformational. Our sense of self has been totally changed, as has our social interaction. People sitting together while texting others has become a common sight, as has people walking or running with headphones in their ears. It is as if we are now going through the day enveloped in our own soundtrack.

Consumption of music has changed from passivity to activity. No longer does one have to buy the whole album to listen to one or two tracks. Now, one can download any tacks one likes from the Internet and compile a playlist. Social media – Facebook, Twitter, Instagram, LinkedIn, Snapchat and a myriad of others – are routinely accessed from mobile devices, so our very sense of a community is now mediated by our mobile devices.

The smartphone has now become, like keys, wallet, credit card, a necessary accoutrement of contemporary living. Even in the downturn, mobile devices and Internet consumption remained a staple fixture of our lives. The modern smartphone is like a mobile office; it allows us to keep in contact, and as screens get larger, documents can be written on smartphones quite easily. With Wi-Fi, the modern laptop (far more portable than the old behemoths that also served as a bicep workout) is no longer the poor relation to the office or home desktop computer; instead, it is often as highly powered and capable of handling everything required of it.

New products using mobile technology and Wi-Fi are being developed all the time, and Ireland has become something of a hub for such businesses, which have quite possibly aided the move out of recession and into a more secure financial place.

KARL DEETER

Mortgages

Mortgages describe a type of financial contract between a 'mortgagee', which is the party doing the lending, and the 'mortgagor', who is the one doing the borrowing. The financial contract is based upon a property transaction where the property becomes security for the loan. During the Celtic Tiger, specifically if you were of legal age and had a pulse, then chances are there was a mortgage product somewhere that would suit you. By 'suit', I mean to the extent that a lender somewhere would grant credit to someone in that position. The traditional model of a salary multiple was put to the side, and loans were available on 'self-certification', and other dubious metrics that helped a lot of people who had no business borrowing leverage up beyond what they could hope to ever repay.

By definition, a mortgage is a loan that is granted in return for the first lien (or ownership right) on a property in order to complete a purchase. This lien is registered on the deed in the Land Registry. When you borrow money from a bank to buy a home, you buy from the seller and simultaneously sell to a bank in exchange for the money to do the deal. The bank then has the first lien as mentioned, while the buyer has beneficial ownership, which means that they get to live there, rent it out or do as they see fit, as long as they pay the loan. When you have equity in a property, say the loan is €50,000 and the house is worth €100,000 and you sell the home, the loan is cleared and you as the 'owner' receive whatever is left over.

Mortgages are one of the cheapest forms of finance, and during the Celtic Tiger this was taken to new heights by banks who offered people fixed margins over the ECB base rate known as 'trackers' (which are covered elsewhere). During the boom years, there were at times 15 or more banks operating in residential lending in Ireland. Today (2019) that number has halved. Lending for property is generally some of the lowest priced available, and although Irish mortgage rates remain elevated relative to other countries, it still remains the case that they are cheap compared to other forms of credit. The mortgage market has changed since the crash, and is now more prudent and new rules limiting a person's ability to borrow will hopefully constrain the ability of people to make financial decisions in the present which could adversely affect them in the future.

In 2015 the Central Bank introduced 'macro-prudential rules' which put a cap on borrowing of 3.5 times income and loan-to-value (LTV) restrictions which, after revision, are 90% for a first time buyer, 80% for everybody else and 70% for investors. A story that is never told is how the mortgage market had become better on its own in terms of underwriting criteria after the crash, as banks had already introduced new sets of rules that really tailored credit towards the person and their ability to repay. However, this was all lost when the macro-prudential rules came, as they acknowledge no personal features to an applicant and use a formulaic solution. That said, there is some scope for differing terms if a person can get an 'exception', but these are limited and banks have been slow to give them out because of how the accounting rules for them work and because of the risks of fines if they do more lending of this type than they are told they can do. There is also a secondary market for mortgages where the banks who write the loans sell them on: in recent years Ireland has seen this activity rise and we now have several companies who specialise in this area of mortgage book sales and others who oversee the ongoing servicing.

JOHN LITTLETON

Murphy Report

In November 2009, during the Celtic Tiger era, the Murphy Report – with the exception of Chapter 19 because of impending court cases – was released after the conclusion of the Irish government's commission of investigation into sexual abuse in the Catholic Archdiocese of Dublin. That commission was chaired by Circuit Court Judge Yvonne Murphy and its 720-page report was one of several on sexual abuse by clergy in Irish Catholic dioceses. In addition, the Ryan Report, released a few months earlier in 2009, focused on physical and sexual abuse in Irish Industrial Schools, orphanages and the Magdalene laundries that had been owned and managed by various Catholic religious congregations on behalf of the State.

The Murphy Report concluded that, whenever dealing with sexual abuse allegations made by a representative sample of 320 complainants' allegations and suspicions against 46 priests between 1975 and 2004, the Archdiocese was more concerned about avoiding scandal and protecting the Church's reputation and assets than about ensuring children's safety and obtaining justice for abuse survivors/victims. Consequently, prior to 1996, complaints to Church authorities regarding sexual abuse by priests were usually ignored. They were certainly not reported to An Garda Síochána (the Irish police service) and other relevant State agencies. Furthermore, alleged offenders were invariably reassigned to other parishes or apostolates without informing colleagues and parishioners about the reason for their removal and transfer. Occasionally, they were temporarily withdrawn from active ministry, sent for psychological counselling and then returned to ministry elsewhere.

Significantly, it is sometimes forgotten that the Murphy Report was also critical of the cover-up of clerical sex abuse and the lack of action taken by the Gardaí who, at senior management levels, had often colluded with Church authorities in not dealing with complaints. On reading the Report itself or on following the media commentary on it, people expressed revulsion and dismay at what had been perpetrated on so many innocent and vulnerable children by priests who ought to have been among the safest and most trusted adults that those children would encounter.

Although the findings of the Report were accepted uncritically by the vast majority of people – including Church authorities – Pádraig McCarthy, a retired Dublin priest, in his book *Unheard Story: Dublin Archdiocese and the Murphy Report* (2013), challenged the Commission's investigative methodology and some of the Report's assumptions and conclusions. He acknowledged the valuable work of the Commission but argued that its Report needed to be critically analysed by stakeholders and commentators so that the facts and figures could not be distorted when being reported and interpreted.

The publication of the Murphy Report during the Celtic Tiger period unquestionably had a damaging impact on Church–State relations and on the status of the Catholic Church in Ireland. However, it was not the causative factor in the Church's overall decline. The seeds had already be sown with the gradual lessening of the authority and relevance of the Church since the 1980s. Nonetheless, the release of the Report and the subsequent public debate confirmed many people's worst opinions of the Church and its role in a modern democratic society.

But also at that time, both Church and State were undergoing enormous change in Ireland. From the perspective of the State, there was an amazing transformation of Ireland from being an under-achieving country to being one of the world's most successful economies and one of Europe's wealthiest nations. The economy was booming – paradoxically, mainly due to a highly educated workforce from church-established schools. Unemployment numbers were low. There was large-scale immigration and salaries were increasing. All these factors combined with the increasing secularisation of Irish society that had begun in the 1960s. More and more people no longer sensed their dependence on God and did not perceive the need for a religious dimension to their lives.

From the perspective of the Church, traditional Catholic teachings about marriage, the family and bioethics were being challenged. Church attendance was declining, especially in urban areas. Vocations to the priesthood and religious life were rapidly dwindling and seminaries were closing. Many people were abandoning the practice of their faith and this was becoming evident in, for example, the ever-increasing number of civil marriages and humanist funeral services. In short, religious beliefs and values were under attack and the Church was desperately searching for suitable pastoral strategies that might stem the tide.

To complicate matters further, the aftermath of the sex abuse scandals and the publication of the Murphy Report seriously compromised the moral authority and credibility of the institutional Church. Its hypocrisy has been exposed and now it is considered by many people to be just another lobby or interest group. Ireland has, at least to some extent, become post-Catholic. However, even with the demise of the Celtic Tiger, the Church continues – albeit in a diminished and humbler form – and the preaching of the Gospel will continue long after the Celtic Tiger has been forgotten.

SEAMUS COFFEY

National Accounts

The national accounts are a set of figures produced by the Central Statistics Office (CSO) that are intended to describe the economy as a whole. The accounts look at the aggregate or overall amount of production, income and consumption in the economy, as well as the stocks of assets and transaction flows with the rest of the world. Internationally, the most widely used measure from the accounts is Gross Domestic Product (GDP), which is a measure of the total value of goods and services produced in an economy in a particular time period, usually a year. For most countries, the output measure of GDP is also a good measure of income and GDP can be used in a variety of contexts.

For Ireland, GDP is a good measure of output but it is a poor measure of income. This is because a very large share of the output produced in Ireland arises in foreign-owned, and particularly US-owned, businesses. Thus, while Ireland benefits from the salaries paid to their employees, the purchases by the companies of goods and services from Irish suppliers, and the tax paid to the government, the net profit accrues to the foreign shareholders, and should not be counted as Irish income.

When such income flows are adjusted for in the national accounts, we get Gross National Product (GNP). This is the income that accrues to the residents of a country. Ireland's GNP has diverged downwards from Ireland's GDP since the early 1970s as the presence of foreign companies in the economy expanded. For 2002, the latest estimate is that Irish GDP was around €135 billion with GNP put at €112 billion. The main reason for the significant difference is that the output of foreign-owned MNCs is included in GDP while the profits from that output are excluded from GNP.

Between 2002 and 2007, this distinction was not a significant issue as most of the output and income growth in the economy was driven by the domestic economy, notably construction investment and household consumption. Over those six years, the volume of GDP increased by an average of 5.2% per annum with average GNP growth of what seemed like an impressive 4.8% per annum. In recent years, there have been even more distortions to Ireland's national accounts arising from issues due to aircraft leasing and intangible assets. In response to this, the CSO have created a bespoke measure of national income that is unique to Ireland's national accounts. This measure is called Modified Gross National Income (or GNI).

In nominal terms GNI rose from €112 billion in 2002 to €165 billion in 2007. This was extraordinary growth in a very short period of time. However, what followed was a crash that was even more extraordinary. By 2009, GNI had fallen to €134 billion and it bottomed out in 2012 at €126 billion. One question worth asking about the national accounts is whether the weaknesses in the economy we now recognise in hindsight were evident in this key set of economic statistics?

An important indicator of the stability of an economy comes from the Balance of Payments component of the national accounts. The Current Account of the Balance of Payments looks at the cross-border flows of trade (imports and exports), income (such as the MNC profits mentioned above) and transfers (like foreign aid and EU subsidies). The Current Account can tell us whether a country is living within its means and a deteriorating Current Account is a good indicator of imbalances building up in an economy.

Here is a quote from a CSO publication from March 2007:

> The fourth quarter of 2006 showed a current account deficit of €839m, half a billion higher than that for the same quarter of 2005, but continuing the trend of reducing deficits during 2006. (CSO, 2007)

While deficits are referenced it is stated that there is a 'trend of reducing deficits' which would go some way to allaying fears about the build-up of significant imbalances up in the economy including in relation to an economy performing above its potential, or what can be described as an 'overheating' economy.

We know the economy was performing above its potential because it came crashing down in 2008. The unsustainable output was supported by a huge expansion in credit, and when that credit tap was turned off in

2008, that output, and associated income, evaporated with the huge falls in national income described above.

If you look at the latest estimates from the CSO you will see a large deterioration in Ireland's Current Account in the run up to 2008. The figures show a Current Account that was in balance in 2004 deteriorating to a large deficit of around €12 billion in 2007 with significant deteriorations in each year.

Why did a deficit equivalent to 8% of national income open up? A key reason was the increase in imports. Imports are goods and services coming into a country and the Balance of Payments records the outbound payments for these goods and services.

There were increased imports for construction activity and household consumption such as new cars, flat-screen televisions and foreign holidays. This was the country living beyond its means. The impact of this can be seen in the figures now which show a rapidly deteriorating Current Account but it was a failure that this was not reflected in the figures at the time.

Would anything different have been done back then if the national accounts did accurately reflect the weakness in the economy? Probably not. But the lesson from an imbalanced economy should inform policy of the future.

National accounts might seem like the arcane reserve of statisticians and economists, and the impact of inaccurate national accounts may have been small in the greater scheme of all the mistakes made up to 2008, but it did contribute to the problems. National accounts are an important input into policy design and not only do we need them to pick up the impact of the known mistakes made in the past, we also need them to be able to pick up the unknown mistakes of the future.

CONSTANTIN GURDGIEV

National Treasury Management Agency (NTMA)

The National Treasury Management Agency (NTMA) was created to provide 'a range of asset and liability management services to government'. These services include borrowing on behalf of the government and management of the National Debt, the State Claims Agency, NewERA, the Ireland Strategic Investment Fund and the National Development Finance Agency. It also assigns staff and provides business and support services and systems to the National Asset Management Agency (NAMA), the Strategic Banking Corporation of Ireland and Home Building Finance Ireland.

During the Celtic Tiger era, the NTMA rode the wave of high economic growth, placing government bonds into the booming markets, underpinned by the Irish economic 'fundamentals'. Green Jerseying was easy: the Dublin story practically sold itself to willing investors, and the NTMA marketing desks at international bond shows were a particular hit, with free Guinness on tap and shrinking debt-to-GDP ratio as macroeconomic appetisers. Growth-obsessed, like the rest of the Celtic Tiger, the NTMA secured a lucrative gig managing the National Pensions Reserve Fund – Bertie Ahearn's savings pot for public sector pensions. From the NTMA's point of view, the job involved outsourcing virtually all front-desk functions to a host of Irish asset management companies, and sitting back to enjoy high returns courtesy of the booming Irish and global economies.

2008 ended the party at the NTMA's offices. However, the crisis also allowed the NTMA to prove its worth in the post-Celtic Tiger era. Since 2009, the NTMA was extremely successful in capitalising on the ECB's quantitative easing and the subsequent improvement in the Irish economy. The Agency successfully sold tens of billions worth of Irish government bonds, often in extremely challenging markets, and managed quite well the re-profiling of the sovereign debt by extending debt maturities and swapping more expensive debt tranches for cheaper ones. The Irish exit from the

Bailout and the repayment of the IMF and bilateral debts incurred during the crisis was in part due to the NTMA's work.

The agency's role as the back-office partner to NAMA is an arms-length relationship that is likely to be one of just two questionable parts of its legacy in the post-crisis recovery, with the second one being the role of the NTMA in 'extinguishing' €25 billion worth of the Anglo and INBS bailout bonds that were temporarily stashed with the Central Bank as the part of the infamous 'Prom Night' IBRC liquidation in February 2013. Not that either one of these parts is going to cost the NTMA leadership any sleep: the agency staff is among the highest paid in the entire Irish public sector, with 136 of its 556 total staff earning in excess of €100,000 in 2018.

DARRAGH FLANNERY

Neary, Patrick

Patrick Neary was the prudential director (2003–6) and CEO (2006–9) of the Irish Financial Services Regulatory Authority (IFSRA) within the Irish Central Bank. The IFSRA was responsible for micro prudential supervision of individual banks in Ireland, and as well as other financial service providers. His role, as the head of the financial regulatory authority, in the lead up to the banking crisis in Ireland in 2008, has been the subject of much debate and featured in numerous reports, inquiries and court cases that have examined the crisis.

Neary resigned from his position in January 2009, at the time facing criticism for the 'hidden loans' scandal within Anglo Irish Bank. Anglo was nationalised (at an eventual cost to the taxpayer of over €30 billion) in December 2008. At the same time, 'the hidden loans' scandal arose after it was discovered that Sean Fitzpatrick, then CEO of Anglo, had been transferring loans of up to €87 million off the bank's book to conceal them from shareholders. It was claimed that staff at the regulator's office first learned of this practice in January 2008, but did not inform the Department of Finance or take any action of its own. The Report of the Committee of the Authority examining the internal communication of matters relating to loans to directors of Anglo Irish Bank Corporation, found there had been a communications break down in the organisation, which resulted in a lack of action by the regulator's office. The same report also noted that the issue could have been identified sooner if the existing information from Anglo's quarterly returns had been supervised to a greater degree. Neary faced further controversy with regard to Anglo Irish Bank in the 'Project Maple' deal. This deal surfaced in mid-2008, whereby 10 investors (The Maple Ten) were approached by the bank and offered loans in return for equity within the bank; a practice that later resulted in two directors of Anglo being found guilty of 10 counts of providing unlawful financial assistance to investors. The court case surrounding this deal also led the sitting judge, Martin Nolan, to heavily criticise the role of Mr Neary within the scandal.

The actions of Mr Neary as the CEO of the financial regulator in the lead up to the crisis have also been examined within prominent reports such as the Honohan Report (2010) and the Nyberg report (2011). The former provides some useful insight, suggesting that the financial regulator 'relied on the deferential view that, as long as there was a good governance structure, decisions of the people actually running the banks could normally be trusted to keep the banks safe and sound, and their decisions did not need to be second-guessed. Voluntary compliance was the preferred enforcement strategy'. More specific to Mr Neary, the report also notes that 'furthermore, in internal communications between the Chair and CEO of the FR in mid-2006 the question of what could be done to address the general problem of an acceleration in the growth of lending and credit growth was raised. There were doubts that the principles-based approach combined with moral suasion would be able to solve these problems. Nevertheless, the FR and the Authority did not appear willing to consider employing more effective forms of intervention to resolve the problem'.

It is also noteworthy that Mr Neary was present at a meeting in government buildings on the night of September 29, 2008, when the decision by the Irish government to guarantee all banking liabilities totalling €440 billion was made. This decision and the contents of the meeting of the 29th has since been the focus of much attention and criticism, particularly within the context of the Report of the Joint Committee of Inquiry into the Banking Crisis (2016). Some notable contributions within this inquiry relating to Mr Neary include former Taoiseach Brian Cowen's evidence that 'Mr Neary and Mr Farrell, from the regulator's office, outlined their serious concerns. I recollect that they were of the view that something significant had to be done immediately to stabilise the situation. In that respect, they spoke of the need for introduction of a Guarantee'. Mr Neary himself stated, 'I didn't believe that any institution was insolvent on the date of the guarantee. Based on the information available to us'.

The same inquiry also noted that Mr Neary assured the nation on RTÉ's *Prime Time* in October 2008 that Irish financial institutions were 'well capitalised' in comparison to European banks and expressed confidence that loan losses would be manageable. He stated to the inquiry: 'Well, I think that, with hindsight, and based on what emerged since in relation to those portfolios, that that assessment was optimistic'.

Overall, Mr Neary, in his capacity as the head of the financial regulator prior to the banking crisis in Ireland, will arguably be most noted for a lack of oversight that helped contribute to the largest bailout in Irish history.

DARRAGH FLANNERY

Negative Equity

Negative equity is the term used when the value of an asset is below the outstanding debt of the asset. In the context of the Irish economy, this concept became prominent within the housing sector as property prices fell by over 50% on average across the period 2008–13 (Byrne et al., 2018). Such a sudden fall in property prices inevitably led to a rise in cases of negative equity for homeowners in Ireland, rising from 9% of households in 2008 to 30% by 2010 (Duffy, 2010). This peaked at 36% (~240,000) and 55% (~50,000) of residential and buy-to-let loans respectively in 2012 (Central Bank of Ireland, 2018).

At the household level, being in negative equity may have no material impact if the owner intends to own the property for a number of years; in this case, they may simply wait for the price of the property to increase again in the future. However, the existence of negative equity can have significant implications for a household if they need to sell the property, perhaps due an inability to service the debt arising from an unexpected income shock such as unemployment. In this scenario, selling the house will not cover the debt owed, and so the lender has a level of bad debt to take on, or the borrower must use savings to clear the debt or possibly even declare bankruptcy. This has clear implications for the broader economy, particularly if seen on a large scale. For homeowners, having to declare bankruptcy, as they are unable to clear their mortgage debt, may have implications for their ability to gain credit well into the future. From the lenders' viewpoint, if they write down the value of the mortgage (their asset) to reflect the lower market value of the house(s), balance sheet and solvency problems may become an issue. This in turn may adversely affect lending in the wider economy, as banks may contract credit availability to businesses and households in order to brace themselves for anticipated losses. Furthermore, negative equity can be a significant driver of mortgage arrears and default. For instance, households that suffer an income shock (through sudden unemployment) and are in negative equity are unable to use the equity in the property to borrow and cover repayments in the short term. If this then leads to significant levels of mortgage default, similar issues for the bank's balance sheets and credit markets will arise.

Duffy (2010) elaborates on these and other undesirable consequences of negative equity within an economy. For example, households in negative equity, even with a full ability to service the existing debt, may consume less goods and services, as they no longer have the ability to generate funds through re-mortgaging. These households may also 'feel' less wealthy, reducing consumer confidence and negatively affect consumption decisions in the economy resulting in a greater tendency for people to engage in precautionary savings. Negative equity may also reduce the mobility of people, as those with a lower house price relative to their mortgage may be less likely to sell their property and move elsewhere. This may also lead to greater rigidity in the labour market as people in negative equity have a tendency to stay in their current properties and thus may not avail of job opportunities in different geographical areas.

Given the well-documented experience of Ireland over the past eight to 10 years with regard to bank lending, mortgage arrears and consumer spending, it is fair to suggest that the property crash and ensuing levels of negative equity experienced by households had a significant impact on the economy. However, given the recent rebound in property prices in Ireland, the Central Bank has estimated that the overall share of property loans in negative equity had fallen to 8% or 57,000 loans by the end of 2017 (Central Bank of Ireland, 2018) with a further reduction in this figure expected.

LORCAN SIRR

Neoliberalism

Neoliberalism is a political and economic philosophy which promotes the 'market' as the key driver of social and financial wellbeing. It was a key component, if not the ultimate driver, of the years of the Celtic Tiger. General principles of neoliberalism include:

1. privatisation of state assets;
2. deregulation of economic sectors;
3. openness to investment flows.

Many commentators argue that for almost 30 years, governments internationally have become increasingly seduced by an agenda that has sought to place 'the market' at the heart of economic life. At the core of neoliberal ideology is the belief that open, competitive, and unregulated markets, liberated from all forms of state interference, represent the optimal mechanism for economic development. Neoliberalism comprises a range of ideas and a theory of economic practices, which propose that the human well-being is best advanced by liberating individual entrepreneurial freedoms and skills within an institutional framework characterised by strong private-property rights, free markets and free trade. It is a somewhat unfortunate term because the word 'liberal' is often used to describe actions which are socially progressive.

During the Celtic Tiger, Ireland developed its own particular version of neoliberalism, as outlined by Kitchin et al. Irish neoliberalism is a mixture of American ideology comprising minimal state intervention; the privatisation of state services; public–private partnerships; developer/speculator-led planning; low corporate (and individual) taxation; limited regulation; and clientelism, with European social welfarism and its developmental state; social partnership; welfare safety net; high indirect taxation; EU directives and obligations. That particular neoliberal model has far from disappeared in Ireland and in other European countries

DEREK HAND

Novels of the Celtic Tiger

The advent of the Celtic Tiger celebrated the marketplace along with the newly minted middle classes who now happily inhabited that marketplace. Interestingly, the Celtic Tiger's arrival, and departure, has given its name to only one literary medium: the novel. One reason for this is that, since its emergence in the seventeenth and eighteenth centuries, the novel form, more so than either poetry or drama, has always been more resolutely tied to the vagaries of the marketplace and the bourgeoisie who find themselves there.

The colonial and post-colonial model that fitted the Irish experience of failure and under-achievement for so long now no longer applied, as success became the barometer of measuring value and worth. Many novels were celebrated simply for the prizes and the awards they won, rather than for their literary merit. A diverse range of responses to the Celtic Tiger's arrival, and its subsequent economically devastating departure, can be found in novels as varied as Kevin Power's *Bad Day in Blackrock*, Deirdre Madden's *Time Present and Time Past*, Rob Doyle's *Here are the Young Men*, Paul Murray's *Skippy Dies* and *The Mark and the Void*, Anne Enright's Booker prize-winning *The Gathering*, Éilís Ní Dhuibhne's *Fox, Swallow, Scarecrow*, Claire Kilroy's *The Devil I Know*, and Donal Ryan's *The Spinning Heart*.

One noticeable consequence was how many novelists called their reader's attention to this shift. A note of comic bewilderment is struck in Roddy's Doyle's 2007 novel *Paula Spencer*, when Paula's sister Carmel seeks to persuade her of the benefits of buying an apartment in Bulgaria:

> – It's an investment, Paula.
> – Oh. Yeah.
> When Bulgaria joins the EU the value of those apartments will go through the fuckin' roof. An investment.
> – An investment. They used to talk about *EastEnders* and their husbands.

This new economy demands engagement, its opportunities heralding a widespread transformation of everyday life for the Irish.

Anne Haverty's comic novel *The Free and Easy* (2006) articulates brilliantly much of the context and the literary response to the arrival of the Celtic Tiger. It lampoons the Dublin art scene in which an artwork's physical size is a key determinant of its cash value. Land development and the buying and selling of property, at home and abroad, provide the backdrop to this story of New Yorker Tom Blessman, who comes to Dublin on a mission to spend the fortune of his Irish émigré great-uncle. In novels of the past, the tourist typically discovered an Ireland and an Irishness always already exotic and strange. Now, though, Blessman finds not the fantastic, but rather the dully familiar. A character suggests: 'Of course it must be disappointing to come all this way and find we're exactly the same as everyone else'.

However, there is entertainment in the hyper reality of the version of Irishness now on display: 'But there's always the theme park aspect. That's an area that's really thriving'. What this novel captures particularly well is how staggeringly self-conscious people are about this moment of success. As a film director puts it in an interview that Blessman reads:

> The rain, the drunken father [...] all that sob stuff, the mangy dog, all that shite, it's over. It's over historically, it's over cinematically [...] But I want to look at real stuff, you know? I want to look at the present, the positive, something we can all relate to. Love, money, multiplicity of choices. We're global now, we're multicultural, let's celebrate. We're done with whingeing, right?

The desire to 'jettison the past' – the past of failure, of trauma and of poverty – becomes a simple narrative trajectory in itself. It is not enough to be successful, it is not enough to embrace the new world and the new culture and economics that come with it; instead, this must be expressed forcefully, and not just once, but again and again. In other words, the Celtic Tiger demands a new story and that story is precisely one about how 'new' everything is. Telling that story makes it real, as real as the new buildings and the new golf courses springing up all over the city and its suburbs.

In this way, the Celtic Tiger novel navigates a course between the local and the global, between the boring known and the exciting new. Despite its success in the literary marketplace, the self-consciousness on display in these novels is actually a manifestation of an inherent anxiety about all this change and newness.

SEAN BARRETT

Nyberg Report

The Report by Peter Nyberg, titled *Misjudging Risk: Causes of the Systemic Banking Crisis in Ireland*, was commissioned by Finance Minister Brian Lenihan in September 2010. Nyberg was then Director General of the Financial Markets Department at the Ministry of Finance of Finland, having previously worked at the Bank of Finland and at the IMF. Chapter 1 of the Nyberg states that 'the Report aims to provide answers on why a number of institutions, both private and public, acted in an imprudent or ineffective manner, thereby contributing to the occurrence of the Irish banking crisis' (p. 1).

The Nyberg Report states that:

> it could be argued that bank management in Ireland, like many banks elsewhere in the world, had forgotten the very nature of credit. Providing credit is not a sale of bank services; it is the acquisition of a risky asset. The appropriate prudential focus of such a transaction is therefore limiting and mitigating risk (or, at the very least, understanding the real risk and pricing it accordingly) rather than expanding sales. This apparent inability, some might say unwillingness, of Irish banks to remember this basic principle of banking was a major cause of the banking crisis in Ireland. The problem was further exacerbated as many banks appear to have emphasised and valued loan sales skills above risk and credit analysis skills. (p. 50)

Nyberg found 'little appreciation – both domestically and abroad – of the fact that Irish economic growth and welfare increasingly depended on construction and property development for domestic customers, funded by a growing foreign debt' (p. iii).

In addition to the banks themselves, Nyberg examined the role of external bodies such as bank auditors, the Department of Finance, the Financial Regulator and the Central Bank. He reported that each had also contributed to the banking crisis. He describes the external auditors of Irish banks as 'the silent observers' (p. vi). He notes that in Ireland 'banks had to be rescued from closure by government guarantee in some instances not more than six months after being given clean audit opinions' (p. vi). Nyberg found that 'PwC reported that on the basis of information presented to them by management, all the institutions were solvent at end-September 2008' (p. 83). The government guarantee was given on September 29, 2008.

Nyberg described the public authorities as 'the enablers' of the Irish banking crisis (p. vii). He found that 'The Department of Finance, discouraged from interfering in the work of the independent Financial Regulator and Central Bank, remained seriously underweight in professional financial expertise and engagement. The Commission (Nyberg was the sole member) considers it likely that the lack of overall analysis and responsibility in so many Irish institutions may have allowed a number of warning signs to go undetected' (p. 97). The Department of Finance being 'seriously underweight in professional expertise' echoed an earlier critique in the Wright Report of December 2010 which found 'in a cadre of 542 staff, the Department had only 39 economists trained to Masters level or higher ... 39 economists in the Department of Finance is extraordinarily low by international standards' (pp. 44/5).

Nyberg criticised strongly the roles of the Central Bank and the Financial Regulator in the banking crisis in Ireland. 'The Central Bank had a pivotal position, itself contributing to overall financial stability and being able to direct the Financial Regulator', but 'did little to alert banks or other authorities to the growing foreign debt or to potential stability risks from the property boom or the overheating economy' (p. vii). Nyberg further states that 'the Central Bank was not powerless; it had the right to direct the activities of the Financial Regulator and it could advise the government. There are, however, no records of such direction or advice or even efforts at such'.

Nyberg makes specific criticisms of 'the enablers' in relation to their non-supervision of zombie banks. 'The problems in Anglo and INBS in particular, were not hidden but were in plain sight of the Financial Regulator and the Central Bank. The funding of Anglo was obvious from its balance sheet and the concentration to the more speculative part of the market was generally known. Similarly, INBS's expansion into development lending was also clearly documented and governance problems in the bank were widely known by the authorities' (p. vii). Nyberg also noted 'the lack of economics skills in the Financial Regulator', lack of leadership in both the Regulator and the Central Bank and a 'solid lack of understanding of stability issues at most management levels' (p. viii).

Nyberg recommended 'reducing and delimiting at least the part of the banking system that may be subject to the various types of government support'. He sought to 'markedly limit bonus and pay for management in both banks and authorities'. He recommended that 'bank auditors should have a regular compulsory dialogue with the client's senior management and boards on the bank's business model, strategy and implementation risks' (p. x).

Nyberg is a useful guide to preventing a repeat of policy and regulatory failure in Ireland. The casual dismissal of the IMF recommendations in 2018 on capital investment assessment in Ireland by the National Development Plan and the hospital cost escalation in 2019 indicate resistance to reform.

SEAN BARRETT

Oireachtas Joint Committee Report

The terms of reference for the Inquiry that were agreed by Dáil Éireann on November 25, 2014 and Seanad Éireann on November 26, 2014, stated that 'the subject matter of the inquiry shall be to inquire into the reasons Ireland experienced a systemic banking crisis including the political, economic, social, cultural, financial and behavioural factors and policies which impacted on or contributed to the crisis, by investigating relevant matters relating to banking systems and practices, regulatory and supervisory systems and practices, crisis management systems, and policy responses and the preventative reforms implemented in the wake of the crisis.

The members of the Joint Committee were deputies Ciaran Lynch (chairman), Pearse Doherty, Joe Higgins, Michael McGrath, Eoghan Murphy, Kieran O'Driscoll and John Paul Phelan, and Senators Sean Barrett, Michael D'Arcy, Marc McSharry, and Susan O'Keefe. The committee held 95 public hearing sessions over 49 days, had private meetings on 57 days, and interviewed 131 witnesses. The witnesses included bank representatives, bank auditors and regulators, senior public servants, people from the construction sector, media commentators, economists from Ireland and abroad, and members and former members of the Oireachtas, including Taoiseach Kenny, former Taoisigh Ahern and Cowen, and senior figures in the Fine Gael, Fianna Fáil, the Green Party, Labour and the Progressive Democrats. The Inquiry report covers three volumes, namely, Volume 1: The Report; Volume 2: The Inquiry Framework; and Volume 3: Evidence. The Report covers 11 chapters and contains 78 findings and 35 recommendations.

There are 11 chapters in the *Banking Inquiry Report* and they may be summarised as follows: Chapter 1, 'The Banks': This chapter contains 13 findings and 10 recommendations. The main findings are that 'when the crisis broke in 2008, banks had already moved very far from prudent lending principles in their dealings with the property development sector in favour of a riskier asset value based lending model'. Commercial real estate lending 'was concentrated among a small number of debtors and in many cases was inadequately secured by paper equity and personal guarantees'. Also, 'there was a culture of excessive executive remuneration in the banks'. The Inquiry recommended experience in financial skill sets and compulsory training appropriate to banking including risk and governance and regular reviews of the internal audit function in banks.

Chapter 2, 'External Auditors': The report notes that KPMG, EY, and PwC dominated the audits of Irish financial institutions for extended unbroken periods. The Inquiry report supports the 'European Commission's recommendations on audit changes for banking, which include mandatory audit rotation of audit firms (originally a maximum engagement period of six years with some exceptions was proposed but this was subsequently increased to 10 years), compulsory tendering for audit services, prohibition on audit firms providing non-audit services and European supervision of the audit sector should be implemented'.

Chapter 3, 'The Property Sector': This section noted that 'many developers had become heavily reliant on bank debt to fund their developments', and that, 'as the property boom took hold, reliance on informal "desktop" and "drive-by" valuations, which did not involve any physical inspection of a property, became more prevalent'. The Joint Committee recommended that 'a detailed and comprehensive property price register should be introduced'.

Chapter 4, 'State Institutions': This chapter is heavily critical of the Central Bank, the Financial Regulator and the Department of Finance. The Bank and the Regulator were aware 'as early as 2003', of the reliance of Irish banks on the property sector, but neither 'intervened decisively at the time or on the years prior to the crisis'. The Department of Finance did not form an independent review on some of the risks identified in IMF, OECD and European Commission reports, but engaged in 'editing and reducing the risks highlighted in the international reports and in speaking notes for the Minister'. The recommendations concerning this chapter included greater expertise in financial stability, and prudential regulation on the board of the Central Bank and the banking division on the Department of Finance and better recording, minuting and documentation of meetings in the civil service. Also recommended was an independent Budgetary Office, increased public access to advice provided by civil servants and special advisors.

Chapter 5, 'Government Policy and the Oireachtas': In this chapter the Report notes significant long-term expenditure commitments made on the back of unsustainable transaction-based revenue streams; particularly tax incentives, extended without sufficient analysis of the costs, benefits and impacts which fuelled an already strong construction industry during most years from the mid-1990s up to 2006. All the main political parties advocated pro-cyclical policies in the years leading up to the crisis, especially in the 2007 general election. The Report recommended effective oversight by Oireachtas committees to improve accountability.

Chapter 6, 'Preparation for the Crisis: July 2007 – September 29, 2008': In August 2007, the NTMA decided to stop placing deposits in any Irish bank. The Minister for Finance directed the NTMA to place deposits in AIB, BOI, IL&P and EBS on December 19, 2007 and in Anglo on December 21, 2007. Further instructions were issued in August 2008 and by then NTMA had €790m on deposit in Irish banks. The Central Bank and Financial Regulator sought liquidity support for other banks but 'it is unclear if this approach was ever communicated to the Government'. No independent deep dive investigation of the banks had been commissioned by the authorities before September 2008. Crisis management preparations 'never advanced to a level capable of dealing with a major bank crisis'. The Inquiry recommended that the powers of the Minister for Finance relating to directions to the NTMA should be reviewed.

Chapter 7, 'The Guarantee': The key findings of this chapter were that Department of the Taoiseach did not keep minutes of the meetings on the night of the guarantee; that the draft press release prepared by the Central Bank covered only deposits and interbank lending; that the ECB had made it clear that no Eurozone-wide initiative was coming and the Sovereign was to ensure that no bank was to fail; and that the government 'was advised by the Central Bank and Financial Regulator that all six banks were solvent on the night of the guarantee'.

Chapter 8, 'Post-Guarantee Developments': The Inquiry found that the PwC Project Atlas Report (September/October 2008) did not reveal the true extent of the capital requirements of the banks because official forecasts for the economy did not materialise, there was insufficient time for loan analysis given the fragility of the banking system and the Report was based on the banks' management accounts and not on independent verification of the loan books.

Chapter 9, 'NAMA': The National Asset Management Agency acquired property development loans from Irish banks with original asset values of €88b, for which it paid €54b. The Inquiry noted in its evidence that 'the acquisition of good loans as well as the bad, was not well received by all borrowers'. The Inquiry recommended that NAMA should continue to be reviewed.

Chapter 10, 'Ireland and the Troika Programme': The Inquiry found that the IMF bailout was under consideration from September 2008 and that the ECB threatened on November 19, 2010 to cease ELA support for Irish banks if Ireland did not enter a bailout programme.

Chapter 11, 'Burden Sharing': The IMF favoured imposing losses on senior bondholders and the NTMA prepared a report on burden sharing with junior and senior bondholders. The Inquiry found that the ECB position 'on imposing losses on senior bondholders contributed to the inappropriate placing of significant banking debts on the Irish citizen'. The Inquiry recommended that 'the Irish government should seek to have the relevant European statutes examined to allow the ECB to participate in parliamentary inquiries'. The President of the European Central Bank, Jean Claude Trichet, refused to appear before the Inquiry in the parliament building at Leinster House in Dublin, but chose instead the Europhile Institute of European and International Affairs, with the parliamentarians in the body of the hall at the Royal Hospital in Dublin. This was the low point in the work of the Joint Committee. The final witness to the Inquiry, Finance Minister Michael Noonan, stated in evidence that he was told by Mr Trichet that 'a bomb will go off in Dublin' if Noonan's proposals to burn bondholders were implemented. The EU contributed to the Irish banking crisis and economic collapse by serious design faults in the euro currency. The abolition of the Irish currency removed an economic signal in that the exchange rate would have incorporated the impact of the large foreign borrowing by Irish banks as they moved from customer deposits as their lending base. The free movement of capital from large to small economies was not evaluated as the ingredient of a property price boom leading to a banking system overwhelmingly based on property sales. Banks were inadequately regulated both by the ECB and the Irish authorities. Interest rates inappropriate to Ireland were imported to the Irish economy. There is no exit mechanism from the euro currency.

Ireland sleepwalked into the currency without analysis and with the ex-post justification that the euro was a political rather than an economic project.

The hearings of the Joint Committee were shown live on television. This allowed the citizens to see the principal actors of a crisis that is estimated to have cost Irish taxpayers €64b. A wide range of incompetence in banking, bank auditing and regulation, and in public agencies, was exposed to the public view. The operation of the Inquiry was restricted by the requirement that questions to be asked by the parliamentarians be submitted in advance to the Inquiry team lawyers and that no supplemental questions could be asked. There were also issues of capture between the Inquiry administration staff and the parliamentarians, which required the latter to reassert that it was a parliamentary committee report. The Inquiry Report adds to the literature on how reckless behaviour in financial institutions and weak public sector regulation amounting to non-supervision by the permanent government of the senior bureaucracy signalled the end of the Celtic Tiger era. The regulatory capture achieved was virtually effortless because the agencies were so inept. The Inquiry also illustrates a serious moral hazard aspect of the Irish banking crisis, in that the burden was successfully transferred to taxpayers as a whole by the private and public sector bodies, which caused the problem in the first instance. In many fields, the reform of Irish economic policy in response to the banking crisis seems more apparent than real in retrospect. Should we actually wish to avoid a repeat of earlier debacles, the Joint Inquiry Report into the Irish Banking Crisis is a good place from which to start.

FABRICE MOURLON

Peace Process: A French Perspective

In the 1990s, the Peace Process in Northern Ireland that would lead to the signing of the Good Friday Agreement in 1998 developed at the same time as the economy in the Republic of Ireland experienced an unprecedented boom, which encouraged cross-border cooperation. The Common Travel Area (1923) agreement between Ireland and the UK, which allowed free movement of people, together with the integration of both countries into the European Single Market (1993), guaranteeing free circulation of goods, paved the way for more economic exchanges. The positive impact of the EU Structural and Cohesion Funds, the investment in quality education and the setting-up of low corporation tax rates fuelled Foreign Direct Investment in the Republic of Ireland – especially from the US – boosting new sectors such as ICT, high-tech, life sciences and financial services. The over-reliance on foreign investments also meant that the financial crisis of 2008 hit the Irish economy hard. It would appear to be improving again if the economic data is anything to go by.

During the Peace Process, Northern Ireland also enjoyed US investment and benefited from the EU Programmes such as PEACE (1995–2020) and INTERREG (1991–2020). Political developments from the mid-1980s on created a favourable context for the resolution of the conflict. The republican movement led by Gerry Adams eschewed violence to adopt a political approach. SDLP leader John Hume played a decisive and crucial role in developing a peacemaking model promoting dialogue between the various traditions in Ireland and building 'harmonious relations' with Britain. He gradually secured the support of the US by engaging in a dialogue with its successive Presidents, from Jimmy Carter to Bill Clinton. At home, a series of talks with Adams would form the basis for a pro-nationalist agenda.

The shift among the Irish-American diaspora away from a pro-Republican support towards a peaceful solution of the conflict contributed to the Clinton administration's involvement in the Peace Process by the early 1990s. Behind the scene negotiations led the Irish and British governments to publish the Downing Street Declaration (1993), which recognised the right of the people of the island of Ireland to 'bring about a united Ireland' on the basis of consent. After an exhausting process entered into by all parties and assisted by direct involvement of the British, Irish and American administrations, the Good Friday Agreement gave Northern Ireland the tools for political stability with the creation of local institutions, North–South and British–Irish bodies. It recognised the legitimacy of both traditions in the north and enshrined the principle of the right to self-determination for the whole of Ireland. US Senator George Mitchell, Tony Blair and Bertie Ahern were instrumental in bringing Northern Ireland's political parties to negotiate, thus alleviating Unionists' fears over cross-border cooperation and Sinn Féin's mistrust of local institutions. While the Good Friday Agreement dispensations were implemented with the UUP and the SDLP forming the first devolved government, the issues of decommissioning, demilitarisation and policing continued to mar the fragile political consensus.

Nonetheless, the peace dividend yielded almost immediate fruit, with major investment in the Greater Belfast Area development of Victoria Square shopping centre, the Titanic Quarter, and the Cathedral Quarter. The Northern Irish economy experienced rapid growth in the service and manufacturing sectors, benefiting also from the spectacular economic prosperity sparked by the rise of the Celtic Tiger in the Republic. As a result, tourism became a vibrant sector in Ireland north and south, with the Irish Tourist Board promoting the country's cultural heritage, scenery and welcoming atmosphere in foreign countries. The Irish diaspora was also instrumental in celebrating Irish culture abroad, as can be seen in the huge popularity of St Patrick's Day on the global stage.

However, the results of the referendum on Brexit in 2016, and the ensuing long drawn-out negotiations, have destabilised cross-border cooperation. Despite the optimistic report of the Joint Committee on the Implementation of the Good Friday Agreement released by the Houses of the Oireachtas in 2017, which encouraged the economic reunification of the country, the debate on Brexit reignited old fears among unionists in Northern Ireland and antagonised the two communities there. The fragile consensus that had developed since the return of the devolved institution in 2007 with a power-sharing arrangement between Sinn Féin and the DUP, has regularly been derailed by various disagreements on issues such as welfare reform, flags and emblems, the Irish language and dealing with the past. This led to the breakdown of the local institutions in 2017.

The Peace Process assisted economic growth and successes in the Republic of Ireland and Northern Ireland. However, the economic stability could be threatened by the challenges associated with Brexit.

MICK FEALTY

Peace Process and Anglo-Irish Relations

In terms of Anglo-Irish relations, the Tiger years are synonymous with the most successful years of the Northern Irish years when Bertie and Ahern and Tony Blair made peace in Northern Ireland a top priority for both the Irish and British administrations. A report on a survey for the British Council in 2003, noted how the two men seemed to 'work well together, are in the same age bracket and they seem to be in one line of thought'. This close alignment followed almost a century of British–Irish discord.

The technology boom, which drove the Irish economy, peaked in 1996, and came roughly midway between the ceasefires of 1994 and the historic compromises, contained within the Belfast Agreement. The convergence of British and Irish interests along with Ireland's increased capacity and resources provided both countries with an opportunity 'to make a lasting settlement of the Northern Ireland question a more attainable option'.

The Belfast Agreement replaced the territorial claim on Northern Ireland in Articles 2 and 3 with an aspiration 'to unite all the people who share the territory of the island of Ireland, in all the diversity of their identities and traditions'. The north–south and east–west strands of the Belfast Agreement also established a framework for cooperation and agenda-setting through cross cutting bodies including at the most senior international level, the *British–Irish Intergovernmental Conference.*

However, both governments invested heavily in the idea that allowing parties of the former extremes, the DUP and Sinn Féin, to drive the reshaping and control outworking powersharing institutions of the new Northern Ireland, would bring an end to conflict. The conference which followed the lengthiest collapse of Stormont at St Andrews in Scotland in October 2006 ignored inputs from the smaller parties, and established what became an effective duopoly between the DUP and Sinn Féin.

The departure of the first of the two key players in the shape of British Prime Minister Tony Blair in June 2007 heralded the end of any sustained interest at senior level in the nascent Northern Irish political process on British side. The departure of Ahern the following May combined with the sudden and catastrophic crumbling of the Celtic Tiger in the Republic's domestic banking crisis of Autumn 2008.

With the financial strictures imposed on the incoming government by the Troika, all existing commitments were honoured, but the political focus on the Irish side was absorbed in wider European Affairs and Northern Ireland's periodic crises attended to on a priority only basis.

JUSTIN CARVILLE

Photography

The ubiquity of the photographic image in the visual culture of the Celtic Tiger was such that its effects on Irish society's perception of the period has largely gone unnoticed. In its variegated forms, photography was mobilised by architects, planners, property developers and the print media to both aestheticise the physical and social transformation of urban and suburban life, and also to normalise visual consumption of unfettered property development as an expression of future prosperity. Virtual environments were constructed by architects and planners to envision property developments through post-photographic digitally generated images, that although not produced through a camera lens, took on the characteristics of the photographic image. These images adorned building hoarding that was wrapped around marquee property developments in city centres, and advertising billboards promoting the future promise of housing developments in suburbs and rural towns.

Through these everyday forms, photography increasingly became part of the scenography of the Celtic Tiger, which took on an intensified photographic appearance. Photography was also a major feature of broadsheet weekly property supplements which codified for readers the visual characteristics of property porn that propagated the myth of the property ladder as a symbol of social and economic mobility. The speculative and aspirational sentiments of the Celtic Tiger increasingly became crystalised through photography as people increasingly bought future property developments based on images.

While photography was embedded in a visual economy that not only constructed images of property development, but also shaped how they should be perceived, it also became a medium through which to forensically explore the social and spatial transformation of the Celtic Tiger years by documentary photographers and artists. The mid-1990s saw a number of significant developments in Irish photographic culture. In 1995 the Gallery of Photography, Dublin, which had been established in 1978, moved into the state's first purpose-built photography gallery, as part of the regeneration of Temple Bar as the city's cultural quarter. In addition, photographic education was transformed from an industry apprenticeship model to a more critically framed visual arts practice model, with the establishment of two honours degree programmes. As a result, Irish photography of the Celtic Tiger period began to reflect both the influences of global photographic movements in documentary and art photography, and the effect of post-modern and post-colonial critical theory in the photographic exploration of the cultural politics of identity and space.

Two projects made a significant intervention into the photographic culture of the period. The first was the German photographer Axel Boeten's series *Traffic Island*, exhibited in the Gallery of Photography in 2003. Boesten's series combined portraits of young Irish workers with photographs of the spatial environments of international call centres in newly constructed business parks. Ostensibly a project about new alienated forms of labour emerging out of Ireland's position in the global economy, Boesten's series identified the visible forms of foreign investment in the rectilinear forms of suburban office buildings which jarred against the landscaped environments of out-of-town business parks. Mark Curran's dual projects *Site* (the construction of the M50) and *Prospect* (the IFSC) brought together in the exhibition *Southern Cross*, incorporated formal portraits of labourers and office workers along with photographs of construction sites and the glass and steel of IFSC office buildings. Although of two discrete sites, the bringing together of the two projects attempted to draw out the tensions of fixed and productive capital that were configuring the Celtic Tiger landscapes.

In the following years much Irish photography took on a spatial bent as numerous photographers turned attention to the transformation of physical space through the building boom and state-run infrastructure projects. The term 'topographical-turn' was coined to describe the characteristics of this work, drawing attention to the aesthetic and political influence of the American New Topographic movement of the 1970s, but also the surface of topographical change being the visible manifestation of deeper political and economic processes that remained imperceptible to the eye. Dara McGrath's 2003 series *By the Way*, which portrayed the intermediary spaces between suburban housing estates and the M50 road network in North Dublin, and Martin Cregg's long-term series *The Midlands*, which documented the empty business parks and emerging ghost estates on the outskirts of regional towns, were prominent examples of the topographical turn in Celtic Tiger photography.

While the term 'Celtic-Tiger photography' has been used to classify photography of this period, the neologism post-Celtic Tiger photography has also emerged to describe this work. The term is strategic in that it seeks to incorporate both the work from the mid-1990s until the economic crisis of 2008, and the work of photographers who have photographed the continued spatial effects of its aftermath. Projects such as Liam Devlin's *Space to Love/Space to Shop* (2008), Anthony Haughey's *Settlement* (2011), and David Farrell's ongoing long-term project on Ireland's ghost estates, *An Archaeology of the Present*, documented the spatial transformation of the Celtic Tiger period and its residuum that continues to mark Ireland's topographies.

SHAEN CORBET

PIIGS Countries

PIIGS is an acronym for five of the most economically weak Eurozone nations during the European debt crisis, namely Portugal, Italy, Ireland, Greece and Spain. The group were mostly known for their weakened economic output and financial instability, which heightened doubts about the nations' abilities to pay back bondholders and generated substantial fear that any of the countries could default on their debts. The term itself appears to have been modified by the *Financial Times* throughout 2009 and 2010 through the addition of a second 'I' to the term PIGS.

The term originated in the 1970s and 1980s with the increased integration of the EU economies, and it was often used in reference to the growing debt and economic vulnerability of the southern European countries, all of which are peripheral to both Germany and France. The addition of a second 'I' represented the addition of Ireland to the group, as the Celtic Tiger economy began to collapse and the probability of a bailout increased. Although Ireland would have been widely considered as a peripheral, economically problematic country throughout the 1970s and 1980s, the Celtic Tiger era elevated perceptions of the country's economic prowess. Since the establishment of the euro as their currency, this group have been unable to employ independent monetary policy to help counteract the widespread damage caused by the financial crisis in 2008.

The economic troubles of the PIIGS nations reignited debate about the efficacy of the single currency employed among the Eurozone nations by casting doubts on the notion that the European Union can maintain a single currency, while attending to the individual needs of each of its member countries. Critics point out that continued economic disparities could lead to a breakup of the Eurozone. In response, EU leaders proposed a peer review system for approval of national spending budgets in an effort to promote closer economic integration among EU member states. It is widely considered that when responding to the European economic crisis, a new approach within the European Union is required. To satisfy the needs of 27 exceptionally different member states, the simplistic 'one-size- fits-all' approach may no longer be the most efficient solution, particularly as there are exceptional differences to the challenges that each member state faces, particularly those of the PIIGS.

The slow-moving Brussels administration at the centre of the European project appears to be unable to characterise and solve the multitude of differing issues it faces. The recent rise of populist and extremist movements can, in part, be explained as a response to the 2007 financial crisis, with even more pronounced evidence presented in the European periphery. In this age of social media-driven mistruths and alternative-truths, the speed of political spectrum change appears to have overcome the structure within which it was designed to be contained. It is widely considered that, within the PIIGS nations, the stress and anger associated with broad austerity implementation in the period after the European financial crises, along with exceptional levels of immigration, have been key drivers that have caused each European member state to enter a period of inward reaction. The left wing movements of Europe have found success by appealing to those most affected by austerity, with dramatic growth in Greece, Ireland, Portugal and Spain. The most prolific examples are identified as that of SYRIZA in Greece, Podemos in Spain and the Anti-Austerity Alliance (Solidarity) in Ireland. Nationalist parties have also received significant support through a combination of dissident voices opposing austerity measures and immigration.

The rise of right-wing parties has been correlated with the promotion of populist Euroscepticism, combined with continuous anti-immigration commentary and opposition to multi-cultural integration. One example of such ultra-nationalism is witnessed in the growth in support for the Greek party Golden Dawn, which obtained 18 seats out of 300 in the Hellenic parliament despite an ideology of neo-Nazism and fascism. The party have been linked with the use of Nazi symbolism and have represented political rhetoric possessing dangerously similar characteristics to that of the German Nazi party.

The UK Independence Party was one of the driving forces supporting the decision for the United Kingdom to leave the European Union and the right-wing movement in France forwarded by National Front, a nationalist party that uses populism to promote its anti-immigration and Eurosceptic stance also share similar, but somewhat less extreme views. These political shifts are evidence of the deep-rooted effects sourced in peripheral European membership and being an unfortunate member of the PIIGS group.

EOIN FLANNERY

Poetry

Poetry might seem a long way from the centre of Irish society's priorities during the Celtic Tiger, and its aftermath, but poetry resolutely precedes and outlasts all such periodical economic and social cycles. Contrary to the sterile imaginative horizons of Ireland's economic boom, in form and content, poetry recognises and embraces multiple futures, and it eschews the delimited mindscapes of unidirectional consumerism. The hollowed-out and dispiriting value system regnant during the Celtic Tiger is anathema to the empathy and generosity embodied by the best of poetry. There is real value to be appreciated when one is alive and open to what the American poet and critic, James Longenbach, terms, 'the virtues of poetry'.

Poetry must itself be challenging as it confronts the challenge of registering as an effective and an affective medium in on-going public debates in Ireland. This very contention is apparent in a piece in *The Irish Times* by Fintan O'Toole, where he moves away from his more sustained anatomisations of the iniquities of Ireland's erstwhile political and financial elites to focus on the role of culture in the post-Celtic Tiger era. For O'Toole 'the boom was resolutely unpoetic,' while 'its hard-faced greed' offered 'an impossible challenge to the lyricism that is the first resort of Irish writing' (2011).

Irish poetry did respond to the hypocrisies and the inequities of the 'boom' years in Ireland with frustration, irony, and black humour. We can intuit from O'Toole's argument that art and culture became commoditised during the Celtic Tiger years and, in addition, the idioms of Irish creative expression were too often warped by the imported and reifying codes of global capitalism. Where culture was not commoditised, it was alienated from Irish society, as the self-reflexive, often critical, function of public art was no longer relevant in a culture defined by consumption and self-congratulation. Indeed, we can see evidence of creative scrutiny in poetic reflections and critiques of the Celtic Tiger period in Ireland by Paul Durcan, Dennis O'Driscoll, Rita Ann Higgins, Dave Lordan, Derek Mahon, Alice Lyons, Iggy McGovern, and Kevin Higgins. These works were written, variously, during the 'ascendancy' of the Celtic Tiger, and after its decline, and represent a range of poetry that responds to social dislocation, moral hypocrisy, cultural inauthenticity and ecological 'ruination'.

In his 2004 collection, *The Art of Life*, Paul Durcan's 'The Celtic Tiger' is striking for the manner in which it 'voices' poverty, exploitation and violence in juxtaposition to material wealth and personal security. The opening section gives a voice to a young woman from a lower-class background – a socio-economic profile that was, and continues to be, denied but that fully deserves a countervailing platform when one reflects on the Celtic Tiger years. Indeed, what is notable from the opening of the poem is that there is no mention of consumption, property speculation or financial largesse. In this way the lengthy first section of 'The Celtic Tiger' seems to be out of sync with the anticipated theme or focus of Durcan's title. In several respects, with its attention to gender, motherhood, abandonment and institutional religion, Durcan's poeticisation of the Celtic Tiger chimes with Rita Ann Higgins's renditions of Ireland's newly affluent society.

'Too many plugs and switches in the room,' John Updike writes at the opening of his poem, 'New Resort Hotel, Portmarnock,' thus capturing, metonymically, the culture of wasteful excess that prevailed during much of the Celtic Tiger years. Updike's poem is part of a triptych of Petrarchan sonnets grouped under the title, 'A Wee Irish Suite,' and appeared in his 2009 collection, *Endpoint and other poems*. It is Updike's ironic take on the Celtic Tiger that proves most effective in this short poem, concentrated, primarily, in the octet, where he writes: 'Too many outlets for the well- / connected businessman, too much Preferred / Lifestyle, here in formerly lovely Eire'. Notwithstanding the potentially grating nostalgia of the final clause, again it is the vision of excessive connectivity without actual connection that exercises Updike's poetic irony. He condenses this in his selection of phrases, 'Too many' and 'Too much', which repeat and echo, in turn, the opening enunciation of the poem. Accumulation, liquidity and consumerist impulses do not seem to be symptoms of historical progress in Updike's snapshot of Ireland, but, rather, are those of cultural and social vertigo. For Updike, there is a dishonesty and a shallowness to Ireland's transient embrace of hyper-consumerism. While some of his rhetoric skirts perilously close to a lamentation for a more 'authentic' Irish culture, his cursory poetic intervention is an instructive *international* poetic perspective on Celtic Tiger Ireland, and chimes with those in circulation by the aforementioned selection of Irish poets.

CHARLES LARKIN

Political Economy

Political economy is the traditional term associated with the study of the economic and financial conditions of a country. The term is most closely associated with Adam Smith, David Ricardo and John Stuart Mill, who authored works on the subject. Political economy sought to integrate what are now distinct disciplines of psychology, jurisprudence, philosophy, economics and political science into one body of knowledge.

Since the mid-twentieth century, economics became a more distinct science based upon mathematical modelling and empirical analysis. Political economy as a term became part of a series of subdisciplines within economics, sociology and political science, most notably as economic policy studies, social policy studies and international or global political economy with further specialisation based upon schools of thought and methodology.

In the case of global political economy, these divisions are based along national lines, as in the US and UK schools of thought. Since the Global Financial Crisis of 2008–13, there has been a renewed interest in the consolidated discipline of political economy with the opening of a department at King's College London in 2010.

NA FU

Professional Service Firms

During the 1990s, Ireland attracted significant foreign direct investment (FDI) which is evidenced by the amount of multinational companies who set up in Ireland. Both MNCs and domestic firms needed accounting and legal services. Such increasing demands in professional service promoted the fast growth in scale and significance of professional service firms in Ireland during the Celtic Tiger.

Academically, professional service firms (PSFs) are defined by Greenwood and his colleagues as 'those whose primary assets are a highly educated (professional) workforce and whose outputs are intangible services encoded with complex knowledge'. Examples of PSFs are accounting, law, consulting and architecture firms. PSFs are knowledge-based or knowledge-intensive organisations. However, they are different from knowledge-intensive firms as their knowledge output is highly customised. In other words, both the services provided by PSFs and the processes involved are customised or tailored to individual customers' needs. In this way, pharmaceutical and software companies are categorised as knowledge-intensive firms, but are not professional service firms, as they sell the same products/services to all customers and do not tailor them for individual clients as PSFs do.

PSFs are knowledge intensive and highly dependent on people. Their input is knowledge embedded in their professional workforce, and their outputs are expert knowledge in the form of customised solutions for their clients. There are three types of capital resources to maintain the PSFs' competitive advantages: human (knowledge, abilities and skills of individuals), social (who you know, relationships) and organisational (efficient organisational system, process and culture) capital resources. Together, it is labelled 'intellectual capital'.

PSFs mainly adopt the partnership form of governance where professionals experience a higher degree of autonomy than they would typically enjoy in conventional bureaucratic structures. Some PSFs, for example, the Big Four accounting firms, have shifted towards the corporate structure, but still attempt to imitate elements of the partnership form. Even employing the corporate structure, PSFs have relatively few levels of hierarchy. With regard to financial structure, many PSFs bill by the hour (or partial hour), day, or an estimated number of days to complete the project.

Taking the example of accountancy, a traditional professionalised and regulated sector; in Ireland, accounting firms mainly employ chartered accountants. These were the first accountants to form a professional body, initially established in the UK in 1854. All accounting firms having chartered accountants are facilitated and managed by the institution of the Chartered Accountants Ireland (CAI). CAI is the largest and longest established accountancy body in Ireland, and has over 18,000 members and 6,500 students. The Chartered Accountants Regulatory Board is a body established by the Institute of Chartered Accountants in Ireland to regulate its members, in accordance with the provisions of the Institute's bye-laws, independently, openly and in the public interest. It has firm information for over 1000 accounting firms located across Ireland. Due to the fast development of MNCs as well as the internationalisation of Irish domestic firms, other regulations and accounting standards had begun to be used in Ireland, including the Association of Chartered Certified Accountants (ACCA), the Institute of Certified Public Accountants in Ireland (CPA), the Chartered Institute of Management Accountants (CIMA), and the Institute of Incorporated Public Accountants (IIPA). Most of the Irish accounting firms are small and medium sized. The Big Four accounting firms during the Celtic Tiger period were KPMG, Ernst & Young (EY), Deloitte, PricewaterhouseCoopers (PwC) and Arthur Andersen. Arthur Andersen Ireland merged with KPMG in 2002.

Overall, PSFs had experienced fast development during the 1990s and 2000s. PSFs employ highly educated workforce and provide knowledge-intensive service to their clients. People are the most valuable resource for PSFs to be successful. PSFs have contributed to the knowledge-based economy during the Irish Celtic Tiger time period and beyond.

CONSTANTIN GURDGIEV

Progressive Democrats

The Progressive Democrats was a political party born out of the widespread public disillusionment with corruption that characterised those at the forefront in Charles Haughey's Ireland. It went on to preside, as an ideological crutch to Bertie Ahern's parish-pump politicking and governance-rules-bending Fianna Fáil, over the creation of the Celtic Tiger and its destruction. As such, one might as well argue that the Progressive Democrats were a cure that made the Irish disease of mis-governance and poor leadership incurable.

The PDs were launched in December 1985 by Des O'Malley and led by a group of ex-Fianna Fáil and Fine Gael politicians who were broadly supportive of a liberal (if not moderately libertarian) social policy agenda, including liberalisation of divorce, contraception and other progressive social policies, while advocating classical liberal positions on economic deregulation, privatisation and low taxation. Originally, the PDs also supported fiscal conservativism and welfare reforms aimed at incentivising higher labour force participation and lower social welfare dependency.

Although founded to contain the Fianna Fáil's corruption and parish-pump politics, the PDs ended up as junior partners in coalition governments with Fianna Fáil in 1989–92 and 1997–2009. Proving that the lap dog's power corrupts no less than absolute power does, the PDs have punched well above their electorally rather invisible weight. During the Celtic Tiger days, the party pushed through a pro-business, low tax economic agenda and presided over the systemic dismantling of regulatory constraints in banking and finance. Meanwhile, its partner in government was actively pursuing the 'green jersey' agenda that promoted abandonment of regulatory enforcement constraints on Irish banks and property markets, as well as unrestricted fiscal spending and investment to support the so-called Social Partnership arrangement of the state-connected organisations and institutions. The combination of the PDs' pro-business ideological stance, and Fianna Fáil's crony corporatism first sustained the Celtic Tiger boom post-1997, and then saw two major financial and asset bubbles bursting – the dot.com bubble crash of 2001–2, and the property bubble crash of 2008–10.

In the wake of the latter crisis, the PDs were dissolved in November 2009, having left a lasting, but controversial legacy as the only major party in Ireland's modern history to ever put forward an ideologically based political platform.

CONSTANTIN GURDGIEV

Property Boom

The house price boom of 1996–2007 was the Celtic Tiger's slow-motion, train crash-like reckoning with Ireland's unalterable historical obsession with property as the main investment asset class, and as the Holy Grail of domestic economic development.

Following a mini-boom in 1977–9, when house prices in Ireland rose at an average rate of 10.9% per annum, the 1980s saw a decade of house price contractions, with an average annual rate of price decline of 3.7% between 1980 and 1987. From there on, and through 1995, house prices grew broadly in line with economic expansion, clocking an average annual rate of growth of just under 3%. Fuelled by tax cuts, property investment incentives and the gradual abandonment of lending constraints in the banking sector, the Celtic Tiger property boom properly took off in 1996, with an average annual growth rate through 2007 of 9.68%. Although the house price inflation rate peaked early in the property boom cycle (averaging 15.75% per annum over 1997–2001), house prices peaked in 2007 at three times their levels back at the start of the boom 12 years earlier.

Much of this boom in house prices was accompanied by similarly spectacular rollercoaster gains in the commercial property segment and in broader property investment. Buy-to-lets mushroomed in the later stages of the boom, as did purely speculative, casino-odds-like buy-ins by Irish investors (from senior civil servants to taxi drivers) into foreign property syndicates. By 2004, Irish business media was full of advertisements for off-plan sales of Bulgarian and Hungarian apartment schemes. One well-known commentator on the Irish economy and financial advice guru was out selling Cape Verde, a small African country, 300 miles west of Senegal, as the 'new Canaries'.

Few saw the end of the bubble coming early enough for the regulators to react. In the early 2000s and throughout the crash, David McWilliams has consistently warned of the dangerous over-valuation of Irish residential and commercial properties. In 2004, Constantin Gurdgiev estimated that Irish housing prices were approximately 40% overvalued, based on Irish economic fundamentals. In summer 2007, Morgan Kelly wrote a now famous article published alongside the ESRI's *Quarterly Economic Commentary*, which suggested that the 'same people who told us we would have a soft landing are saying we will crawl out ... we have bottomed out. We have not. We are very far from the bottom of the property market'. However, Irish media and the majority of Irish analysts – from economists, to banking experts, to property market researchers – and virtually all Irish officials in charge of economic policy, remained oblivious to the dangers of the property asset bubble inflating in their back yards.

The bust that followed the property boom has been equally impressive. From their peak in 2007, house prices fell more than 53% by the time the market hit the bottom in 2012. Eleven years after the start of the crash, Irish residential property prices were still 19.3% below their 2007 levels. Based on the data from the Bank for International Settlements and the CSO, at the end of 2018, Irish house prices were only back to the levels of mid-2005.

None of which, of course, deterred Irish investors and households from piling back into property markets once the recovery took hold in 2014. Between 2014 and 2018, Irish residential property prices appreciated at an average rate of 11.3% per annum, with double digit growth recorded every year, save 2016. The early signs of a new property price bubble emerging out of the ashes of the old one are, ironically, virtually identical to what has happened in the past: property sections and advertising in newspapers are growing once again, just as the media *kommentariate* is talking up the virtues of property ownership, and party conversations in the posher suburbs of Dublin are drowning once again in the chatter about vacation homes and investment rentals. The absence, for now, of the Irish travel groups scouring distant Eastern European countries for cheap apartments to buy is about the only part of the pre-2008 boom still missing. However, if history is any guide to the future, it will not be missing for long.

PASCHAL DONOHUE

Public Finances in the Celtic Tiger

Ireland experienced an economic boom during the Celtic Tiger decade from the mid-1990s. The employment rate rose from 54% in 1995 to 65.5% in 2004 – higher than the EU25 average of 63% that year. In the mid-2000s, the construction sector directly accounted for one in every eight persons employed, symptomatic of imbalances emerging in the economy.

The pick-up in economic conditions and, in particular, the convergence of Irish living standards to (and subsequently beyond) European norms from the second half of the 1990s, resulted in substantial migration inflows. From 1996 to 2009, average net inward migration averaged 37,000 people each year. Inward migration peaked in 2007, with inflows in net terms of 105,000 people. This was thanks, in part, to flows from those Member States that joined the EU in May 2004.

At their peak of just over €47 billion in mid-2007, taxation receipts had effectively doubled from the levels at the beginning of the decade. As turnover in the residential and commercial property sector increased abruptly during the mid-2000s, with both sectors ultimately moving from 'boom' into 'bubble' territory, transaction-based taxes (i.e. stamp duties on property transactions and capital taxes) rose. As a result, receipts from this category increased from 8% of total receipts at the beginning of the decade to 16% in 2007.

The flawed policy of using these highly cyclical, transaction-based taxes to finance both a narrowing of the income tax base and increased public expenditure (which in nominal terms doubled over the period 2000–7) lay at the heart of the collapse of the public finances from 2008. The 'tax rich' construction bubble also artificially inflated other revenue headings such as income tax receipts, which were distorted by excessive employment in the house-building sector. In addition, VAT receipts were inflated by the exceptional high level of new house building which amounted to over

90,000 units at its peak. Similarly, corporation tax receipts were artificially boosted by the highly profitable property-related activities in the banking and construction sectors.

The global financial crisis and the bursting of the construction bubble led to a contraction in GDP growth in 2008–10 (–4.8% in 2008, –9.4 in 2009 and –1.4 in 2010). The corresponding increase in unemployment resulted in enormous losses in income tax revenues and a large increase in social welfare payments. Total tax receipts declined by one third to a low of just over €31 billion in mid-2010. All taxation sub-heads were adversely affected by the collapse in domestic demand reflecting the fact that the construction bubble had pervaded numerous sectors of the economy.

The journey since then has undoubtedly been difficult but the economy is now in much better shape. The public finances have stabilised, our tax base has been broadened, we are close to full employment, progress is being made in improving our public services and our economy is one of the fastest growing in the EU. Last year, Ireland ran a small Exchequer surplus in cash terms, the first underlying surplus since 2006.

Employment, consumer spending and other economic indicators all continue to expand and, in doing so, generate tax revenue streams. In 2018, tax revenues of €55.6 billion were collected with taxes for 2019 forecast at €58.445 billion.

The transformation of the public finances is rivalled only by the transformation in the labour market. The unemployment rate has fallen from a high of 16% in 2012 to 5.4% in March of 2019. There are now more people at work than ever before. Further gains in employment are in prospect in 2019, with the number in employment expected to increase by 50,000 (2.2%). Wages are forecast to grow by over 3% in each year between 2019 and 2023. While these are very positive developments, they can create challenges also, as we move towards full employment.

The Irish economy is growing strongly and sustainably. The priority now must be to learn from the past, build on the success of recent years, continue to invest in our public services and, as a small and very globalised economy, enhance the country's resilience to withstand external shocks.

BRIAN LANGAN

Publishing

The Celtic Tiger years marked a period of transition for the publishing industry in Ireland. Through the 1970s, 1980s and early 1990s, there had been a gradual shift from a relatively traditional, indigenous focus to a more progressive and outward-looking stance that saw Irish writing as a force for change, reflecting the opening of the economy itself.

From the mid-1990s, there was a consolidation of long-established Irish publishers such as Gill & Macmillan and Mercier Press, combined with the fresh approach of relative newcomers such as Lilliput, The O'Brien Press, Poolbeg and New Island. When the economy began to take off, many of these publishers started to push out the boundaries of what Irish publishing could do. For instance, Poolbeg Press was instrumental in driving the 1990s boom in 'commercial women's fiction', exemplified by writers such as Maeve Binchy, Patricia Scanlan, Sheila O'Flanagan, Marian Keyes, Cathy Kelly and Cecilia Ahern.

UK publishers had long held an interest in Irish writers, and in the 2000s three of the biggest global publishers set up publishing offices in Ireland, with Penguin Ireland and Hodder Headline Ireland (later Hachette Ireland) both established in 2002, and Transworld Ireland founded in 2008.

These 'Anglos', as they became known, quickly established a strong sense of competition that had, arguably, been lacking among Irish publishers. Most indigenous publishers rose to the challenge. For instance, Gill Books, having rebranded after a management buyout at Gill & Macmillan, have recently had a number of huge successes, matching and at times surpassing their international competitors.

Technology and globalisation also affected Irish publishing during the Celtic Tiger years, though this initially resulted mostly in changes in processes and markets. One casualty of technological changes was the indigenous printing industry, with companies such as ColourBooks closing as a result of competition from European and Asian printing companies.

A number of other challenges saw fortunes ebb and flow through the Celtic Tiger years and beyond. In the early 1990s, the collapse of the Net Book Agreement, which had previously fixed book prices across retail outlets in the UK and Ireland, saw the rise of discounting, which inevitably favoured larger publishers, larger bookshop chains and supermarkets. This, alongside the emergence and rise of Amazon, ultimately led to the closure of a number of smaller independent bookshops, as well as the Hughes & Hughes chain, and some branches of Waterstones and Borders.

Another result of these changes was that the 'big books' dominated available shelf-space each year, with smaller publishers and titles struggling for visibility during the key selling period from September to December. This also created some opportunities for certain genres to thrive during this period. As well as the aforementioned commercial fiction (including the über-Celtic Tiger character of Ross O'Carroll-Kelly), sports books often dominated annual bestseller charts, while children's and young adult titles saw a massive resurgence, largely driven by the Harry Potter phenomenon.

Interestingly, while the early years of the Celtic Tiger saw some books on the economic phenomenon itself (including Paul Tansey's *Ireland at Work*, Paul Sweeney's *The Celtic Tiger* and Ray MacSharry and Padraic White's *The Making of the Celtic Tiger*), some of the biggest titles of the era arrived in the mid-2000s and took broader views of the changes in Irish society, two of the most notable being Diarmaid Ferriter's *The Transformation of Ireland 1900–2000* and David McWilliams' *The Pope's Children*. And, perhaps inevitably, public interest in the Irish economy grew stronger when it faltered, with the early years of the recession marked by a swathe of books with titles such as *Ship of Fools* (Fintan O'Toole), *The Bankers* (Shane Ross) and *The Banksters* (David Murphy and Martina Devlin).

While Irish literary fiction has always had a disproportionately strong influence internationally, with authors such as John McGahern, William Trevor, Edna O'Brien, John Banville and Seamus Heaney leading the way, the Celtic Tiger years witnessed a resurgence in interest in Irish literary fiction, with global successes for new and emerging writers like Anne Enright, Sebastian Barry, Emma Donoghue, Colm Tóibín, Joseph O'Connor, Roddy Doyle and Kevin Barry. However, it was not until the recession years that the lives of ordinary Irish people during and after the Celtic Tiger were examined in fiction by writers such as Donal Ryan, Lisa McInerney, Eimear MacBride, Sara Baume, Mike McCormack and, most recently, Sally Rooney.

While the Celtic Tiger years witnessed major changes in Irish publishing, in retrospect these were just a prelude to the massive changes since its demise. The recession itself coincided with the acceleration of technology and globalisation, exemplified by the increasing dominance of Amazon, the rise in eBooks, book piracy, subscription models and self-publishing, as well as competition from other art forms and, of course, the preponderance of the Internet and social media. The Irish books market fell by 35% in value terms between 2008 and 2013, yet the period since has seen a recovery and many positive changes to a resilient industry.

But that's a story for the sequel.

CHARLES LARKIN

Quinn, Sean

Sean Quinn was born on December 5, 1947, in Derrylin, County Fermanagh. He is an Irish businessman who was once the richest man in Ireland, with a net worth of €4.722bn in 2008, according to the *Sunday Times* Rich List. Sean Quinn, along with other members of his immediate family, was the owner of the privately owned Quinn Group. He is considered by many in the popular media as 'patient zero' of the Irish financial crisis that ultimately led to the collapse of Anglo Irish Bank, the Bank Guarantee, the Troika Bailout and the eventual economic contraction that lasted approximately a decade, which sunk the economy into an acute recession bordering on depression, expanded unemployment by 10% and nearly broke the Eurozone.

Quinn was one of the 'Maple 10', otherwise known as the 'Anglo Golden Circle'. He personally held approximately 10% of the shares of the Anglo Irish Bank, and a further six members of the Quinn family were also heavily invested in the Anglo Irish Bank. Quinn in July 2008 wrote to the CEO of the bank, David Drumm, advising that this was an 'ill advised' strategy. Anglo Irish Bank's internal documents showed that the transaction caused Quinn to make a collective loss of €955m. Ultimately Quinn came to owe Anglo Irish Bank €2.8bn at the point of nationalisation in January 2009. Mr Quinn sold his position in Anglo Irish Bank through contracts-for-difference (CFDs) which he had allegedly built up secretly. Quinn's family took approximately 15% of ordinary shares, while the 'Anglo Golden Circle' bought the 10% stake with loans from Anglo Irish Bank to help support the share price of Anglo Irish Bank. This was one of the many aspects of 'crony capitalism' that became associated with the use of 'light-touch' regulation in the Irish financial and property sector during the first decade of the twenty-first century.

In March 2010, the Quinn Group was placed under the control of a receiver, with Quinn Insurance no longer considered a viable entity by the then Financial Regulatory, Matthew Elderfield. In April 2011, a receiver was appointed to Sean Quinn, and his personal position and that of his family in the Quinn Group was ended. The Quinn family and Sean Quinn ceased to have any ownership or role in the Quinn Group. The Quinn Group was renamed Aventas in November 2013. Sean Quinn was declared bankrupt in Northern Ireland in November 2011, but this was annulled subsequently. Quinn was declared bankrupt in the Republic of Ireland (which has a longer discharge period than the UK) in January 2012.

Quinn was imprisoned from November 2, 2012 to January 3, 2013, for contempt of court. This related to non-cooperation with court orders, and to a €455m asset-stripping scheme set across several countries (including but not exclusively Russia, Cyprus, Czech Republic, India, and Ukraine).

The Quinn Group was a major employer (approximately 7,000 jobs) in County Cavan, where he had extensive local support. This created a tension between Quinn supporters and the authorities in Dublin, where there was widespread outcry at the financial positioning of the Quinn family, and the exposure of the Quinn Group in the collapse of Anglo Irish Bank. Sean Quinn firmly blames the 'underhand' takeover of his companies in 2011 on Anglo Irish Bank in court statements.

Since the liquidation of the Irish Bank Resolution Corporation (IBRC) in February 2013 the Quinn family has been taking legal proceedings against the Irish State since the legislation closed off any further litigation against the IBRC. Litigation at the High and Supreme Courts by Quinn and his family continues as of June 2019. A conservative estimate of the litigation costs is at €25m and rising, with no clear end in sight.

DEIRDRE FLYNN

Referendums

Over the course of the Celtic Tiger (1995–2008) Ireland held a baker's dozen of referendums: 13 in total. However, while bail restrictions (16th amendment, November 28, 1996) and the International Criminal Court (23rd amendment, June 7, 2001) might be long forgotten, there are five (well technically 4) referendums that really stand out over the 13-year period. In fact, some were so good we had to run them twice.

The Celtic Tiger began with the contentious divorce referendum on November 24, 1995. Divorce was outlawed by the constitution, and a previous referendum in 1986 was rejected by 63.5% of the population. The 1995 referendum was definitely a marker of change in Irish society, as the country began the process of separating church and state, which has continued with the marriage equality referendum in 2015 and the abortion referendum of 2018. The latter was not easily passed, and the debate was highly divisive, with slogans like 'Hello Divorce, bye bye Daddy', and 'Divorce Kills Love' on the 'No' side. Weekly sermons from the pulpits told of the evils of divorce, and the church and special interest groups like Youth Defence campaigned for a 'No' vote. Old and New Ireland were separated by this issue, and there was a clear urban–rural divide in the 'Yes' result. The referendum passed by the slightest of margins – 9,114 votes – or 50.28% to 49.72%. If it had not been for the stronger support in the Dublin city and county constituencies, along with five constituencies outside the Pale, the referendum would not have passed. The legislation introduced allowed for divorce if the couple were separated and living apart for the last four out of five years; this latter clause was removed in 2019 by another referendum. The 36th amendment in 2019, which allows for the period of separation to be decided by legislation, was passed by 87%, showing how far Ireland has come since the 1995 debates.

Three years, and three referendums later, one of the most politically significant referendums was passed by a 94.4% majority – the referendum to ratify the Good Friday Agreement on May 22, 1998. Although turnout was just 56.3% on the day, there was clear support for this historic agreement – now under threat from Brexit – which allowed all people on the island of Ireland to be part of the Irish nation.

One amendment, or two referendums, are sure to be remembered as not so 'Nice'! On June 7, 2001 Irish people rejected the Treaty of Nice by 53% and were asked to return to the polls for a very similar referendum 18 months later, which this time passed by 62.9% after 'concerns' about Irish neutrality and abortion rights were addressed in specific wording changes. Nice may have been the first referendum we had to take twice, but after the Celtic Tiger had left our shores, Ireland was again faced with another European treaty referendum twice, namely the Lisbon Treaty in June 2008 and October 2009. The deteriorating economic situation clearly convinced Irish voters that they needed Europe more than Europe needed it, from whence the change of mind.

One referendum that has current implications for Irish society is the 2004 Citizenship referendum. This referendum asked voters to remove the automatic right to Irish citizenship at birth, something that had been inserted as part of the Good Friday Agreement in 1998. Over the course of the Celtic Tiger, Ireland had seen huge increases in inward migration and people seeking asylum and this referendum highlighted (as Ronit Lentin has pointed out) how it created something of a racist state. Those who were helpful to our economic expansion were welcome, but others were not, and Irish identity was now being defined in racial terms. The campaign suggested that pregnant women were coming to Ireland as citizenship 'tourists', and placed pregnant migrant women at the centre of the debate. The referendum held on June 11, 2004 passed by 79.2% after a turnout of just under 60%. Journalist Vincent Browne, writing in *The Irish Times* in 2007, called it a low point in Irish history, while Fintan O'Toole said in 2006 that the state is using structured racism to divide migrants into good and bad people.

CONSTANTIN GURDGIEV

Regling-Watson Report

During the heydays of the pre-2008 boom, the Irish establishment's modus operandi with respect to hiring senior foreign officials into key positions at the top of the public sector's executive and regulatory pyramid, was to seek specialists who were happy to lavish praise on the Celtic Tiger's achievements. With the onset of the crisis, however, this approach has given way to the one where foreign experts are being brought in to state unspeakable (by the Irish officialdom's standards) truths.

Commissioned in February 2010, and published in May that year, the Regling-Watson Report, officially titled as 'A Preliminary Report on The Sources of Ireland's Banking Crisis', was commissioned with exactly this purpose in mind.

The main findings from the report include a summary of things known well in advance of its publication, such as the fact that the Irish financial crisis was a combination of mutually reinforcing domestic and global shocks, and that the pro-cyclical nature of Irish fiscal policies prior to the crisis increased vulnerability of the Irish economy. The report also highlighted the weak (to put it mildly) governance and risk management practices in the domestic banking sector, and how these weaknesses spilled over into the government's misguided response to the shocks relating to the collapse of the Anglo Irish Bank. The report also, predictably, blames the Irish crisis on the 'plain vanilla property bubble' that was exacerbated by the banking sector's role in fuelling same, and the concentrated nature of Irish banks' financial exposures to the property sector.

While all of these (and other) report findings were correct, the Regling-Watson report contributed virtually nothing new to our understanding of the causes of the crisis, its evolution and the lessons that should be learned from the Irish experience. Speaking to the media after the report's publications, then Minister for Finance Brian Lenihan said: 'There's nothing in

Mr Regling's report that surprises me. I've had to live with these problems since I became Minister for Finance'.

In simple terms, the Regling-Watson report was official Ireland's document of record that put the blame for the collapse of the Celtic Tiger onto virtually every institution (private and public) within the Irish economy, but allocated no individual liability. As a result, the Report helped the State to escape the need for pursuing direct investigation and punishment of key individuals who have headed up Irish financial services regulatory and supervisory authorities, shaped Irish financial regulation and policies, or presided over the Irish financial institutions in the run-up to the crisis.

KARL DEETER

Repossessions

While the history of Irish mortgage arrears (which at time of writing is a decade old and still going strong) will warrant a book of its own one day, the story of repossessions is interesting to the extent that there were constant warnings of a 'tsunami' of them that never actually arose. This was, and is, the best equivalent of an economic version of the story of Chicken Little who ran around screaming that the sky was falling. When it came to repossessing homes, Irish banks have shown a reluctance to do so, and this came from their own decisions in part because they knew that holding on for as long as possible is a solution of sorts (asset prices do tend to recover rather than go down and stay down).

The Central Bank initiated what is in this analyst's view, one of the most critically ill-thought pieces of regulation in 2009 when, under the guidance of Governor Patrick Honohan and Deputy Governor Matthew Elderfield, a one-year ban on repossessions was introduced. From that moment, there was an acceleration in an already deteriorating arrears vista because all possibility of recourse was temporarily removed. The idea had been tried and failed miserably in Hungary in the past, and it soon proved the same in Ireland as the relationship between arrears and unemployment decoupled. This was followed by restrictions in collections which came about as the 'MARP' or 'mortgage arrears resolution process' which formalised the way people in arrears should be treated. This much needed approach was then hampered by restrictions in a lender's ability to contact a person with a distressed mortgage to only three times per month. While the banks had been abusing the lack of rules in this area, this change made it increasingly difficult to resolve anything.

The courts rapidly filled with cases and the judiciary did their part to defend borrowers, which has also helped to keep repossession numbers in Ireland at very low levels. The Circuit Court rules brought in a practice direction adjournment, which meant that the first time someone appeared in court, they were automatically adjourned and this typically meant another six-month wait. The combined forces of anti-bank sentiment, frustrated borrowers, political class intervention, judicial ruling and Central Bank regulation, came together to ensure that arrears rose, but also did not result in people being evicted from their homes in large numbers. Repossessions in Ireland are viewed by financial institutions as being near impossible to obtain. To date, over 100,000 resolutions have been put in place. Arrears peaked in September 2013 at about one in eight loans (12.9%) being in arrears: since that time these figures have more than halved to 6%.

The long-term arrears, loans greater than two years behind, peaked in 2015 at 38,000 loans and since then they have come down to around 30,000. Long-term arrears warrant special attention in two respects: firstly, no other country in the world has them because homes are repossessed by the time a person is two years behind, while the second point of interest is that despite having so many solutions in place, the resolution of these problematic loans remain stubbornly ongoing, which indicates either an inability for Irish institutions and laws to deal with them, or that there are other plans in place for these homes because a loan can be effectively performing while also in arrears. In many cases, we do not know because it is thought that as many as 40% of long-term mortgage arrears cases are not engaged or providing the banks with information required to reach a resolution (McCann Central Bank 2018).

HARRY WHITE

Riverdance

'Refulgent, majestic, ready to fall': Richard Ellmann's supremely perceptive reading of Oscar Wilde on the unwitting edge of catastrophe also summons for me the rueful and ruinous aftermath of the Celtic Tiger. The vertiginous descent into economic chaos, abject financial loss and a proverbially national depression that suddenly ensued upon 15 years of unbounded success seemed all the more shocking on account of its brutal swiftness. The strings seemed suddenly false, and the cosmopolitanism (in humiliating retrospect) ill-founded and ersatz.

But even from the ashes of this sorry remembrance, the Phoenix-like ascent of *Riverdance* appears yet as the anthem of a new age, destined though this was to ignominious collapse. Anyone who remembers those seven minutes during the interval of the European Song Contest on April 30, 1994, will scarcely dispute that *Riverdance*, even in its brief incipience, took the nation's breath away, and astonished all of Europe by virtue of its heraldic brilliance and revelatory power. Here was a reconstructed identity for Ireland that was immediately persuasive. The surpassing intelligence of this reconfiguration, this newly imagined and immaculately executed artwork, was its emblematic virtuosity of expression. *Riverdance* privileged the combinative genius of its own technique, its own faultless exactitudes. It represented Irish music and dance from the high altitude of its formidable (but effortlessly achieved) demands and deliverances. Its unfolding sequence of choral and choreographical episodes gave no quarter to the invitatory commonplaces of popular culture: it sought no participation other than the acclaim it immediately induced. The rhetoric of *Riverdance* was (and remains) akin to that of a *corps de ballet*, or of an Irish *Rite of Spring*. Like the art object in Wallace Stevens's 'Anecdote of the Jar', it did not give of bird or bush. Above all else, it invented the genre to which it belongs.

It may seem to many that *Riverdance* now sails indefinitely into a future which contradicts the Ireland it once memorably portended. But that is the fate of any work of art which survives its originary circumstances, its own historical adjacencies and intimacies. The spectacular success of *Riverdance* – on Broadway, in the West End, and across the globe – has perhaps eclipsed these intimacies, and in particular that sense of annunciation and of cultural regeneration which its early performances conveyed with unerring (if ineffable) clarity. Like the greatest of Wilde's plays, its currency no longer depends on those political, social and cultural forces which brought it into being. It continues to excite and divide critical opinion (another hallmark of its aesthetic intelligence) and to inspire imitation (a phenomenon which nevertheless affirms the singularity of the original). But its inherent dependencies are another matter. In the case of *Riverdance*, it is an especially arduous undertaking to keep the show (literally) on the road. The stewardship of *Riverdance*, much of which has fallen to its composer, Bill Whelan, is exceptionally time-demanding and (one imagines) draining. I have spoken to Whelan about this, and to some of the musicians who have given years of their lives to this enterprise, and such conversations have led me to the conclusion that however vast the success which continues to accrue to *Riverdance*, its merest artistic requirements (including a corps of exceptionally accomplished Irish dancers) are above the ordinary.

Imagine, since I've already mentioned it, the demands on a single company of continuously keeping *The Rite of Spring* in circulation in multiple troupes of dancers and musicians around the world. Such an undertaking is surely worth a moment's scruple. In the case of both works, the music has led a life of its own, independent of the choreography for which it was originally written. But *Riverdance* as a work of art cannot really survive this sundering, because its choreography is so completely and so strategically attached to the work's composite meaning. Its representative prowess – a vision of Ireland in the kaleidoscopic swirl and shapely intelligence of music and dance – remains collaborative and co-dependent. In this collaboration, the transcendent condition of *Riverdance* is likely to abide, just as the work itself survived the sudden aftermath of deep recession. Its aural and visual signatures now connote humane optimism rather than ebullient triumph and are all the better for it. Even if the Celtic Tiger now co-exists in the public imagination as an episode in Irish economic history and as a cultural myth shaped by the morose downturn which followed, it is mistaken to read *Riverdance* simply as the defining epigraph to this era. Its claims to our attention are greater, because the work itself reimagined and extended the legitimacy of Irish art. *Riverdance* flies past the net of economic and cultural remembrance which once ensnared it and perpetuates this legitimacy through its own visionary condition of being. Its existential originality and expressivity are of no less significance than its capacity to define Ireland musically.

EAMON MAHER

Ryan, Donal: *The Spinning Heart*

The Tipperary author Donal Ryan (1976–) is undoubtedly best known for his debut novel, *The Spinning Heart*, winner of Book of the Year at the Irish Book Awards in 2012. This novel deals with how a rural community in Co. Tipperary is forced to come to terms with the fall-out from the collapse of the Celtic Tiger and the failure of the local developer, Pokey Burke, to pay his workers' stamps, an omission that leaves them impoverished when the company goes bankrupt. His foreman, Bobby Mahon, reflects on how they could all have been naïve enough to believe that the self-serving Pokey, whose own father finds it hard to love him, was a 'legitimate' businessman. Then again, the construction game does not require too much intelligence, as Bobby reflects: 'You don't need brains to shovel shit and carry blocks and take orders from red-faced little men who'll use you all day and laugh at you all night and never pay in your stamps'.

Ryan does an excellent job in capturing the misery of those who were front line casualties of the collapse. Mahon feels he has let many people down: his wife and family; those who worked under his supervision; the people who purchased houses at inflated prices and were forced to live in a ghost estate with few amenities and houses that were barely habitable. One of these, Réaltín, bought at the height of the boom and is bemused when Bobby asks her if the 'C2' boys had called into her: 'Self-employed workers,' he explained, 'sub-contractors, foreign workers who were only taken on by builders if they registered as self-employed. That way the builders hadn't to pay the proper rates: stamps, tax, pensions or what have you'. One of the scams that characterised the lack of regulation during the construction bubble is foregrounded here.

Apart from its undoubted literary qualities, *The Spinning Heart* captures something of the *Zeitgeist* of post-Celtic Tiger Ireland, particularly the anger and disappointment at the trauma inflicted on ordinary decent people, while those mainly responsible for the crash appeared to be escaping relatively unscathed. The way in which the novel is narrated by different characters, each of whom encapsulates a human story, provides a great insight into the struggle of day-to-day existence of these people. Their dilemmas are not always associated with financial problems: we also come to know their hopes and fears, their regrets about failed relationships, or the loss of loved ones, all of which combine to produce a snapshot of a community at a time of genuine crisis. The observation of the young girl Millicent illustrates the impact the crisis is having on families: 'Mammy told Daddy *I* was a better earner than *him* because *I* bring in a hundred and fifty euros a month and he brings in fuck all'. The humiliation for her father at being told that the Children's Allowance brings in more money than what he earns is keenly felt by the daughter, who knows that her parents' marriage is under serious strain.

There is also much frustration in evidence at how the media are covering the crisis. A sub-contractor called Denis cannot abide the 'whingers' who ring up Joe Duffy moaning about whose fault it all is: 'Fellas that never done a day's work in their lives, besides spouting shite about how everyone is wrong except them. They'd make you puke'. A Garda called Jim sees a real urban-rural divide, and senses that only the former is being given any air time: 'I blame them bigmouths on the radio and the television for a lot of this hysteria that's after overtaking people. They fatten on the fear of others, them bastards'. Jim is also concerned at the rumours that are circulating about pensions being cut.

At the end of *The Spinning Heart*, a young child who has been abducted by a pair of amateur criminals is recovered unharmed, which prompts Bobby's wife Triona to sound a note of hope in the last line of the novel: 'What matters only love?' One has the sense of a community slowly emerging from the wreckage of their lives and rediscovering the things that might sustain them into the future: love, community spirit, resilience, a sense of their inherent worth, a reappraisal of what truly matters. But this does not detract in any way from the raw anger that is expressed about how a situation was allowed to develop which left so many ordinary people exposed to the greed and mismanagement of unscrupulous businessmen and women.

CATHERINE MAIGNANT

Ryan Report

Following the *Ferns Report* (2005), The *Report of the Commission to Inquire into Child Abuse* or *Ryan Report* (2009), shook the foundations of Irish society by exposing the lofty ideals of twentieth-century Catholic Ireland as being somewhat fraudulent. Dealing mostly with allegations concerning some 60 Industrial Schools and reformatories run by religious orders under the supervision of the Irish Department of Education, it identified over 800 abusers in more than 200 institutions. It also revealed that Church and State collusion from the early days of the Irish Free State had served to occlude the heinous reality of the abuse visited on children in such institutions and the subsequent cover-up by Church figures, politicians and local authorities. It laid bare the cruelty and the misery, the shame and the guilt that the system engendered.

With the Ryan Report, Celtic Tiger Ireland contributed to disrupting the flawed ethical compass that nationalist Ireland had established. In the age of human rights, wealthy, educated Ireland cast a critical eye on its murky past, to a time when the poverty-stricken country's poorest and most vulnerable children were denied the most basic human rights. That the situation should have persisted until the turn of the twenty-first century was particularly disturbing.

As is so often the case, the media were central to the debunking of myths by disclosing unpalatable truths which led to the first legal actions by former inmates of Catholic institutions. Mary Raftery's TV series, *States of Fear*, released on RTÉ caused such a shock that in April 1999, questions were raised in the Dáil and Taoiseach Bertie Ahern felt compelled to 'make a sincere and long overdue apology to the victims of childhood abuse for our collective failure to intervene, to detect their pain, to come to their rescue'. The Commission to Inquire into Child Abuse Act was subsequently set up in 2000. Under the initial leadership of Judge Mary Laffoy (1999–2003), the commission's remit was to meet victims, investigate allegations of abuse made to its members and establish the responsibility of the institutions concerned. An indication that the critical process was no easy task can be gauged by the fact that Ms Justice Laffoy eventually resigned after criticising the state for its lack of cooperation and interference in the work of the Commission. It was her successor, Mr Justice Séan Ryan, who brought the investigation to completion in 2009, patiently gathering scathing evidence that the Commission published in a five-volume, 2,000-page report that shattered the country.

The commission concluded that 'physical and emotional abuse and neglect were features of the institutions' and that 'sexual abuse occurred in many of them, particularly in boys' institutions' (*Ryan Report* 6.01). Very severe corporal punishment was the norm, which fostered a climate of fear, as 'children lived with the daily terror of not knowing where the next beating was coming from' (*Ryan Report* 6.11). Sexual abuse is presented as endemic in boys' institutions, ranging from 'improper touching and fondling to rape with violence' (*Ryan Report* 6.20). The case of the child who was 'tied to a cross and raped whilst others masturbated at the side' was widely commented on in the media. Neglect was the norm everywhere. 'Food was inadequate' and 'witnesses spoke of scavenging for food from waste bins and animal feed' (*Ryan Report*, 6.32). Inadequate clothing, bedding, heating and hygiene facilities resulted in children being cold, ill clad, dirty and unkempt. Education was scarce and, where available, its standards were poorer than in average schools. Finally, emotional abuse in the form of humiliation and degradation was endemic and 'witnesses spoke of being belittled and ridiculed on a daily basis' (*Ryan Report* 6.39).

The report also makes it clear that both the religious congregations and the Department of Education were aware of the situation. Abuse seems, in fact, to have been systemic. Covering up was the rule, in particular with regard to sexual abuse, 'with a view to minimising public disclosure and consequent damage to the institution and the Congregation. This policy resulted in the protection of the perpetrator' (*Ryan Report*, 6.20), who was simply transferred to a different institution, where he could quietly resume his abusive practices. Like the rest of the Irish society, the Department of Education was submissive and deferential towards the Church, and its system of inspection 'was fundamentally flawed and incapable of being effective'

(*Ryan Report*, 6.06). It allowed the abuse to continue. Worse, if we are to believe John Banville, writing in *The New York Times* (May 22, 2009), everybody knew and kept quiet.

No prosecutions followed the release of the report. Outraged or embarrassed religious tried to lay the blame on excesses of power and sexual frustration connected to a flawed theology, but this was insufficient to counter the devastating effects of the report, especially as the *Murphy Report* (also in 2009), the *Cloyne Report* (2011) and two later official reports (2013 and 2014) only confirmed the conclusions of the *Ryan Report*. Even if the issue is particularly meaningful in the Irish context where it raises questions about the foundations of national identity, it should also be connected to similar revelations across the world, a reminder that Celtic Tiger Ireland embraced globalisation and its side effects, for better or for worse.

SHAEN CORBET

Saint Patrick's Day Massacre of Shares

The St Patrick's Day Massacre of 2008 has traditionally been observed as the tipping point of the subprime market in the United States. Perhaps somewhat ironically, it had taken place as the then Taoiseach, Bertie Ahern, was handing over the traditional bowl of shamrocks to then US president George Bush, who had taken the opportunity to attempt to reassure market participants. The collapse followed the firesale of the investment bank Bear Stearns at a price of $2 per share to a consortium of JP Morgan Chase. Incredibly, the bank had traded at over $70 one week earlier, presenting evidence of the speed at which financial conditions had decayed.

Although there existed much evidence that Bear Stearns had been dangerously exposed to the rapidly deteriorating US subprime market, markets had been struggling to deal with grasping the 'hard truths' central to the impending collapse of such a core financial institution. In June 2007, Bear Stearns had actually proceeded to bail out its own High-Grade Structured Credit Fund, presenting a collateralised loan in excess of $3 billion. On March 14, 2008, the situation had further deteriorated to the point where the Federal Reserve Bank of New York agreed to provide $25 billion to support Bear Stearns, while creating a separate holding company to accept assets. This cash was designed to provide liquidity to the bank that financial markets had refused to provide. On March 16, 2008, Bear Stearns then signed a stock swap with JP Morgan Chase acting as a part-provider of liquidity finance.

This deal was considered to be vital in an attempt to mitigate what would otherwise have been a chaotic unwinding of investments, most likely leading to sharp detrimental impacts to the wider real economy. However, on March 17, 2008, the second-largest underwriter of mortgage-backed securities, Lehman Brothers, proceeded to collapse in value by almost 50%, based on rumours that it would be the next bank to collapse – it did eventually collapse in September 2008. Further rumours had also spread about the rapid deterioration of Alt-A and subprime portfolios in Fannie Mae and Freddie Mac, whose primary purpose was to provide a liquid secondary market for mortgages. Financial market contagion quickly transferred across the world, leading to sharp falls across Asia and Europe.

The sequence of the previous events must also be considered. Rumours of the Bear Stearns bailout began on Friday, March 14, with much negativity surrounding financials. When the market closed for the weekend, further rumours began to circulate about an impending takeover of Bear Stearns which then came to fruition on Sunday, March 16. This incredible level of uncertainty led to a market panic when the Stock Exchange opened on Monday, March 17, therefore leading to the broad declines and substantial contagion observed. Contagion effects were observed where investors could trace financial interlinkages between international financial institutions and subprime lending. Further, investors then began to ask question about the fair value and true health of other international housing and mortgage markets. Iceland was one country that experienced such repercussions; Ireland was another.

The St Patrick's Day Massacre acted as the first major signal of oncoming strife, as the Irish Stock market began to fall to its lowest level observed in the three previous years, with Anglo Irish Bank falling in excess of 15%. €5 billion was wiped off the value of Irish stocks predicated on fears about broad economic health, with many worried that the country was facing a deterioration in growth rates and elevated unemployment. Further fears had been expressed about the health of the Irish export market, with sharp deteriorations observed in the currencies of a number of our largest trading partners. The extreme financial market volatility did not stop on March 17, however. On March 19, federal regulators allowed Fannie Mae and Freddie Mac to take another $200 billion in debt in what was observed as a last-ditch attempt to save the US economy from the detrimental effects. Both institutions were bailed out in September 2008 by the US Treasury Department. The St Patrick's Day Massacre simply acted as a moment of realisation for international financial markets that the unthinkable was about to happen.

CONSTANTIN GURDGIEV

Second Houses

In the later stages of the Celtic Tiger, second houses (owner-occupied properties acquired for the purpose of vacations and leisure time), became the symbol of household wealth and membership in the ever-expanding club of families who were 'winners' in the New Ireland. Fear of missing out on the property boom that fuelled purchases of buy-to-rent properties in the 2000–7 period, also drove up the demand for holiday homes.

The boom in second homes started around 2000–1, when both foreign and rural domestic properties saw growth in marketing campaigns in the Republic on foot of rising prosperity. By 2006, a bubble of its own, distinct to the primary residencies price bubble, emerged in the demand for second homes by Irish investors. As Irish taxi drivers, Gardaí, nurses and other middle-class households raced to take out equity loans against their primary residences and buy-to-let properties, Irish buyers flocked to bid on holiday apartments and houses in such exotic, and often questionable – in terms of property rights of foreign buyers and other markets' fundamentals – destinations, such as Cape Verde, Dubai, Bulgaria, Romania, South Africa and even Brazil. By 2006, Irish buyers of foreign real estate were spending well over €1 billion per annum on second homes abroad. The market got a significant boost with the maturity of the €14 billion in the Special Savings Incentive Accounts (SSIA). At the peak of this speculative rush to 'invest' offshore, Prestige Properties – a leading Irish market investment intermediary for brokering sales of properties abroad – published its first 'International Hotspots Index', which showed Warsaw as the top destination for Irish investors in second homes, followed by Florida, Cape Verde, the Algarve and Bulgaria.

In the Republic, Celtic Tiger era government policies that promoted housing development as a central pillar of rural economic growth support strategy created a mini-boom in what has since proven to be unsustainable rush-to-build and second homes investment bubbles. The legacy of this bubble are the unfinished, abandoned construction sites dotting the Irish rural landscape since the 2008 bust. In 1991, based on the data reported by Norris et al. (2010), the share of second homes in total housing stock rose from 1% in 1991 to 3% in 2006, with over 90% of these new second homes constructed in the largely rural and peripheral regions. Almost one in five (18%) of these second homes were vacant in 2006 – a number that is similar to the vacancy rates for second homes in Spain, Portugal and Italy, where foreign buyers markets were more developed than in Ireland.

In contrast to these destinations, however, second homes located in Ireland were more likely to be owned by households with mortgages still outstanding on their primary residences. This higher exposure of the Celtic Tiger second home markets to risk of excessive leverage likely contributed to the severity of the Irish property bust, especially in rural areas.

IDA MILNE

Shopping Trips to New York

The hotel concierge at the Philadelphia hotel whispered conspiratorially: 'Lady, go to Franklin Mills tomorrow. You Irish really love those bargains!' as he staggered up to my room with the day's loot. It was March 2008. Hotel concierges are experts and they knew, as US tourism statistics record, that the Irish passion for US shopping had been reaching unprecedented levels. I was a travel journalist specialising in the North American market from Ireland. My employer, the business travel newspaper *Travel Extra*, had given me the rather catchy title of shopping correspondent. This reflected the significance of US shopping to the Irish travel trade. Shopping was the ultimate consumerist manifestation of the massive expansion in travel during the Celtic Tiger, as Irish people got more confident in their passion for travel, and as their disposable income increased. Several travel companies specialised in shopping trips to cities with direct flight access from Ireland, and to the growing numbers of luxury brand discount outlet villages.

If transatlantic shopping had been an Olympic sport towards the end of the Celtic Tiger, the Irish would have had a strong chance of a medal. NYC and Company, the official destination marketing organisation and convention and visitors bureau for the five boroughs of New York City, claimed that they were receiving 291,000 Irish visitors a year by 2007, placing Ireland sixth in their international visitor chart. The typical shopping trip, according to those NYC and Co statistics, consisted of four females, with each spending about 2,400 euro.

Chelsea Premium Outlets' Woodbury Common became a household word; other popular venues for Irish shoppers included the Wrentham Village complex, near Boston, Massachusetts and the Philadelphia outlets. Certain American brands were particularly in demand: for example, Irish teenagers wanted Ugg boots and Abercrombie and Fitch hoodies. Their mothers and aunts sought cut-price or fake Prada and Gucci handbags in New York's Century 21 Chinatown, discount Christian Louboutin shoes from Neimann Marcus Last Call, jeans and other staples from Macey's and the outlets.

In 1990, Irish residents made an estimated 107,000 transatlantic trips, according to the Central Statistics Office. By 2000, this number had more than doubled to 242,000. The peak came about 2008, with 520,000 Irish residents were going across the Atlantic for an average of 11 nights. Transatlantic figures fell significantly as the Tiger tottered, to 403,000 outward bound trips by residents in 2009, and dropped to a relative nadir of 305,000 in 2011. The figures never went down to the pre-Tiger years. Times might have been tough, but the Irish had gotten the taste for it and were not fully letting go.

The Irish travel to the US was just part of the massive travel expansion during the economic boom. In 1990, Irish residents made 1,798,000 trips out of the country, again according to CSO estimated figures. By 2000, the number had expanded to 3,783,000, but this was a tiny figure compared to the 2008 figure of 7,833,000 million trips. The number dropped significantly to 7,021,000 in 2009, with the average stay going down to 8.1 nights, compared to stays abroad of more than 12 nights in the Celtic Tiger peak. By 2011, the brakes on travel were really on, slowing to just 6,293,000 trips.

While extra disposable income is a key component of the massive increase in Irish foreign travel, the picture is complex, for a variety of factors. For one thing, the US shopping travel, predominantly by women, probably reflects the growing numbers of women at work – with more discretionary income – as the new century progressed. CSO figures show that employment rates for women reached 60% by 2008, compared to 48% in 1998.

Another factor is that comparing travel in the 1990s with travel in the 2000s is not comparing like with like. Travel journalist Eoghan Corry, a leading commentator on travel trade, argues that because there were major changes in the way travel was bought and sold in Ireland in this period, the reasons behind the massive increase in Irish foreign travel are more complex than a simple explanation that people had more money to spend: 'A lot of what happens in travel is about fares and access. Average fare prices dropped so much that in 2006 they were less than half of what they had been in 1996'. He points out that the number of flight destinations out of Dublin over the course of the Celtic Tiger tripled. The abolition of the Shannon stopover, and the expansion of Ryanair were important, he says. 'When a country has money, airlines and travel companies come flocking to offer you new routes and curated new experiences. And flock they did'.

SHAEN CORBET

Short Selling

While stock markets, housing markets and pretty much all other types of markets continued to appreciate substantially throughout the Celtic Tiger period, few investors considered mechanisms through which one could profit from falling prices. The practice of short selling is best described as an investment or trading strategy that speculates on the decline in a stock or other securities price. It is an advanced strategy that is advised to be undertaken only by experienced traders and investors.

Short selling is a very suitable as a tool to speculate on an impending fall in value, and investors or portfolio managers may use it as a hedge against the downside risk of a long position in the same security, or a related one. Hedging is a more common transaction involving placing an offsetting position to reduce risk exposure. In short selling, a position is opened by borrowing shares of a stock or other asset that the investor believes will decrease in value by a set future date, known as the expiration date. The investor then sells these borrowed shares to buyers willing to pay the market price. Before the borrowed shares must be returned, the trader is betting that the price will continue to decline and they can purchase them at a lower cost. The risk of loss on a short sale is theoretically unlimited since the price of any asset can climb to infinity.

Also, short-selling stocks require a margin account, similar to that used by traders of contracts for difference, and usually incurs interest charges based on the value of the stock that is held short. Irish stock markets have quite a chequered history when considering the process of short selling. At the start of the collapse in value of Irish banking institutions, it was widely reported that significant short positions had begun to accumulate, as both domestic and international traders observed a considerable opportunity to profit from what had appeared to be substantially inflated share prices. We must consider that Anglo Irish Bank had traded at €17.31 on May 24, 2007. In December 2008, the Irish government announced plans to inject €1.5 billion of capital for a 75% stake in the bank, while both the Dublin and London Stock Exchanges immediately suspended trading in Anglo Irish's shares, with the final closing share price of €0.22 representing a fall of over 98% from its peak. It was widely reported that there were eight shares short for every one share long at this time, indicative of the substantial pressures that the bank was under.

The Central Bank of Ireland now impose a regulation stating that public disclosure of significant net short positions in shares pursuant to Article Six of the Short Selling Regulations is illegal. Such a rule is needed to mitigate situations such as that identified in September 2008, where Eminence Capital and Lansdowne Partners declared that they possessed short positions in Anglo Irish Bank worth approximately €840m, while Adelphi Capital, a London-based hedge fund, disclosed a short position in Bank of Ireland worth approximately €230m. These positions were announced shortly after the imposition of a broad shorting ban on financial stocks on September 19, 2008, designed to match similar measures that had been imposed in the UK. The regulator also required the daily disclosure of existing short positions in financial companies of more than 0.25%.

On the day in which the shorting ban was imposed, trading levels were identified as being exceptionally heavy, with almost 74 million shares traded as hedge funds looked to cover the short positions that they had accumulated and long-only institutions made a return to investing in Irish banks. On the first morning of the shorting ban, financial stocks were up over 30% while the ISEQ exchange was up almost 25%. The bank had results in a clear alleviation of downward pressure.

Since the collapse of the Celtic Tiger, the Central Bank of Ireland has been responsible for the implementation of regulation (EU) No 236/2012 of the European Parliament, and the Council of March 14, 2012 on short selling and certain aspects of credit default swaps. The regulations are designed to mitigate such issues as those described, but also increasing the transparency of short positions held by investors in certain EU securities while reducing settlement risks and other risks linked with uncovered or naked short selling. Regulatory improvements are designed to ensure that Member States have clear powers to intervene in exceptional situations to reduce systemic risks and risks to financial stability and market confidence arising from the process of short selling.

CONSTANTIN GURDGIEV

Single Currency

Ireland entered the euro in 1999, having previously participated in the European Exchange Rate Mechanism (ERM) since March 13, 1979. On January 1, 1999, the Irish Punt (*Punt Éireannach*) was formally replaced by the euro for non-cash usage, and on January 1, 2002, Ireland switched to euro coins and banknotes as the country's new official legal tender. The process of phasing out the Punt, and its replacement with the euro, was very fast and relatively painless. The Punt value was fixed at conversion at 0.787564 Irish pounds to the euro, and the introduction of the euro was associated with the loss of theoretical monetary autonomy by the Central Bank of Ireland. At the time of changeover, the main fear among the public and the majority of Irish analysts was that the new currency would lead to a steep increase in inflation rates. Average consumer price inflation in 1990–7 was running at 2.43% per annum, which reflected higher growth rates in the first stage of the Celtic Tiger.

In 1998–2001, average inflation was significantly higher at 3.28% per annum, and this rose to 4.23% (average annual rate) over 2002–3. There is no actual evidence to support the claims, occasionally made in the Irish media at the time, that the higher inflation rates immediately following the euro adoption could be attributed to the introduction of the single currency. End-of-year inflation rates for 2000–2 for Ireland were 4.81%, 4.31% and 4.52%, respectively. In other words, on the year of euro introduction, inflation was slightly below the year average prior to the switchover.

Where the common currency did have a material impact, however, was in the significant decline in the cost of credit. During the first stage of the Celtic Tiger (through 1997), Irish mortgages rates averaged 9.35%, in 1998–2001 the average was 5.91%. In 2002, the Irish mortgage rate fell to 4.7%, and the decline continued into 2004. Between 2002 and 2007 – the period of the unsustainable property boom – Irish mortgage rates averaged

4.39%, a decline of more than half on the 1992–7 average. The decline in commercial property and land acquisition debt was similarly dramatic. The monetary policy conducted by the ECB simply did not fit the rapidly growing and overheating Irish economy. The end result was a massive binge in personal debt, primarily funnelled into property prices, engendering a massive in scale and historically unprecedented property boom.

The single currency, and the one-size-fits-all monetary policies of the Euro area, were simply not designed for addressing structural imbalances building up in the Irish economy. In 2002–7, the Irish economy grew at roughly 2.65 times the rate of growth in the Euro area economy in real terms, and Irish inflation outpaced Euro area inflation by a third. As Irish lenders pursued an increasingly reckless approach to issuing new loans for property purchases, and as interest rates continued to fall, the Celtic Tiger economy turned Celtic Garfield: the property and construction sectors' contribution to Irish GDP rose, and private consumption reached unsustainably high levels, all fuelled by cheap and readily available credit.

The bust that followed was equally spectacular, and made more painful by the lack of monetary and fiscal autonomy, both driven by the common currency rules. Irish bank bailouts and the ensuing austerity were made, in part, necessary by the force of the ECB's commitment to not allowing any Euro area banks to undergo liquidation during the crisis. Repayment of banks' debts to international creditors was also the direct outrun of the ECB's policies and decisions. In a way, the single currency was poorly designed and mismanaged both on the way up (the Celtic Tiger era), and on the way down (the post-Celtic Tiger bust).

Despite this, the deeper and more structural roots of the Irish crisis of 2008–12 lay outside the common currency zone and its institutions. The Euro, both prior to the crisis and since the onset of the recovery, has played a major role in facilitating Irish exports and the Foreign Direct Investment inflows into the country. Instead of looking accusingly towards Frankfurt, Ireland has only its own regulatory and political elites to blame for the severe excesses of the late Celtic Tiger era and the misery these brought about during the Global Financial Crisis and the Great Recession.

LORCAN SIRR

Social Housing

Right in the midst of the Celtic Tiger, Part V of the Planning and Development Act 2000 introduced a requirement for developers to allocate 20% of their units for sale in developments of more than five units to the local authority at a reduced price for use as social and/or affordable housing. The then Minister for the Environment, Noel Dempsey, deserves a paragraph in Irish housing history for this innovative (for Ireland) move. This was an almost continental-style policy move that put an onus on the private sector to contribute to social housing provision whilst also trying to ensure a degree of social mix. Not everybody was impressed with Noel Dempsey's commitment to social justice, however, and it wasn't long until his successor, Martin Cullen, neutered the requirement by allowing developers to provide alternative land or money instead of actual housing. The upshot was that instead of delivering 20% social housing, between 2002 and 2011 less than 4% of all housing built was social housing: this was 9,393 houses in total, only 3,757 of which (or 2.7% of the total housing output for the period) were for local authorities.

Even in the heady years of the Celtic Tiger, there was a considerable need for social housing. The downside of Dempsey's plan was that it took pressure off local authorities to keep building social housing that in turn took pressure off government to keep funding local authorities to do so. Another flaw was the reliance on private sector house-building activity, so when private sector output fell, therefore, so did social housing output, just when an increase in demand for social housing can be expected.

In 2015, these Part V requirements were reformed. To have a Part V obligation, developments now have to be of 10 or more units, and the 20% requirement has been reduced to 10%. The option of buying out the Part V agreement has been removed, as has the option of providing land on alternative sites outside the local authority area.

A consistent criticism of the Part V mechanism, apart from its reliance on market activity, is that as most housing scheme developments are built in urban areas, it means that purchasers of these will be paying for social housing provision twice over – once in their own development, and again in taxes to fund social housing in rural areas where most housing developments are small or one-off builds and therefore don't include social housing. This brings the burden back to the local authority again, and nationally to the taxpayer. The capacity to build houses during the Celtic Tiger was hugely diminished by the crash and the chronic shortage of social housing in Ireland currently is attributable to the policies adopted by successive governments to divest themselves of their responsibility in this area.

SHAEN CORBET

Sports

Ireland has developed a significant reputation for its ability to compete above its weight across a range of sports, an amazing feature for a country with a pre-Celtic Tiger population of approximately 4 million people. This achievement was even more impressive considering that soccer, being the most-played and broadly the most supported game in the country during this time, had to compete with hurling, football, rugby and a range of other interests such as boxing, basketball, athletics, horse-racing and Formula One. Across these individual sports, Irish fans had also gained a strong international reputation as both a vibrant and exceptionally mobile group.

As rugby fans in recent years, in the midst of the exceptional success of the national team and the four provinces, might fail to recall, Ireland until then had not been consistently successful. Although largely considered to be associated with the decision of the English teams not to compete in 1999, Ulster won their first European cup at a politically charged Lansdowne Road in the presence of many of those involved in the development and completion of the Good Friday Agreement. This also acted as the starting point for what has been a 20-year upward trajectory of Irish rugby.

The very next year saw the start of Munster's decade-long fairytale, which resulted in two European Cup wins in 2006 and 2008, releasing the shackles of two very tight losses in both 2000 and 2002. It is probably the 2006 final which will forever last in the memories, not only for the sheer intensity and emotion of the day, but perhaps for the exceptional fan base that made the trip to Cardiff, estimated to have been far above 120,000, without mentioning the incredible crowds that gathered at venues across the country to view the game. At this time, it would have felt that money was freely available for such a 'disposable-type' of expenditure, the same being said in 2008.

The European Cup, or Heineken Cup of the time, was very much reliant on Irish support due to the much evidenced inability of other teams to fill stadiums, such as that observed in Leicester's 2001 and Toulouse's 2003 wins. The success of Leinster in the era since the collapse of the Celtic Tiger has also occurred in tandem with the incredible achievements of the Irish national team, which has become one of the top-ranked teams in the world. In the 1990s and early 2000s, beating the New Zealand All Blacks was considered to be an achievement far beyond the reach of an Irish team. It is now an expectation of the current team, which is testament to the development of the sport in Ireland.

The Celtic Tiger created quite a significant breaking point in the provision of sponsorship deals, with many reduced and some even cancelled in the aftermath of collapse. One of the areas where this was most evident at grass-roots, was in rugby as seen in reduced attendance in the Celtic League and re-branded Pro12/Pro14 competitions, and indeed even at the level of the All Ireland League.

In soccer, fresh off the back of an incredible performance in the 2002 World Cup, sadly marred by internal politics, the growth of the game in Ireland was evident. Television revenues, and the way in which fans interacted with the game, was one of the key drivers of this substantial growth. Much attention had been paid by Irish fans to teams in the English leagues; however, a core group of fans remained committed to the League of Ireland. However, in the aftermath of the Celtic Tiger attendances had fallen sharply from over 330,000 in 2008 to below 270,000 in 2012. Such reduced footfall had substantial effects on team revenues, further reducing the potential for future success.

In Formula One, we had the Jordan team until 2005. In 2008, we had the incredible boxing successes of Kenny Egan, Paddy Barnes and Darren Sutherland, with boxing acting as the cornerstone of our Olympic achievements for some time after, mainly spurred by the Gold Medal won by Katie Taylor and some other sports such as horse jumping and walk racing. Much of the decline of Irish athletics had been attributed to the sharp cuts in funding provided to athletes who were for the most part solely dependent on such funds.

The sports that appear to have suffered the most in the aftermath of the collapse of the Celtic Tiger were Gaelic football and hurling. At an inter-county level, attendances sharply fell for rounds in advance of provincial finals and games closer to September in both codes. The GAA, which had largely attempted to increase the depth of games through the introduction of the 'back door' system, had been widely observed to be taking advantage of fans through a quite acute pricing structure. This generated substantial damage and turned away a broad number of price-sensitive fans. However, the core of the damage to both hurling and football occurred at the levels below as county championship teams began to struggle to provide regular competition due to the absence of players within the community. This had been caused by mobility issues as younger professionals having to move from isolated rural regions to cities for employment, particularly after the collapse of the Celtic Tiger.

CONSTANTIN GURDGIEV

SSIA

The Celtic Tiger's SSIAs were the financial cure to the disease that made that particular malady incurable. The SSIAs, or the Special Savings Incentive Accounts, were created in the Finance Act 2001, with the explicit purpose of controlling rampant increases in money supply and the resulting inflationary pressures in the economy. In 2000, end-of-the-year consumer price inflation in Ireland rose to 4.806%, up on 1.08% recorded a year before. This rate of inflation was threatening the Irish position vis-à-vis the Euro area targets on the eve of the euro adoption (see Single Currency section), and required a drastic counter-measure to be taken by the government. Thus, under the SSIA scheme, termed savings accounts could be opened in Irish banks between May 1, 2001 and April 30, 2002 that provided a 25% state savings 'bonus' for every euro deposited by the savers. The maximum contribution per person was set at €254 per month.

With all SSIAs maturing in May 2006–May 2007, €14 billion worth of fresh savings funds became liquid at the very peak of the housing market bubble. Unsurprisingly, 2006–7 were marked by a re-acceleration in house price inflation, and in general consumer price inflation. The SSIAs maturity also helped Fianna Fáil to retain a majority in the Dáil, following the general election of 2007, allowing it to form a new coalition government with the Green Party and the electorally bruised Progressive Democrats.

In the end, SSIAs were the financial steroids that pushed the already unfit Irish economy over the cliff. By late 2007, Irish property markets started showing signs of severe fatigue, with volumes of sales and new completions slowing down. In less than 12 months following the SSIAs maturity cliff, the Irish economy was in a tailspin.

EOGHAN SMITH

Suburban Literature

The mass expansion of housing during the Celtic Tiger was principally suburban, so it is no surprise that a substantial body of suburban literature was produced during these years. Although the suburbs are often negatively associated with homogeneity, dullness, and uniformity, suburban Irish literature during the Celtic Tiger was as rich, varied, and vibrant as the period it emerged from. While it is not possible to provide a comprehensive survey of suburban literature here, a number of trends are discernible.

In general, literature about the suburban working classes tends to expose increasing social deprivation in a time of unprecedented economic growth. One of the most prominent writers of the suburbs during the early years of the Celtic Tiger is Roddy Doyle. Based on Kilbarrack on Dublin's northside, Doyle's Barrytown is perhaps the most famous fictional suburb in Irish writing, and was the setting for comedic, if socially conscious, pre-Celtic Tiger works such as *The Snapper* (1990), *The Van* (1991), and *Paddy Clarke Ha Ha Ha* (1993). Doyle's later works set in working-class suburbs of north Dublin, such as *The Woman Who Walked into Doors* (1996) and *Paula Spencer* (2006,) uncover hidden, violent realities of suburban life. Equally, if not more so, dark portrayals of Irish working-class suburban life were replicated by other writers. Dramatists such as Mark O'Rowe and Dermot Bolger in their plays *Howie the Rookie* (1999) and the 'Ballymun Trilogy' respectively focused on the left-behind working classes, offering stark and shocking portrayals of alcoholism, drug abuse, sexual exploitation, and violence during a period of both massive social investment and economic expansion.

For the suburban middle classes, who were both the principal drivers and beneficiaries of the Celtic Tiger, more genteel crises centred on the secrecy, hypocrisy and deception that lie hidden behind bourgeois facades, as in Anne Enright's *The Gathering* (2007) and Eilís Ní Dhuibhne's *The Shelter of Neighbours* (2012), for example. A more scathing intervention into hubristic middle-class privilege was Kevin Power's novel *Bad Day in Blackrock* (2008), an excoriation of the entitled south Dublin DART-line suburban middle class. Plays such as *That Was Then* (2002) by Gerard Stembridge and *Shiver* (2003) by Declan Hughes set about exploring the complicit relationships between the upwardly mobile suburban middle classes and the wider economy in which they operated and exploited for personal gain, and provided real-time critiques of the ethical complexities of the new economic and social dispensation. And perhaps the best known representative of this group of people is Paul Howard's hugely popular satirical creation, Ross O'Carroll-Kelly, the Celtic Tiger poster-boy, southside snob and all round rugby bore who provided a running commentary in *The Sunday Tribune* and, later, *The Irish Times*, on the hubris of the Celtic Tiger. However, more serious criticisms of suburban blindness emerged; by the end of the 2000s, the widespread environmental damage caused by suburban expansion was recognised by literary artists such as poet Paula Meehan, whose poetry collection *Painting Rain* (2009) powerfully captured how the economic need to sustain continual property development was changing the Irish landscape through rampant ecological destruction.

A good deal of suburban literature has emerged since the collapse of Celtic Tiger in 2008, most of it retrospectively critical in their exploration of speculative property development. Notable examples of this genre include Claire Kilroy's *The Devil I Know* (2012), Donal Ryan's *The Spinning Heart* (2013), Paul Murray's *The Mark and the Void* (2015) and Dermot Bolger's *Tanglewood* (2015). The collapse of the suburban dream for would-be housebuyers has also provided Irish writing with one of its most fruitful new tropes: the ghost estate. These unfinished suburban developments stand as a physical reminder on the landscape of the failure of the Celtic Tiger economic model. Visual artists such as Aideen Barry, Vera Klute and Valerie Anex have exploited the image of the ghost estate as a powerful visual metaphor for the ruinations of the property market, and literary artists have also seen gothic potential in these abandoned developments, as in Conor O'Callaghan's *Nothing on Earth* (2016). In these works, the Celtic Tiger has maintained a phantom presence in Irish literature long after it has departed. For these artists, the Celtic Tiger was not simply a phase in Irish economic and social history; instead, the ghost estate is a spectre of suburbia that continues to haunt long after its death.

FRANCES COPPOLA

Target2 Balances

Target2 is the Euro's real-time gross settlement system. All Euro payments, except for physical cash, settle via Target2. That includes exports from one Eurozone country to another; transactions in Euro-denominated financial instruments such as bonds and stocks; remittance payments from foreign workers in, say, Germany, to their families in other Eurozone countries; movement of bank deposits from one country to another ('capital flight'). All of these payment types are settled via Target2.

Since every payment has a payer and a payee, the total flow of money across Target2 nets to zero, but the bilateral flows between Eurozone countries do not. There can be a net inflow to, say, Germany, which is balanced by net outflows from, say, Italy, Spain and Greece. If a country has persistent net inflows, it accumulates a positive balance, known as a 'claim', in Target2: similarly, a country that has persistent net outflows accumulates a negative balance, or 'liability', in Target2. You can think of these Target2 balances as an accounting representation of the balance of payments between the countries of the Eurozone. Any country with a current account surplus vis-a-vis the rest of the Eurozone will have a net Target2 claim: conversely, any country with a current account deficit will have a net Target2 liability.

Over time as economic convergence moves forward Target2 balances should fluctuate around zero. However, over the last decade, balances have at times become very large. 'Core' Eurozone countries have accumulated Target2 claims, while periphery countries have accumulated Target2 liabilities. Each time, the underlying cause has been the same: capital flight due to rising risks in periphery countries.

During the Eurocrisis, Germany's net claim on Target2 rose exponentially: the net liabilities of Spain, Italy, Portugal and Greece likewise rose. This led to claims by prominent German economist Hans Werner Sinn argued that this amounted to a concealed bailout of periphery countries.

This was roundly rebuffed. Target2 balances also rose as the ECB embarked on quantitative easing (QE). Soon, the question of whether periphery countries should 'settle' their Target2 balances once again started to rear its ugly head. On the face of it, Target2 liabilities do look very much like debts. But the visible balances in Target2 are only half of the story. What is missing is the private sector flows. When these are included, the system is in balance and there is no need to 'settle' anything.

To take an example when an importer in Ireland buys a consignment of BMWs from Germany, a Euro payment is typically made from an Irish bank to a German bank. This settles via Target2. The German bank's Euro deposits increase by the amount of the payment, while the Irish bank's deposits reduce by the same amount. Thus there has been a net flow of money from Ireland to Germany. This causes an increase in Germany's Target2 claim and a corresponding increase in Ireland's Target2 liability. *Within* Target2, it appears as if Ireland owes money to Germany. But the money has in reality already been paid by the Irish private sector. If the Irish central bank were to 'settle' its Target2 balance by making a Euro payment to the German central bank, as some have argued, Ireland would simply be paying twice.

The size of Target2 balances indicates the degree of fragmentation of the Euro. When they are very wide, in effect, a Euro in Germany is worth significantly more than a Euro in, say, Greece. If Target2 balances were to widen exponentially – or rather, the tidal forces tearing at the Euro become irresistible – the Eurozone could break up. If this were to happen, then the Target2 balances would crystallise, resulting in real debts that the departing countries would in theory need to settle. Or maybe not – the US never settled its gold obligations after President Nixon suspended convertibility in 1971, despite France's colourful attempts to force it to do so.

The long-term solution to the Target2 balances problem is to eradicate persistent economic imbalances between Eurozone countries. This implies a much closer union than is presently the case, including complete banking and capital markets union, risk sharing and fiscal transfers. Politically, this appears a very long way off, though the European Commission continues to promote it as a desirable goal. Target2 balances are likely to remain a thorn in the side for the foreseeable future.

EIMEAR NOLAN

Texting and the Celtic Tiger

Reflect back for a minute to before the Celtic Tiger; if someone informed you that the main mode of communication for Irish people in 2019 would be through their mobile phones, would you have believed them? Probably not. The very notion of having a mobile phone was unthinkable, while the idea of being able to ring or text people at will was a thing of fiction. Interestingly, the first mobile phone was launched in Ireland by Eircell in 1993, Digifone (1997), with Meteor (2001) and 3 (2005) all following within the next 12 years. In that short time span, we evolved into a society that, on average, will pick up our mobile phones 55 times a day to check them. In fact, Irish people are now among the top smartphone users in Europe. Well over three million people today in Ireland own or have access to a smartphone – a number that is set to increase for the foreseeable future. In 2022, it is estimated that there will be 4.06 million smartphone users in the country. In just over ten years, we have evolved from having one home phone line, two if you were lucky, to carrying around portable devices that allow us access to each other on a constant basis.

Prior to the Celtic Tiger, we voice-called our friends and family to catch up, arrange a meeting, or ask a question. Today, our communication with family and friends has shifted from voice calls to text messages. A survey conducted by Deloitte in Ireland showed that most Irish people (68%), communicate with each other via text message on a daily basis, and this is far more than other communication methods such as voice calls, instant messages, emails and social networks. The majority of us see text messaging as the easier option, as it avoids the unnecessary chit-chat that a phone conversation requires, making it a time-saving and a productive method of communication, for the most part. Let's say you have a quick question or want to confirm a time of a get together later on, it is more efficient to send a text than it is to find the opportune time to call someone. They could be working, at the gym, in the cinema or anywhere, and a text message makes communication fast and efficient.

We have come a long way from the first text message option on mobiles where you had to click three times to get the letter 'C' and so forth – a slow and painful process if you can remember it. Today, we have predictive texting, which if used correctly can speed up typing a text, but I am sure we have all been on the wrong side of predictive texts. Some phones allow you to swipe the letters with your fingers, rather that touching each letter of the word. Let's not forget the functionality to speak and your phone/watch converts it into text. Coupled with this, a texting language has also been evolved to speed up the already rapid communication method. For example, IDK – 'I don't know'; ICYMI – 'in case you missed it'; EM? – 'Excuse me'?; and for all the parents out there: PAL – 'parents are listening'! Trying to decipher what these abbreviations mean if you are not familiar with them is almost an impossible task. Thankfully, we have the Internet (on our phones too) to help us with this should we run into difficulty!

VIC MERRIMAN

Theatre of the Celtic Tiger

The Celtic Tiger economy coincided with a moment of remarkable energy in Irish theatre, marked by vigorous interactions between new and revived plays, their critical reception, scholarly discussion, and diversifying audiences. For most of the twentieth century, the National Theatre Society was uncontested as the fount of Irish dramatic writing, and dramaturgy, production choices, scholarship and critical practice largely reflected this. The founding of Druid Theatre Company (1975) and Field Day Productions (1980) brought new vitality, and made possible the Celtic Tiger's diverse theatre worlds. The success, artistic integrity, and drive of Druid and Field Day inspired other artists to pursue distinctive aesthetic projects in dialogue with local circumstances, including, among others, Rough Magic TC (Dublin, 1984), Pigsback TC (Dublin, 1988–96), Gallowglass TC (Clonmel, 1990), Island TC (Limerick, 1988–2008), Meridian TC (Cork, 1991–2009), Corcadorca TC (Cork, 1991), and Blue Raincoat TC (Sligo, 1991). Macnas street theatre company (1986) is synonymous with Galway Arts Festival, and Bickerstaffe Theatre Company (Kilkenny, 1994–2001) gave rise to The Cat Laughs comedy festival. In Waterford, Waterford Arts for All, a community arts movement, engendered Red Kettle (1988), and Waterford Spraoi Festival (1993), which nurtured a range of theatre artists, and staged Jim Nolan's impressive body of dramatic works. Alongside these developments, Field Day (Derry, 1980–2005), Wet Paint Arts (Dublin, 1984–91), Calypso Productions (1991–2007), and Glasshouse Theatre Company (1992–9) articulated a renewed sense of theatre's socio-cultural purpose.

Celtic Tiger Ireland's state-funded theatre space was broadly bifurcated between an established National Theatre and what might be called an emerging Theatre of the Nation; the former prioritised aesthetic development, the latter, social purpose. The commercial theatre sector flourished, in venues such as the Gaiety, Olympia, Tivoli and Andrews Lane theatres in Dublin. The Point Depot (Dublin, 1988–2007) a venue with 8000+ seating capacity hosted large-scale West End transfers, and, on three occasions, the Eurovision Song Contest – 1994 (at which the interval act was Celtic Tiger cultural avatar, *Riverdance*), 1995, and 1997. As art and artists were redefined as an economic 'sector', this was reflected in changes in the membership of boards of arts organisations, including companies and venues. 'Business people' proliferated, and 'business planning' and its administrative burdens began to take up increasing amounts of time and resources available to arts organisations. Marketing began to shape repertoire and casting decisions, and to circumscribe, in some cases, what was required of new writing. Successful companies, although safely anchored by state funding, were encouraged to project themselves as 'risk takers' and 'entrepreneurs' and the commercial success of cultural events such as Brian Friel's *Dancing at Lughnasa* (Abbey Theatre, 1990), Martin McDonagh's *Leenane Trilogy* (Druid Theatre Company, 1997) and Conor McPherson's *The Weir* (Royal Court Theatre, London, 1997) were totems of Ireland Successful. All three productions ran successfully on Broadway, and further proof of Irish theatre's global currency was seen in the extraordinary international success of Enda Walsh's *Disco Pigs* (Corcadorca Theatre Company; Triskel Arts Centre, Cork, 1997), which toured widely, and – like *Dancing at Lughnasa* – was adapted for cinema.

Individual performance events track the Celtic Tiger's trajectory from acceleration to devastation. The eponymous dance scene in *Dancing at Lughnasa* anticipated the exuberance of *Riverdance*, and found a powerful echo in Mary Robinson's presidential invitation, 'Come dance with me in Ireland!' Though its abandon seemed wholly congruent with emerging aspirations to a better and more prosperous future, the Mundy sisters' dance was actually an embodied indictment of the impoverishment of poor rural Irish women, post-independence. However, theatre can seduce as well as inform, domesticate as well as criticise, and the socio-historical context of the 1930s was elided as driving dance tunes possessed Friel's women and their audiences, in equal measure. From Dublin to Broadway, Prague to Sydney, captivated spectators misrecognised their frenzy as a celebration of exuberant life, rather than a cacophonous anguish at its deep frustration. Twenty years later, when the music had stopped, economist David McWilliams's polemical performance/lecture *Outsiders* (Peacock Theatre, 2010) eschewed the constituent ambiguities of dramatic poetry to articulate public indignation at the incestuous corporate, social, and political interpenetration of Irish finance elites. The definitive play of Celtic Tiger Ireland may be Pom Boyd, Declan Lynch, and Arthur Riordan's 'city comedy', *Boomtown* (Rough Magic, 1999). Its unruly satire on a rampant Celtic Tiger economy was originally excoriated, but was revealed (revised, 2009) as a mordant requiem for Celtic Tiger profligacy. Its sung finale, 'Aren't We Great!' is a withering verdict on the self-deluding idea that 'everyone loves the Irish ... We're Irish. Wow!'

RAYMOND KEARNEY

Tourism

Ireland's tourism industry boomed during the Celtic Tiger years. Hotels were full, restaurants introduced second sittings, drink prices rose as the evening wore on, and, at the end of a night, it was next to impossible to get a taxi home.

On the surface, this was a golden period for Irish tourism. With greater flight connections and cheaper air fares, particularly within Europe, our international tourist arrivals grew from 6.31 million in 2000 to 8.01 million in 2007, with overseas visits to Ireland from mainland Europe increasing by over 78%.

At home, as Irish people started to feel wealthier, short breaks within Ireland became increasingly popular and our domestic holiday market grew 74% between 2000 and 2008. Well-known international hotel brands, including the Four Seasons, Westin, Ritz Carlton, Sheraton, Marriott, Clarion, Hilton and, Radisson, began to arrive, underscoring a widespread confidence in the prospects for Irish tourism.

Hosting the Ryder Cup in 2006 confirmed our status as a premium global golf destination, and as a worldwide TV audience watched on, we confidently predicted that our golf visitor numbers would soar. With the Irish Exchequer awash with money, plans were put in place to build key infrastructure to support our tourism sector, including Terminal 2 at Dublin Airport, the Port Tunnel, the Convention Centre in Dublin, Grand Canal Theatre and the Aviva Stadium.

There was huge investment in our motorway network too, and we marvelled at how quickly we could get from Cork to Belfast, or from Dublin to Galway. We also spent over €400 million changing our rail fleet from one of the oldest in Europe to one of the most modern. Just as we were approaching full employment and 'staff needed' signs began to appear in restaurants and shop windows, Eastern European workers, primarily Polish, arrived to fill the gap.

Believing that the good times would roll on forever, we ignored the first warning signs when they began to appear. In 2004, the OECD pointed out that the growth in visitor numbers was not 'necessarily translating into profitability for individual enterprises, particularly those in the west' and identified that 'substantive change was required in key areas of government policy, in the delivery of that policy by the tourism state agencies, in the work of industry representative bodies, and at the level of individual enterprises'.

Meanwhile, visitor surveys began to show that an increasing number of overseas visitors regarded an Irish holiday as representing poor value for money, with the price of car-hire, food and drink coming in for particular criticism.

The competitiveness issue was compounded by the fall in the value of sterling and the US dollar – the currencies of our two most important markets – against the euro, by 20% and 40% respectively. This resulted in the number of holidays visits from the UK and North America remaining static at almost 1.7 million visits and 0.7 million respectively from 2000 to 2007.

Tourism in the West of Ireland was significantly impacted by the new trend towards city breaks. Touring-based holidays fell out of favour and the number of travellers using sea ferries as a mode of travel dropped from 24% in 2000 to just 12% in 2007. Whereas at the beginning of the Celtic Tiger period, two out of three of all nights spent by holiday visitors to Ireland were in the West, by the end, the share of bed-nights spent along the western seaboard was estimated at just over half.

At the same time, there was a sharp rise in the number of hotel bedrooms in Ireland – from 40,000 in 2001 to 59,000 in 2008 – and this was facilitated by the availability of associated capital allowances for tax purposes. No consideration was given to the impact such a huge increase in supply would have on the viability of existing operators, and by 2008 hotels were indebted to the tune of €4.1 billion. In fact, a 2009 report recommended that the sector should prepare for the orderly elimination of 15,000 rooms.

Back to the present, and Ireland is again experiencing strong tourism growth, facilitated primarily by increased aviation links. By 2037, the global airline fleet is forecast to be 47,990 – more than double the number in 2018 (21,450). Going forward, we will see a marked shift away from the question of how to attract more visitors to how do we manage the numbers we have. We need to move away from the short-term thinking that characterised much of the decision-making during the Celtic Tiger, and focus instead on the strategic issues, namely leadership, governance, environment, R&D, innovation and productivity.

NA FU

Trade Unions

The needs of economic growth and development both nationally and globally during the Celtic Tiger period put a renewed emphasis on business performance and profit. The foundation for any organisation's sustainable success is its people. Sometimes, the ultimate goals for employers and employees are different. Employers seek to maximise the use of resources to achieve high levels of productivity and performance. Employees aim to achieve high performance at work but equally important, work–life balance, satisfactory pay and working conditions. Trade unions are formed to represent and protect the interests of their members, that is, employees.

Trade unions represent employees and negotiate with employers for better pay and work conditions via collective bargaining. According to the Industrial Relations (Amendment) Act 2015, collective bargaining is defined as: 'voluntary engagements or negotiations between any employer or employers' organisations on the one hand and a trade union of workers or excepted body to which this Act applies from the other, with the object to reaching agreement regarding working conditions or terms of employment, or non-employment, of workers'. Collective bargaining was viewed as one of the most effective means to bring employee influence into organisational decision making. During the 1990s, in Ireland, trade unions represented employee interests and helped to enlarge employee voice and influence via the means of collective bargaining, as well as increasing productivity during the Celtic Tiger and reducing time lost to strikes. However, collective bargaining was criticised as it sometimes led to a less co-operative management–worker relationship.

The role of trade unions in employer–employee relationships has attracted increasing attention from the academic world. There have been a number of Irish scholars who made extraordinary contributions to employee relations or industrial relations as well as to the role of trade unions both nationally and internationally. They are Professors John F. Geary (UCD),

Michael J. Morley (UL), Patrick Gunnigle (UL), Paul Teague (QUB), Tony Dundon (UL), William Aidan Kelly (UCD), and William K. Roche (UCD). Their work significantly helped organisations to establish and maintain good relationships with their employees via working with trade unions.

In the later 1990s and early 2000s, organisations, particularly multinational companies, started to adopt the strategic human resource management practices which helps them to attract, motivate, and develop top talent. One of the key HR practices is employee involvement and participation. Organisations provide opportunities for employees to speak up, share their opinions for making better decisions related to them and their organisations. Given the development of technology, the information exchange and communication between organisations and employees became more regular and fruitful. By adopting consultation with employees in decision-making, organisations promote employee participation which has been found to be a critical factor for employee motivation and retention.

According to the ETUI Benchmarking Working Europe 2012, Trade Unions' density has declined between 2000 and 2009 in 27 EU countries. Trade unions will have to make changes to suit to the new working environment, a point underlined in the statement from 2013 Report of the Commission on the Irish Trade Union Movement by the Irish Congress of Trade Unions, the largest civil society organisation on the island of Ireland, representing and campaigning on behalf of 800,000 working people:

> We must build a strong, vibrant and effective trade union movement to articulate and progress the rights of workers at a time when these rights are being oppressed to a degree unprecedented in modern times.

CHARLES LARKIN

Troika

The 'Troika' was the colloquial term used to describe the combined officials of the International Monetary Fund, European Central Bank and European Commission that designed, executed and administered the €85bn bailout package for Ireland.

The Troika had quarterly meetings with Irish officials as part of the conditionality of the bailout. They would follow those meetings with an initial press conference, outlining what progress they felt had, or had not, taken place as part of the Irish reform and fiscal restructuring programme.

Reports by the International Monetary Fund and the European Commission would then follow. Both the International Monetary Fund and the European Commission continued post-programme monitoring for two years after the December 2010–December 2013 programme was completed. The initial public faces of the Troika were Ajai Chopra (IMF), Istavan Szekely (European Commission) and Klaus Masuch from the European Central Bank.

EUGENE O'BRIEN

U2

I can remember being in Dublin in 2003 at a book launch in the Irish Film Centre. Getting there early, and wandering around Temple Bar, I was struck by two things. One was the variety of ethnic food that was now on offer in Dublin and which was very popular. The other was that from what seemed like every bar in the area, U2's *How to Dismantle an Atomic Bomb* was blaring. One of the most popular tracks was 'Vertigo', and this could well be seen as symbolic of the Celtic Tiger. Vertigo suggests a condition of dizziness and lack of balance. Such dizziness is often caused by looking down from a great height. The driving rhythm and the lyrics were redolent of the time, 'a feeling's so much stronger than a thought' and the location could well describe the dizzy heights of the Celtic Tiger:

> Hello, hello (*hola*!)
> I'm at a place called Vertigo (*dónde está*!)
> It's everything I wish I didn't know
> Except you give me something I can feel, feel!

The use of Spanish conveyed the global feel of the new Ireland, and the notion of a cultural dizziness at the sudden transformation from the poor relation of the European Community to now being the poster boy of economic development and growth was captured by seeing Celtic Tiger Ireland as a 'place called Vertigo'. It is a place which is uncertain (the Spanish question means 'who is it?' or 'who is he?') but which provides satisfaction of desire by giving something that 'I can feel'. Analysing the lyrics is useful, but it is the driving guitar beat that makes the song seem to sing the mood of the Celtic Tiger. and if one were being acerbic, the countdown at the beginning of the song: '*Uno, dos, tres, catorce*' which translates as 'one, two, three, fourteen' could stand for the idiosyncratic regulation practices that were being employed in the banking sector, practices that would ultimately bring this period to a shuddering end.

So in many ways, U2 could be seen as providing the soundtrack to the Celtic Tiger. This period was a time when Ireland, to paraphrase Robert Emmet, had taken its place among the nations of the earth. It seemed that we had gone form a pretty backward economy, bypassed the slow *embourgeoisement* that characterised a modernist economy and moved straight to a postmodern form of economy with resultant success.

At another level U2 were an embodiment of a newfound sense of Irish cultural confidence. For years, it was American and British artists who flooded Irish airwaves and TV programmes, and if one wished to hear Irish music, generally this would be found on home-produced programmes on RTÉ or on programmes made about Ireland and Irish issues on other channels, but now, U2 were being played as parts of the soundtracks of global television shows, and Irish people watching seasons 2 and 3 of *Friends*, for example, would have heard the haunting guitar riffs and lyrics of 'With or Without You' on November 16, 1995 ('The One with the List'); January 30, 1997 ('The One where Monica and Richard are Just Friends') and the iconic February 13, 1997 episode ('The One where Ross and Rachel Take a Break').

For Irish people to hear music from an Irish rock group being played on such a world wide platform signalled a confidence in Ireland as a place in the world, as opposed to a poor relation of the European community, dependent on structural funds to bring us to some form of modernity. Culturally, the ubiquitous sound of U2 provided a cultural confidence that seemed to go hand in hand with the new economic confidence of our growling tiger economy. During this period, U2 songs could be heard in *Entourage*; *Cold Case*; *Scrubs*; *Sons of Anarchy*; *The Simpsons*; *The Sopranos*; *Cold Case*; *Ugly Betty*; *CSI Miami*; *The Office* (US edition), while the following films also featured songs from the band: *The Devil Wears Prada*; *Vanilla Sky*; *Lara Croft Tomb Raider* and *City of Angels*. 'Beautiful Day' is heard when, in season 7, episode 17 of *The West Wing*, Matt Santos wins the presidential election on April 9, 2006.

As a symbol of how Ireland had become a confident, globalised and financially and culturally aware place, the sounds of U2 were pervasive. Across a global media, they replaced the folk and ballad songs which had hitherto indicated Ireland, with their own brand of rock music which signified a more postmodern, assertive country. Whereas generations of Irishmen and women had emigrated to America to work, these four Dubliners went to America to play stadium tours. Things, indeed, had changed during the Celtic Tiger.

CONSTANTIN GURDGIEV

Unemployment

During the Celtic Tiger Era, unemployment presented Fianna Fáil, and its coalition partners, with an opportunity to flex their policy muscles, proving that no problem can resist the force of cash being thrown at it. During the era of organic growth (as opposed to property and construction bubble-fuelled growth), Irish unemployment reached its historic low of 3.6% in 2000. At the same time, the Irish labour force participation rate steadily rose from the mid-56% mark in the mid-1990s, to 59.6% in 2000, with gains in both male and female participation, based on the data from the National Households Survey reported by the CSO. Thereafter, spurred on by the tax incentives that favoured a two-working adults' households, consistent rises in the cost of living, and the booming domestic economy (including the property bubble inflation and increases in public spending), the Irish labour force expanded into 2007, reaching the highest annual participation rate of 64.08%. In that year, the male participation rate peaked at 73.725% and female participation rose to 54.55%. Unemployment was slightly more elevated at 4.6%, but still below the full employment rate.

The collapse of the Celtic Tiger, starting with the 2008 Financial Crisis, reversed much of the gains achieved during the boom era. Irish unemployment peaked at 14.7% in 2012, when participation rates collapsed to 59.9%, erasing the gains made during the later stage of the Celtic Tiger. Male participation declined a whopping 6.125% on 2007 levels, while female participation was down just under 2%.

Falling unemployment during the Celtic Tiger also had a collateral effect. Self-employed, especially self-employed with employees, are the early-stage entrepreneurs who underpin the new firms' formation in any economy. During the Celtic Tiger, the share of self-employed and self-employed with employees entered an irreversible decline. Over 1998–2007, the likelihood of an Irish employed person being self-employed dropped from 18.3% to 16%. The downward trend continued in the post-crisis recovery period. The share of self-employed with employees in the total employment has fallen from just under 6% in 1998 to 4.7% by the end of 2011.

LORCAN SIRR

Unfinished Estates

A rather 'one dimensional and simplistic' (Kenna, 2009) approach to housing policy and supply led to a significant oversupply of housing when mortgage lending dried up in 2008. This oversupply was evident in the 620 estates in which 50% or more of the housing units were unoccupied, under development or unfinished. These were known as 'ghost estates' due to the lack of occupants. 86 of these developments had 50 or more housing units.

There were several reasons why Ireland ended up with an oversupply of housing – with most of this oversupply somewhat perversely in areas where diminishing or no demand had ever existed – and the biggest reason was poor planning practice by local authorities. According to certain commentators, what emerged was a pattern of housing development that ran counter to what one would have expected or hoped for in the context of good planning. Essentially, a number of local authorities did not: heed good planning guidelines and regional and national objectives; conduct sensible demographic profiling of potential demand; or take account of the fact that much of the land zoned lacks essential services such as water and sewerage treatment plants, energy supply, public transport or roads.

Instead, planning permissions for housing development and the zoning and re-zoning of land to residential use were facilitated by the abandonment of basic planning principles by elected representatives on the local and national stage, often driven by the demands of local people, developers and speculators. 'Site-farming' became prevalent, as farmers sold random plots of land for the construction of one-off housing which they knew would get planning permission given the free-for-all building climate and ignoring of good planning practice. Not only did central government fail to adequately oversee, regulate and direct local planning, it actively encouraged its excesses through tax incentive schemes including the flaunting of its own principles as set out in the National Spatial Strategy through policies such as decentralisation, itself a classic example of the often evidence-free and careless politically driven ideology of the Celtic Tiger years.

After some speculation as to how many such estates existed in Irish towns, cities and countryside, the then Department of Environment, Communities and Local Government (now the Department of Housing, Planning and Local Government) undertook a nationwide survey in 2010. The National Survey of Housing Developments reported that there were 2,846 documented unfinished estates in Ireland, present in every local authority, of which only 429 were still active (Housing Agency 2010). The highest proportions of 'empty' unoccupied developments were in western and midland counties. Counties such as Cork, Leitrim, Longford, Sligo and Roscommon had particularly high rates of housing oversupply in comparison to their populations.

Planning permissions for housing developments contained conditions requiring the lodgement with the planning authority of a security for the purposes of providing funding for the satisfactory provision of public infrastructure (not the development) in case of default by the developer. In many instances this security was in the form of a cash deposit, an insurance policy or a construction bond. Since 2011, local authorities across the country obtained approximately €63 million from securities lodged during the Celtic Tiger era to complete essential public infrastructure within unfinished housing developments, including roads, water services, public lighting and amenity areas and where breaches of planning conditions have occurred.

There have been numerous knock-on effects of the phenomenon of unfinished estates. Many of the builders of these estates were not professional developers, but tradespeople who, subsequent to the crash, emigrated to find work elsewhere, leaving the estates incomplete. These tradespeople are now in high demand in Ireland as a labour shortage threatens a housebuilding recovery. The rehabilitation of unfinished housing in these estates also caused housebuilding completion numbers to be artificially inflated as houses built, in some instances years previously, were finally connected to the electricity grid many years later and thus counted as a new house as per the house-counting methodology. The artificial inflation of housebuilding completions – in part caused by unfinished estates – has caused the counting system to be reviewed and the GDP figure for 2017 to be questioned as more accurate completion statistics became available.

PADDY PRENDERGAST

Universities

'Hire them before they hire you', was the brilliant and iconic slogan used by the Industrial Development Authority in the years just before the Celtic Tiger began to roar. The caption accompanied a group photograph of graduates that formed part of the state agency's international advertising campaign: 'The Young Europeans'.

The IDA was already pitching successfully for mobile foreign direct investment. However, capitalising on Ireland's increasingly well-educated workforce was an inspired addition to the campaign. It helped convey the impression that Ireland, as a young and vibrant EU member state, was ready to take on the world economically. Of course, the country did lead the way in economic growth for a decade or so. This lead was backed up and cemented by increasing state investment in higher education, where enrolment rose at an unprecedented rate.

The growth in student numbers in those years was quite extraordinary. In the 1991/2 academic year, there were 76,809 full-time undergraduate and post-graduate students in the Republic of Ireland, but this had almost doubled to 145,7890 in January 2009. The numbers have continued to grow to 183,696 in the 2017/18 academic year.

The abolition of tuition fees by Education Minister Niamh Bhreathnach helped fuel the growth in student numbers, even if that decision did not help her or the Labour Party in the subsequent general election in 1997. In the boom years, there was money from the State to compensate the universities for the loss of the fees revenue, but that began to dry up during the recession that began in 2008.

What also eventually began to dry up was the funding available under the remarkably successful Programme for Research in Third Level Institutions (PRTLI). It was launched in 1998, following a pilot programme in science and technology. Over three cycles some €605m was expended, with 30% of this money coming from Chuck Feeney's Atlantic Philanthropies.

Ireland owes Chuck Feeney an immense debt of gratitude as the man who helped to end the country's abysmal record of investment in research and development. When one looks at the fine research centres on university campuses around the country now, it is hard to remember that until a few decades ago our investment in this lifeblood of a modern university and a successful economy was one of the worst in the developed world.

The economic dividend from this investment in research, and in the resulting enhanced skills base, was obvious during the Celtic Tiger years, with new industries springing up, immigration rising and unemployment falling. Researchers flocked to our shores wondering why our booming economy was comparing well with those of the Asian Tiger countries and asking what part did higher education play in this economic 'miracle'. Without the sustained investment in higher education and research over the boom years, the effects of the downturn would have been much worse for Ireland.

Today, the IDA continues to emphasise the importance of such investment in its unstinting efforts to attract foreign investment, as does Enterprise Ireland in trying to 'grow' indigenous industry. *Plus ça change.*

CONSTANTIN GURDGIEV

'We all partied'

Uttered by the then-Minister for Finance, the late Brian Lenihan Jnr during an interview on RTE's *Prime Time* on November 24, 2010, the phrase came to symbolise the Irish elites' response to the causes of the crisis. The extended quote, however, offers a glimpse into Lenihan's deeper, and more nuanced view. 'I accept that there were failures in the political system. I accept that I have to take responsibility as a member of the governing party during that period for what happened. But let's be fair about it. We all partied'. Lenihan strikes a tragic figure in the history of the Celtic Tiger. Conflicted by his earlier government positions, and suffering from failing health, he took the poisoned chalice of running the Department of Finance at the peak of the crisis. He did so with integrity, albeit in the absence of serious expertise, and made multiple mistakes. Nevertheless, his policy errors were largely forced, framed or nudged by forces external to Ireland, such as the reluctance of the ECB and the EU leadership to address the roots of the crises that befell Ireland.

Taken out of its context, 'We all partied' conveys – correctly – the arrogance of the Irish leadership at the time of the crisis. Taken within the context of the broader acknowledgement of the state leadership's failures, it narrates – again, correctly – a real sense of what the later years of the Celtic Tiger came to symbolise: a nearly total abandonment by the governments, the regulators and the banking and business elites of their duty of care for the ordinary residents of Ireland. That abandonment, framed into economic forecasts and musings by an army of complacent academics and financial and state sector yes-minister minstrels, propelled Irish society towards careless borrowing and binge consumption, reckless investments in property and banks shares, and fuelled the bubble that burst in 2008.

An added irony relevant to Lenihan's quote is that in the same November 2010 interview, the Minister solemnly promises the public that those who drove the country into the crisis will face punishment. In hindsight, the Minister was partially correct: in the end, punishment for the Celtic Tiger excesses was loaded onto the shoulders of the ordinary people, while those who truly partied in the Celtic Garfield era of financial excesses have ended up in cushy new jobs or in a sweet retirement.

Thus, some have partied more, some have partied less. The former got to keep their toys and the latter got clobbered with the bill.

BRIAN MURPHY

Wine Culture

Ireland's relationship with wine changed considerably during the Celtic Tiger years. Up to relatively recently, wine was often perceived as the preserve of wealthier, more elite groups in Irish society. However, the new millennium brought change, and according to the Irish Wine Association, wine sales almost doubled from 4.5 million cases in 2000 to 8.2 million cases five years later. During this period the country underwent what wine writer Jean Smullen referred to as a 'democratisation of wine'. The factors that contributed to that democratisation are not unique to Ireland, but were certainly more pronounced in this country because of the Celtic Tiger boom. Returning emigrants who had been working in high-status jobs, with commensurate salaries and career structures, were more discerning, and demanding, when it came to matching good food with wine.

The Celtic Tiger period also saw a rapid growth in food media in terms of content that frequently involved discussions and segments around wine and wine recommendations. The popularity of New World wine, with simple to understand flavours, and clearly labelled bottles, also helped make wine more accessible. This was reflected in the fact that both Australian and Chilean wines came to dominate sales in Ireland while France, despite its reputation as the home of wine culture, ranked only third in popularity.

The rise of the female wine market has also been an important factor in our changing relationship with wine. Despite recent calls for moderation, much of the wine consumed at home still comes through the weekly supermarket shop, which is still predominantly controlled by women. 80% of wine is now purchased from sources like supermarkets and off licences, with only 20% purchased in bars and restaurants. Our wine market is largely varietally driven, and the Celtic Tiger bore witness to the rise in popularity and subsequent decline of many different grape varieties. We saw the dominance of the ubiquitous bottle of Chardonnay or Shiraz, the rise of a crisp glass of Sauvignon Blanc, an oaked Cabernet Sauvignon, or perhaps a delicate Pinot Noir. Preference was increasingly based on grape variety rather than brand. Sparkling wines like Prosecco became popular, although they now appear to be losing ground, as we wait for the next fashionable drink to take centre stage.

Celtic Tiger Ireland was introduced to other aspects of wine culture. We had the rise in popularity of dedicated magazines such as *Food and Wine*, along with a plethora of newspaper articles reviewing, contemplating and promoting wine. Accredited wine courses expanded across the country and wine writers and enthusiasts such as Tomás Clancy, Jean Smullen and Martin Moran, came to the fore. Many excellent restaurants emerged during this period, and began to employ dedicated sommeliers as consumer knowledge and interest increased.

At the end of the Celtic Tiger period, wine sales in Ireland stood at just over 8 million cases. As a luxury product one might have expected these sales to fall dramatically once the economy crashed. However, despite a slight dip, they remained strong. In part this was driven by what has been described as the trend for 'cocooning'. For both budgetary reasons and perhaps the desire to avoid overt displays of wealth, there was a considerable rise in people staying in, and creating dining experiences at home. One of the consequences of the building boom was the improvement in Ireland's housing stock and, despite being negatively leveraged, many homes were often well suited to home entertaining. An array of retail options facilitated the trend for 'cocooning' with companies like Tesco and Marks and Spencer, among others, heavily promoting dine-in ranges with the ubiquitous bottle of wine included.

Despite the demise of the Celtic Tiger economy, good wine is now part of our drinking culture and is viewed by many as an integral part of contemporary diets. Dedicated wine bars are on the increase, Irish pubs are improving their selection of wines and wine is increasingly seen by the Irish as a food partner, and not as a food primer. It would be fair to say that wine in Ireland has finally become 'democratised'.

SHARON TIGHE-MOONEY

Women and the Church

The economic rise of the Celtic Tiger was preceded by the cultural fall of the Catholic Church with the revelation, in 1992, about the popular bishop Eamon Casey fathering a son. This was followed swiftly by the exposure of the fathering of two children by the singing priest, Michael Cleary. These seismic cultural shocks were soon engulfed by the recounting, in 1994, of the decades of abuse perpetrated by the Norbertine priest, Brendan Smyth in the UTV documentary, *Suffer the Children*. This was followed by the detailing of the sustained abuse suffered by children in Irish Church-run industrial and reformatory schools over a 50-year period in Mary Raftery's *States of Fear*, broadcast by RTÉ in 1999. To this dismal list was added the details of the punitive lives of women incarcerated in Magdalene Laundries, the high death rates of their children and more recently, although first reported to the Vatican by Sr Maura O'Donoghue in 1994, the widespread abuse of nuns and vulnerable women by priests on every continent.

While much has been written about the crisis in the visible cultural fabric of Irish society, the role of women, as the former unofficial propagators of the faith, and the consequences for the faith of the renouncing of that role, has been less well documented. Catholic Church thinking has long divided the world into private and public spheres, with decision making, leadership, business and the worldly affairs of the public sphere vested solely in men. Women were associated with the private sphere of the home, a view reflected by the Irish State in the Constitution and consolidated by a raft of legislation limiting the autonomy of Irish women. It is, in fact, in this sphere, where the transformation in the religious cultural fabric in society has occurred.

In a study conducted by sociologist Betty Hilliard in Cork City in 1975, women, in responding to general questions about their lives as mothers, inadvertently revealed the significant influence the Church had held over the institution of motherhood. When a selection of the group was revisited in 2000, there had been a significant change in attitudes to church teaching in the intervening 25 years. Women had begun to reflect on their experiences in relation to their reproductive lives and, 'A widespread reaction amongst participants in this study to their treatment by the church in relation to marital sexuality was anger,' which prefigured altered mind-sets and attitudes brought about by the new prosperity and more open media channels of the Celtic Tiger. This anger fuelled a sea change in attitudes in terms of deference to the church and its personnel as well as to the obligation of full acceptance of church dictats.

Pre-1994, the number of Irish women in the labour force was low, compared to their European counterparts. However, during the Celtic Tiger period, the Irish female workforce grew almost five times faster than was happening in the rest of Europe. Tax individualisation meant that women were incentivised to continue in careers after giving birth to their children (indeed, many had no choice but to do so). With independence and prosperity comes confidence and during this period, many long-running campaigns in areas in which women's autonomy was particularly affected were successfully accomplished. Additionally, women's growing self-determination meant that many were less likely to accept constraints on their freedom. In other words, the economic independence and enhanced educational opportunities led to a situation where women saw their role differently within society and within the Catholic Church.

While many women in Hilliard's study related that they no longer took on the role of propagator of the Catholic faith in the home, others acknowledged that the scandals had, in fact, undermined that role in any case. In other words, the scandals directly influenced how the faith might be practised, or not, in the next generation. Without the yoke of cultural obedience, as well as the toppling of the church from its pedestal, the next generation of women had little incentive to accept the church's monitoring of their lives in the same way as their mothers had done. Additionally, millennials have little interest in giving their time and talents to an institution in which they have no official role as contributors, leaders, or decision-makers.

While many women still attend official religious ceremonies, it is on their own terms. The Catholic Church, whatever its rhetoric, is quite clear about not wanting the contribution of women in any official capacity. However, it is the church's own actions that have ensured that many Irish women no longer perform their former unofficial role as propagators of the faith either.

DEIRDRE FLYNN

Women in the Celtic Tiger

The precise year the Celtic Tiger started changes depending on what academic, critic, economist or journalist you ask. However, one of the major markers of change for women in Ireland was in 1996, when the final 'mother and baby' home closed its doors, putting an end to the decades of enforced incarceration and punishment of women and girls. It was a further 13 years before the Ryan Report was published, detailing the mistreatment of infants, unpaid labour, and physical and sexual abuse of many in those Church and State-run institutions. Survivors are still waiting for justice. The closure of these institutions and the opening of national inquiries has been an essential step in the healing process. A report commissioned by the Dublin Rape Crisis Centre in 2002 highlighted that 42% of women, and 28% of men, in all of Ireland had experienced sexual abuse, one of the highest such figures in Europe.

Despite the suggestion that Ireland, during the Celtic Tiger, was a more liberal and secular place, the constitution tells a different story for the women of Ireland. The 8th Amendment, inserted into the constitution in 1983, meant that the heartbeat of the unborn was deemed to be of equal importance to the health of the mother, and abortion was not available in Ireland in any circumstance, apart from the legally vague clause about there being a real and substantial risk to the life of the mother. Referendums prior to the Celtic Tiger allowed doctors to provide information, and gave women the right to travel to access the necessary medical care. Removing the right to abortion in the case of suicide was narrowly defeated in 1992, and again in 2002, and during this time, and until 2018, those who obtained an abortion in Ireland could be jailed for up to 14 years. According to an article in the *Irish Times* on May 2, 2018 over 74,000 people travelled to the UK to obtain an abortion between 1995 and 2007.

The 2004 citizenship referendum had women at the centre of the amendment, and in particular marking out pregnant women not born in Ireland as not Irish, and being deemed as citizenship tourists. The referendum removed the automatic entitlement of citizenship at birth. Pregnancies of these women were subject to huge scrutiny and racism during the campaign and today children of inward migrants and asylum seekers are still feeling the repercussions of the amendment that passed by 79%.

Section 41 of the constitution from 1937, and still in place today, suggests that Woman and Mother are interchangeable terms and that the most important duties of a 'woman/mother' hybrid are those in the home. The Divorce referendum of 1995 was a very important moment for married women in Ireland, and its passage into law was welcomed by the National Women's Council of Ireland.

It is interesting that during the Celtic Tiger period record numbers of women entered the labour force. According to the CSO, the number of women in work outside the home increased by 128,000 between 1996 and 2000. Despite this, the gender pay gap remained at around 20%. Research from the Irish Congress of Trade Unions highlighted that the lowest paid labour was in industries considered traditionally female. For parents, the increasing cost of childcare, along with the lack of state-sponsored childcare, meant that Ireland had one of the lowest rates in Europe of labour force participation for mothers of children under 5. The gap between rich and poor expanded during the Celtic Tiger really impacting women from lower socio-economic backgrounds, migrant women, and ethnic groups such as Irish Travellers. In 2004, the UN said that Ireland had the highest level of inequality in the EU.

In politics, Mary McAleese replaced Mary Robinson as the second female President of Ireland in 1997. Women called Mary were very popular in politics, and in 1997, Mary Harney, then of the Progressive Democrats, became the first female Tánaiste. Other famous Marys during this period include Mary Hanafin, Mary Coughlan, Mary O'Rourke, Mary Upton, and Maire Hoctor. Yet in the 28th Dáil (1997), only 12% of members were female, increasing to 13.3% for the 29th Dáil (2002).

Other noteworthy women include Veronica Guerin, the crime reporter who was killed in 1996, and in the same year swimmer Michelle Smith won three gold medals and one bronze at the Olympics in Atlanta. (Unfortunately, her swimming career ended with a ban from the sporting authorities for tampering with a urine sample.) Druid Theatre's Garry Hynes became the first female director to win a Tony for *The Beauty Queen of Leenane* on Broadway in 1998. The first female editor of *The Irish Times*, Geraldine Kennedy, was appointed in 2002, and in 2006 Katherine Zappone began her campaign to have her Canadian same-sex marriage recognised in Ireland.

MARY O'DONNELL

Women Writers

Despite the recession being 'over', writing by female authors reacted to and interpreted background events ranging from the tragi-comic excess of the boom years, to the social and economic marginalisation that followed.

But some writers were preoccupied by other themes not quite within the ambit of boom and bust. Compelling writing appeared from Christine Dwyer Hickey (*The Cold Eye of Heaven*, 2011) and Deirdre Madden, for example. The latter's novel, *Time Present, and Time Past* (2013), returns to one of her favourite themes, the relationship between memory and time. Dwyer Hickey's novel also addresses time, and takes the reader in reverse chronology from 2010 to 1940s Dublin, tracing a backwards journey from prosperity to hardship. Meanwhile, in 2015 the gifted Sara Baume produced an isolated man, a one-eyed dog, and a telling sense of place in her debut novel *Spill, Simmer, Falter, Wither*.

More directly focused on the years of economic prosperity and after, is Lisa McInerney's *The Inglorious Heresies* (2015), an award-winning novel set in a violent, drug-infected Cork that shares certain preoccupations that can be seen also in the writing of Claire Kilroy, Danielle McLaughlin, and Dame Edna O'Brien (*The Little Red Chairs*, 2015).

To read any of their work is to sense the mania that afflicted the country, swelling like a carbuncle while we accepted inflated prices as a matter of pride ('Sure, can't we afford it now?') along with Finance Minister Charlie McCreevy's annual bonanza of increased children's allowances, tax relief, and reduced corporate taxation.

Tellingly, 'Money kills the imagination', the narrator of Claire Kilroy's 2012 novel *The Devil I Know*, announces. Tristram, her enjoyable caricature of a wine-soaked double-dealer, hauled home to Ireland to testify about his Celtic Tiger activities, has failed to comprehend the true nature of money. And if, as Kilroy writes, imagination is to be killed by money, then five years earlier, Éilís Ní Dhuibhne's narrator Anna, in the opening pages of her satiric novel *Fox, Swallow, Scarecrow* (2007), perhaps in a moment of authorial prescience, confirms that too much money also leads to smugness. Here, she describes the passengers on one of the city's new trams:

> They were in love with the tram. Confidence and well-being crowned them like an aura, one and all, from a toddler wearing cheerful denim and mini mountain boots to the old ladies in beige raincoats and cute little Burberry hats ...

After the crash, a different tone emerged in the writing – grimmer, darker, less forgiving. One of the best accounts of the devastation it brought is found in Danielle McLaughlin's short story 'In the Act of Falling' (from her collection *Dinosaurs on Other Planets*, 2015). First published in *The New Yorker*, it raises the spectre of a laid-off husband, and regardless of evocative language which places the piece just south of the Irish midlands, brings the reader hard up against the cruel face of the recession from hell.

The protagonist, living in post-recession misery in a now-unheated early nineteenth-century Georgian mansion with depressed husband Bill, and arguably disturbed son Finn, commutes daily to Dublin, distracted by work, distracted by the cataclysmic plunge in fortune that blights their lives. It is this story, rather than any novel, that distils the tragedy that spliced the lives of so many people. Not alone is there a fault line in the socio-cultural landscape of the time, but that fault line criss-crosses the couple's relationship, unavoidably sucking in their child, as another woman who has both time and fundamentalist beliefs at her disposal edges into the scene. The sense of jeopardy is pervasive. Everything is up for grabs – the material things, the signifiers of their once-upon-a-time wealth and achievement – but also the people themselves, including their son. Most important of all, the story stands as a descriptor of irretrievable loss; the loss of peace of mind. The results are neither cosy nor familial. This uncompromising story will endure, I suspect, as a classic work whose subject is loss, as it evokes the ultimate psychological nightmare of desperation that afflicted so many.

It became easy to whip ourselves into a state of accusation for our folly once the golden years had ended. Yet if money is a limited currency for material wellbeing, I'd like to think that some of the literature produced in response to the recession offers a different currency for the imagination, one that is inexhaustibly rich. Through this writing, a new descriptor and signifier has emerged, which returns us to sometimes fabular tales of individuals, betrayal, and of a social underside pitting itself against impossible odds for the retrieval of lost dreams.

Notes on Contributors

MAURA ADSHEAD is Associate Professor in Politics and Public Administration at the Department of Politics and Public Administration, University of Limerick. She was instrumental in the design and establishment of UL Engage and was appointed as the UL Academic Advocate for Engaged Scholarship in September 2015. She is currently chair of the national Campus Engage Working Group on Engaged.

SEAN BARRETT FTCD served as Pro-Chancellor of Dublin University from 2018 to 2019 and a university Senator from 2011 to 2016. He was a member of the Parliament's Committee of Inquiry into the Irish Banking Crisis (2016). He has served on the National Economic and Social Council and on the board of the Journal of Air Transport Management and on OECD and EU advisory bodies on air transport liberalisation and the ending of Europe's airline cartels.

RUTH BARTON is Head of the School of Creative Arts and Associate Professor in Film Studies at Trinity College Dublin. She has written widely on Irish cinema. Her new monograph, *Irish Cinema in the Twenty-First Century*, was published in 2019 by Manchester University Press.

DAVID BEGG is a former General Secretary of ICTU and is currently Chairman of both the Pensions Authority and the Mater Misericordiae Hospital Group. He is author of a book on European Integration published in 2016. He has a PhD in Sociology and is Adjunct Professor at Maynooth University Institute of Social Sciences.

SUSAN BOYLE is a drinks consultant, researcher, writer and performer and an award-winning member of the British Guild of Beer Writers.

JOE BRENNAN is the markets correspondent with *The Irish Times*, having covered the banking crisis with Bloomberg News in Dublin between 2010 and 2016 and the *Irish Independent* between 2007 and 2010. Prior to that, he worked with *The Sunday Times's* Irish edition and spent five years reporting on German equities in Frankfurt for financial newswires.

AOIFE CARRIGY is a writer, journalist and editor specialising in food and drink. She holds an MA in Anglo-Irish Literature from UCD and was undertaking postgraduate research on Cultural Representations of the Irish Pub at Technological University Dublin, Tallaght at the time of her contribution to this publication.

JUSTIN CARVILLE teaches Historical & Theoretical Studies in Photography at IADT, Dun Laoghaire. He is currently working on a book titled *The Ungovernable Eye: Photography, Ethnography and the Racialization of Ireland*.

SEAMUS COFFEY is a lecturer in the Department of Economics in University College Cork. His research and writing focuses on the performance of the Irish economy. He became a member of the Irish Fiscal Advisory Council in 2016 and was made Chair of the Council in January 2017. He is also a member of the external advisory board to the Irish Governmental Economic Evaluation Service and of the council of the Irish Economic Association.

FRANCES COPPOLA is the author of the Coppola Comment finance & economics blog, which is a regular feature on *The Financial Times*'s Alphaville blog and has been quoted in *The Economist, The Wall Street Journal, The New York Times* and *The Guardian*. She is also a frequent commentator on financial matters for the BBC.

SHAEN CORBET works as an Associate Professor of Finance at Dublin City University Business School in Dublin, Ireland. He has previously worked as a commodities and equities trader and as an economist with the Financial Stability Department at The Central Bank of Ireland. He has published a number of research papers in a range of internationally recognised journals and is a member of multiple inter-disciplinary working groups.

KARL DEETER is a business-person and commentator. He helps to run Irish Mortgage Brokers, a business he co-founded, and also writes for several national papers (*The Sun* and the *Sunday Business Post*). He has been songwriting for about 25 years.

PASCHAL DONOHUE is the Fine Gael TD for Dublin Central. He was first elected in February 2011, where he topped the poll. In June 2017 he was appointed as the Minister for Finance, while also holding the position of Minister for Public Expenditure and Reform. He has also served as Minister for Transport, Tourism and Sport and Minister for European Affairs. He is a graduate of Trinity College, with a degree in Politics and Economics.

NEIL DUNNE is Lecturer in Accounting at Trinity College Dublin, and Programme Director for Trinity's Postgraduate Diploma in Accounting. An award-winning lecturer and researcher, he holds a Bachelor of Commerce from University College Cork, a Master's degree in Finance from Trinity, and is also a Fellow of Chartered Accountants Ireland.

MICK FEALTY is founding editor of the *Slugger O'Toole* website, news portal and blog. He has written papers on the impacts of the Internet on politics and the wider media, and is a regular guest at speaking events across Ireland, the UK and Europe.

MARTINA FITZGERALD is the author of the number-one bestseller *Madam Politician: The Women at the Table of Irish Political Power*, which received critical acclaim following its publication in 2018. With almost two decades experience as a senior journalist, she has reported extensively on all recent general elections and referendums – and was RTÉ's Political Correspondent until December 2018.

DARRAGH FLANNERY is Lecturer in Economics at the Kemmy Business School at the University of Limerick. He holds a PhD in Economics from the National University of Ireland and specialises in applied microeconomics, focusing on a range of public policy issues. He has over 20 peer-reviewed publications and a number of on-going research projects related to the economics of higher education.

EÓIN FLANNERY lectures in the Department of English Language and Literature at Mary Immaculate College, University of Limerick. He is the author of four books including *Ireland and Ecocriticism: Literature, History, and Environmental Justice* (2016) and *Colum McCann and the Aesthetics of Redemption* (2011).

DEIRDRE FLYNN is Lecturer in Contemporary World and Irish Literature and Drama. She has worked at University College Dublin, National University of Ireland Galway, University of Limerick and Mary Immaculate College. She has published widely on Irish Literature, Drama, and Culture and world literature.

NA FU is Associate Professor in Human Resource Management, Programme Director for MSc HRM, and Co-Director of Centre for Digital Business at Trinity Business School, Trinity College Dublin. He is an Academic Fellow of the Chartered Institute for Personnel Development. He specialises in strategic human resource management, professional service innovation, and digital transformation of workplace.

MEGAN GREENE is Senior Fellow at the Mossavar-Rahmani Centre for Business and Government (M-RCBG) at the Harvard Kennedy School. She also writes a regular column on global economics for *The Financial Times*, is a member of the Council on Foreign Relations, serves as a Non-Resident Fellow at Trinity College Dublin and sits on the board of directors at NABE, the Irish Parliamentary Budget Office, Rebuilding Macroeconomics and Econofact.

CONSTANTIN GURDGIEV is a 'Polarizing Bear' (*Irish Times*) and an 'international man of mischief' (*Dubliner*). In his free time, he serves as Associate Professor of Finance with Middlebury Institute of International Studies at Monterey, California, and Adjunct Professor of Finance with Trinity College Dublin.

DEREK HAND is Head of the School of English in Dublin City University. His *A History of the Irish Novel: 1665 to the present* was published by Cambridge University Press in 2011. He is also the co-editor of a collection of essays on John McGahern entitled, *Essays on John McGahern: Assessing a Literary Legacy* in 2019.

RAYMOND KEARNEY lectures in international tourism policy at TU Dublin. He has been involved in several pan-European tourism projects and presents at industry conferences across Europe and Asia. He is a Fellow of the Irish Hospitality Institute.

SARAH KELLEHER is a PhD candidate in the History of Art department at UCC and a Government of Ireland Scholar. She is co-director of Pluck Projects, an independent curatorial venture, an editor of *Enclave Review* and an occasional lecturer within the History of Art Department at UCC and CIT Crawford College of Art and Design.

FINOLA KENNEDY is an economist. She lectured in UCD and the IPA. Her areas of research include public expenditure and family change from an economic perspective. She was a member of the Review Group on the Constitution and a number of State Boards, including the Housing Finance Agency (chairperson).

STEPHEN KINSELLA is an Irish economist. He has two doctoral degrees, one in mathematical economics from NUIG; the other in economics from New School New York. He is Associate Professor of Economics at the University of Limerick's Kemmy Business School in Ireland and a columnist with Ireland's *Sunday Business Post*. He has written a number of books about the Irish economy.

ROB KITCHIN is a professor in the Department of Geography and Maynooth University Social Sciences Institute. He is author/editor of 30 academic books and a 12-volume encyclopedia, and was the recipient of the 2013 Royal Irish Academy Gold Medal for the Social Sciences.

BRIAN LANGAN has over two decades' experience in publishing, most recently as editor at Transworld Ireland, an imprint of Penguin Random House, where his authors included Donal Ryan, Hilary Fannin, Colm O'Regan and Conor O'Clery. He is now a freelance editor and literary agent. He is also a published author and is currently writing his second novel.

CHARLES LARKIN is Senior Lecturer and Director of Research of the Institute for Policy Research at the University of Bath. A PhD graduate in

Economics from Trinity College, he has extensive experience in the policy and legislative space in Ireland, and has authored numerous academic articles in economics and finance.

JOHN LITTLETON, a priest of the Archdiocese of Cashel and Emly, is Director of the Priory Institute, Tallaght, Dublin. He has taught theology and religious studies in several institutions in Ireland and the UK. He served as President of the National Conference of Priests of Ireland (NCPI) from 2001 until 2007.

BRIAN LUCEY is Professor of International Finance and Commodities in Trinity Business School, Trinity College and the University of Sydney. A graduate of TCD and Stirling University in Scotland, his research interests are in the areas of commodities, international finance, and international economics.

MÁIRTÍN MAC CON IOMAIRE is Senior Lecturer in Culinary Arts and Food History at TU Dublin, where he chairs the Masters in Gastronomy and Food Studies. He is co-founder and chair of the biennial Dublin Gastronomy Symposium and a Trustee of the Oxford Symposium on Food and Cookery.

JOHN MCDONAGH is Senior Lecturer in English at Mary Immaculate College, University of Limerick. He has written studies on Brendan Kennelly, Michael Hartnett and Paul Durcan.

EAMON MAHER is Director of the National Centre for Franco-Irish Studies in TU Dublin. He is General Editor of two series with Peter Lang, Oxford: Reimagining Ireland and Studies in Franco-Irish Relations. His latest book, co-edited with Derek Hand, is *Essays on John McGahern: Assessing a Literary Legacy* (Cork University Press, 2019).

CATHERINE MAIGNANT is Professor of Irish Studies at the University of Lille (France). She was president of the French Association of Irish studies (SOFEIR) and of the European Federation of Associations and centres of Irish Studies (EFACIS) for a number of years. After writing a PhD on early medieval Irish Christianity, she now specialises in contemporary Irish religious history.

PATRICIA MEDCALF is Lecturer in Advertising and Marketing at TU Dublin. Previously, she was Project Director with branding specialists The Identity Business, and Marketing Consultant with Siemens. In 2004, she published the textbook, *Marketing Communications: An Irish Perspective*. Her PhD thesis analysed five decades of Guinness Advertising in Ireland.

VICTOR MERRIMAN is Professor of Critical Performance Studies, Edge Hill University. His books include: *Because We Are Poor: Irish Theatre in the 1990s* (Carysfort Press, 2011) and *Austerity and the Public Role of Drama: Performing Lives-in-Common* (Palgrave Macmillan, 2019). He was a member of *An Chomhairle Ealaíon*/The Arts Council from 1993 to 1998.

IDA MILNE is a social historian who lectures in European history at Carlow College. She worked for many years as a travel journalist for *Travel Extra*. Her recent publications include *Stacking the Coffins, Influenza, War and Revolution in Ireland, 1918–19* (Manchester Press, 2018) and, co-edited with Ian d'Alton, *Protestant and Irish: The Minority's Search for Place in Independent Ireland* (Cork University Press, 2019).

FABRICE MOURLON is Professor of British and Irish Studies at Université Sorbonne Nouvelle in Paris. He is Editor-in-Chief of the French journal of Irish Studies, *Etudes Irlandaises*. His research interest focus on post-conflict issues in Northern Ireland, small political parties and popular culture as well as alternative economics. His recent book, *L'Urgence de dire: l'Irlande du Nord après le conflit*, was published in 2018 with Peter Lang.

JOHN D. MULCAHY was originally a hotel management graduate, whose international career encompassed fine dining, hotel schools, UN and off-shore catering, gastropubs and wine education, culminating in responsibility for food tourism development in Fáilte Ireland. Currently an independent gastronomy tourism activist, advisor and researcher, he contributes to publications and conferences regularly.

BRIAN MURPHY lectures in the School of Business and Humanities at the Technological University Dublin-Tallaght Campus. He specialises in beverage studies, food and drink tourism and gastronomy. He has published a number of articles on the role of 'place and story' in contemporary food and drink culture.

EIMEAR NOLAN is Assistant Professor of International Business. Prior to joining Trinity Business School she held academic positions in the UK and the USA. Her research interests include expatriate adjustment, cultural intelligence, recruitment and retention strategies, ethics, and the health care sector.

EUGENE O'BRIEN is a senior lecturer, and Head of the Department of English Language and Literature in Mary Immaculate College, University of Limerick, Ireland. He is the director of the Mary Immaculate Institute for Irish Studies and the editor for the Oxford University Press Online Bibliography project in literary theory. His latest books *Patrimoine / Cultural Heritage in France and Ireland* (with Eamon Maher) and *Representations of Loss in Irish Literature* (with Deirdre Flynn).

JOHN O'CONNOR was co-founder of the design practice Information Design in 1985. He is currently Director and Dean of the College of Arts and Tourism, Technological University Dublin.

MARY O'DONNELL's seven poetry collections include *Unlegendary Heroes* and *Those April Fevers* (Ark Publications). Four novels include *Where They Lie* (2014) and the best-selling debut novel *The Light Makers*, reissued last year after by 451 Editions. Her new poetry collection *Massacre of the Birds* will be published in 2020. She is a member of Aosdána, and was recently awarded a PhD at University College Cork.

BRIAN O'NEILL is Director of Research, Enterprise and Innovation Services at TU Dublin and is chair of the Media Literacy Ireland Steering Group.

PADDY PRENDERGAST is Provost and President, since 2011, of Trinity College. A native of Wexford, he is an engineer by training. He has published extensively in biomechanics and more latterly in the areas of university governance and education policy.

KATE SHANAHAN, Head of Journalism and Communications at TU Dublin, is an award-winning journalist and radio and television producer. She is a founder member of Women Leaders in Higher Education and sits on the Research Advisory Board of the European Journalists Training Association.

LORCAN SIRR is a senior lecturer in housing at the Technological University Dublin. He has also written for most major Irish publications, including the *Sunday Times*, where he was a housing columnist, and provides analysis for major media outlets such as RTÉ, CBC (Canada), BBC and Bloomberg. He is author of *Housing in Ireland: The A-Z Guide* published in May 2019.

EOGHAN SMITH is a writer and academic. He has taught at universities and colleges in Dublin, Maynooth and Carlow, and is the Programme Director for Arts and Humanities at Carlow College, St Patrick's. He recently co-edited the collection *Imagining Irish Suburbia in Literature and Culture* (Palgrave, 2018). He is the author of the monograph *John Banville: Art and Authenticity* (Peter Lang, 2013) and a novel, *The Failing Heart* (Dedalus, 2018).

SHARON TIGHE-MOONEY has an interdisciplinary MA in English, Sociology and Theology and a PhD in English from the National University of Ireland, Maynooth. She is co-editor of *Essays in Irish Literary Criticism: Themes of Gender, Sexuality, and Corporeality* (2008) and author of *What About Me? Women and the Catholic Church* (2018).

HARRY WHITE is Professor of Music at University College Dublin and a Fellow of the Royal Irish Academy of Music. His research interests include the cultural history of music in Ireland and concepts of authority and autonomy in early eighteenth-century music in Europe.

Reimagining Ireland

Series Editor: Dr Eamon Maher, Technological University Dublin

The concepts of Ireland and 'Irishness' are in constant flux in the wake of an ever-increasing reappraisal of the notion of cultural and national specificity in a world assailed from all angles by the forces of globalisation and uniformity. Reimagining Ireland interrogates Ireland's past and present and suggests possibilities for the future by looking at Ireland's literature, culture and history and subjecting them to the most up-to-date critical appraisals associated with sociology, literary theory, historiography, political science and theology.

Some of the pertinent issues include, but are not confined to, Irish writing in English and Irish, Nationalism, Unionism, the Northern 'Troubles', the Peace Process, economic development in Ireland, the impact and decline of the Celtic Tiger, Irish spirituality, the rise and fall of organised religion, the visual arts, popular cultures, sport, Irish music and dance, emigration and the Irish diaspora, immigration and multiculturalism, marginalisation, globalisation, modernity/postmodernity and postcolonialism. The series publishes monographs, comparative studies, interdisciplinary projects, conference proceedings and edited books.

Proposals should be sent either to Dr Eamon Maher at eamon.maher@ittdublin.ie or to ireland@peterlang.com.

Vol. 1 Eugene O'Brien: 'Kicking Bishop Brennan up the Arse': Negotiating Texts and Contexts in Contemporary Irish Studies
ISBN 978-3-03911-539-6. 219 pages. 2009.

Vol. 2 James P. Byrne, Padraig Kirwan and Michael O'Sullivan (eds): Affecting Irishness: Negotiating Cultural Identity Within and Beyond the Nation
ISBN 978-3-03911-830-4. 334 pages. 2009.

Vol. 3 Irene Lucchitti: The Islandman: The Hidden Life of Tomás O'Crohan
ISBN 978-3-03911-837-3. 232 pages. 2009.

Vol. 4 Paddy Lyons and Alison O'Malley-Younger (eds): No Country for Old Men: Fresh Perspectives on Irish Literature
ISBN 978-3-03911-841-0. 289 pages. 2009.

Vol. 5 Eamon Maher (ed.): Cultural Perspectives on Globalisation and Ireland
ISBN 978-3-03911-851-9. 256 pages. 2009.

Vol. 6 Lynn Brunet: 'A Course of Severe and Arduous Trials': Bacon, Beckett and Spurious Freemasonry in Early Twentieth-Century Ireland
ISBN 978-3-03911-854-0. 218 pages. 2009.

Vol. 7 Claire Lynch: Irish Autobiography: Stories of Self in the Narrative of a Nation
ISBN 978-3-03911-856-4. 234 pages. 2009.

Vol. 8 Victoria O'Brien: A History of Irish Ballet from 1927 to 1963
ISBN 978-3-03911-873-1. 208 pages. 2011.

Vol. 9 Irene Gilsenan Nordin and Elin Holmsten (eds): Liminal Borderlands in Irish Literature and Culture
ISBN 978-3-03911-859-5. 208 pages. 2009.

Vol. 10 Claire Nally: Envisioning Ireland: W.B. Yeats's Occult Nationalism
ISBN 978-3-03911-882-3. 320 pages. 2010.

Vol. 11 Raita Merivirta: The Gun and Irish Politics: Examining National History in Neil Jordan's *Michael Collins*
ISBN 978-3-03911-888-5. 202 pages. 2009.

Vol. 12 John Strachan and Alison O'Malley-Younger (eds): Ireland: Revolution and Evolution
ISBN 978-3-03911-881-6. 248 pages. 2010.

Vol. 13 Barbara Hughes: Between Literature and History: The Diaries and Memoirs of Mary Leadbeater and Dorothea Herbert
ISBN 978-3-03911-889-2. 255 pages. 2010.

Vol. 14 Edwina Keown and Carol Taaffe (eds): Irish Modernism: Origins, Contexts, Publics
ISBN 978-3-03911-894-6. 256 pages. 2010.

Vol. 15 John Walsh: Contests and Contexts: The Irish Language and Ireland's Socio-Economic Development
ISBN 978-3-03911-914-1. 492 pages. 2011.

Vol. 16 Zélie Asava: The Black Irish Onscreen: Representing Black and Mixed-Race Identities on Irish Film and Television
ISBN 978-3-0343-0839-7. 213 pages. 2013.

Vol. 17 Susan Cahill and Eóin Flannery (eds): This Side of Brightness: Essays on the Fiction of Colum McCann
ISBN 978-3-03911-935-6. 189 pages. 2012.

Vol. 18 Brian Arkins: The Thought of W.B. Yeats
ISBN 978-3-03911-939-4. 204 pages. 2010.

Vol. 19 Maureen O'Connor: The Female and the Species: The Animal in Irish Women's Writing
ISBN 978-3-03911-959-2. 203 pages. 2010.

Vol. 20 Rhona Trench: Bloody Living: The Loss of Selfhood in the Plays of Marina Carr
ISBN 978-3-03911-964-6. 327 pages. 2010.

Vol. 21 Jeannine Woods: Visions of Empire and Other Imaginings: Cinema, Ireland and India, 1910–1962
ISBN 978-3-03911-974-5. 230 pages. 2011.

Vol. 22 Neil O'Boyle: New Vocabularies, Old Ideas: Culture, Irishness and the Advertising Industry
ISBN 978-3-03911-978-3. 233 pages. 2011.

Vol. 23 Dermot McCarthy: John McGahern and the Art of Memory
ISBN 978-3-0343-0100-8. 344 pages. 2010.

Vol. 24 Francesca Benatti, Sean Ryder and Justin Tonra (eds): Thomas Moore: Texts, Contexts, Hypertexts
ISBN 978-3-0343-0900-4. 220 pages. 2013.

Vol. 25 Sarah O'Connor: No Man's Land: Irish Women and the Cultural Present
ISBN 978-3-0343-0111-4. 230 pages. 2011.

Vol. 26 Caroline Magennis: Sons of Ulster: Masculinities in the Contemporary Northern Irish Novel
ISBN 978-3-0343-0110-7. 192 pages. 2010.

Vol. 27 Dawn Duncan: Irish Myth, Lore and Legend on Film
ISBN 978-3-0343-0140-4. 181 pages. 2013.

Vol. 28 Eamon Maher and Catherine Maignant (eds): Franco-Irish Connections in Space and Time: Peregrinations and Ruminations
ISBN 978-3-0343-0870-0. 295 pages. 2012.

Vol. 29 Holly Maples: Culture War: Conflict, Commemoration and the Contemporary Abbey Theatre
ISBN 978-3-0343-0137-4. 294 pages. 2011.

Vol. 30 Maureen O'Connor (ed.): Back to the Future of Irish Studies: Festschrift for Tadhg Foley
ISBN 978-3-0343-0141-1. 359 pages. 2010.

Vol. 31 Eva Urban: Community Politics and the Peace Process in Contemporary Northern Irish Drama
ISBN 978-3-0343-0143-5. 303 pages. 2011.

Vol. 32 Mairéad Conneely: Between Two Shores / *Idir Dhá Chladach*: Writing the Aran Islands, 1890–1980
ISBN 978-3-0343-0144-2. 299 pages. 2011.

Vol. 33 Gerald Morgan and Gavin Hughes (eds): Southern Ireland and the Liberation of France: New Perspectives
ISBN 978-3-0343-0190-9. 250 pages. 2011.

Vol. 34 Anne MacCarthy: Definitions of Irishness in the 'Library of Ireland' Literary Anthologies
ISBN 978-3-0343-0194-7. 271 pages. 2012.

Vol. 35 Irene Lucchitti: Peig Sayers: In Her Own Write
ISBN 978-3-0343-0253-1. Forthcoming.

Vol. 36 Eamon Maher and Eugene O'Brien (eds): Breaking the Mould: Literary Representations of Irish Catholicism
ISBN 978-3-0343-0232-6. 249 pages. 2011.

Vol. 37 Mícheál Ó hAodha and John O'Callaghan (eds): Narratives of the Occluded Irish Diaspora: Subversive Voices
ISBN 978-3-0343-0248-7. 227 pages. 2012.

Vol. 38 Willy Maley and Alison O'Malley-Younger (eds): Celtic Connections: Irish–Scottish Relations and the Politics of Culture
ISBN 978-3-0343-0214-2. 247 pages. 2013.

Vol. 39 Sabine Egger and John McDonagh (eds): Polish–Irish Encounters in the Old and New Europe
ISBN 978-3-0343-0253-1. 322 pages. 2011.

Vol. 40 Elke D'hoker, Raphaël Ingelbien and Hedwig Schwall (eds): Irish Women Writers: New Critical Perspectives
ISBN 978-3-0343-0249-4. 318 pages. 2011.

Vol. 41 Peter James Harris: From Stage to Page: Critical Reception of Irish Plays in the London Theatre, 1925–1996
ISBN 978-3-0343-0266-1. 311 pages. 2011.

Vol. 42 Hedda Friberg-Harnesk, Gerald Porter and Joakim Wrethed (eds):
Beyond Ireland: Encounters Across Cultures
ISBN 978-3-0343-0270-8. 342 pages. 2011.

Vol. 43 Irene Gilsenan Nordin and Carmen Zamorano Llena (eds): Urban and Rural Landscapes in Modern Ireland: Language, Literature and Culture
ISBN 978-3-0343-0279-1. 238 pages. 2012.

Vol. 44 Kathleen Costello-Sullivan: Mother/Country: Politics of the Personal in the Fiction of Colm Tóibín
ISBN 978-3-0343-0753-6. 247 pages. 2012.

Vol. 45 Lesley Lelourec and Gráinne O'Keeffe-Vigneron (eds): Ireland and Victims: Confronting the Past, Forging the Future
ISBN 978-3-0343-0792-5. 331 pages. 2012.

Vol. 46 Gerald Dawe, Darryl Jones and Nora Pelizzari (eds): Beautiful Strangers: Ireland and the World of the 1950s
ISBN 978-3-0343-0801-4. 207 pages. 2013.

Vol. 47 Yvonne O'Keeffe and Claudia Reese (eds): New Voices, Inherited Lines: Literary and Cultural Representations of the Irish Family
ISBN 978-3-0343-0799-4. 238 pages. 2013.

Vol. 48 Justin Carville (ed.): Visualizing Dublin: Visual Culture, Modernity and the Representation of Urban Space
ISBN 978-3-0343-0802-1. 326 pages. 2014.

Vol. 49 Gerald Power and Ondřej Pilný (eds): Ireland and the Czech Lands: Contacts and Comparisons in History and Culture
ISBN 978-3-0343-1701-6. 243 pages. 2014.

Vol. 50 Eoghan Smith: John Banville: Art and Authenticity
ISBN 978-3-0343-0852-6. 199 pages. 2014.

Vol. 51 María Elena Jaime de Pablos and Mary Pierse (eds): George Moore and the Quirks of Human Nature
ISBN 978-3-0343-1752-8. 283 pages. 2014.

Vol. 52 Aidan O'Malley and Eve Patten (eds): Ireland, West to East: Irish Cultural Connections with Central and Eastern Europe
ISBN 978-3-0343-0913-4. 307 pages. 2014.

Vol. 53 Ruben Moi, Brynhildur Boyce and Charles I. Armstrong (eds): The Crossings of Art in Ireland
ISBN 978-3-0343-0983-7. 319 pages. 2014.

Vol. 54 Sylvie Mikowski (ed.): Ireland and Popular Culture
ISBN 978-3-0343-1717-7. 257 pages. 2014.

Vol. 55 Benjamin Keatinge and Mary Pierse (eds): France and Ireland in the Public Imagination
ISBN 978-3-0343-1747-4. 279 pages. 2014.

Vol. 56 Raymond Mullen, Adam Bargroff and Jennifer Mullen (eds): John McGahern: Critical Essays
ISBN 978-3-0343-1755-9. 253 pages. 2014.

Vol. 57 Máirtín Mac Con Iomaire and Eamon Maher (eds): 'Tickling the Palate': Gastronomy in Irish Literature and Culture
ISBN 978-3-0343-1769-6. 253 pages. 2014.

Vol. 58 Heidi Hansson and James H. Murphy (eds): Fictions of the Irish Land War
ISBN 978-3-0343-0999-8. 237 pages. 2014.

Vol. 59 Fiona McCann: A Poetics of Dissensus: Confronting Violence in Contemporary Prose Writing from the North of Ireland
ISBN 978-3-0343-0979-0. 238 pages. 2014.

Vol. 60 Marguérite Corporaal, Christopher Cusack, Lindsay Janssen and Ruud van den Beuken (eds): Global Legacies of the Great Irish Famine: Transnational and Interdisciplinary Perspectives
ISBN 978-3-0343-0903-5. 357 pages. 2014.

Vol. 61 Katarzyna Ojrzyńska: 'Dancing As If Language No Longer Existed': Dance in Contemporary Irish Drama
ISBN 978-3-0343-1813-6. 318 pages. 2015.

Vol. 62 Whitney Standlee: 'Power to Observe': Irish Women Novelists in Britain, 1890–1916
ISBN 978-3-0343-1837-2. 288 pages. 2015.

Vol. 63 Elke D'hoker and Stephanie Eggermont (eds): The Irish Short Story: Traditions and Trends
ISBN 978-3-0343-1753-5. 330 pages. 2015.

Vol. 64 Radvan Markus: Echoes of the Rebellion: The Year 1798 in Twentieth-Century Irish Fiction and Drama
ISBN 978-3-0343-1832-7. 248 pages. 2015.

Vol. 65 B. Mairéad Pratschke: Visions of Ireland: Gael Linn's *Amharc Éireann* Film Series, 1956–1964
ISBN 978-3-0343-1872-3. 301 pages. 2015.

Vol. 66 Una Hunt and Mary Pierse (eds): France and Ireland: Notes and Narratives
ISBN 978-3-0343-1914-0. 272 pages. 2015.

Vol. 67 John Lynch and Katherina Dodou (eds): The Leaving of Ireland: Migration and Belonging in Irish Literature and Film
ISBN 978-3-0343-1896-9. 313 pages. 2015.

Vol. 68 Anne Goarzin (ed.): New Critical Perspectives on Franco-Irish Relations
ISBN 978-3-0343-1781-8. 271 pages. 2015.

Vol. 69 Michel Brunet, Fabienne Gaspari and Mary Pierse (eds): George Moore's Paris and His Ongoing French Connections
ISBN 978-3-0343-1973-7. 279 pages. 2015.

Vol. 70 Carine Berbéri and Martine Pelletier (eds): Ireland: Authority and Crisis
ISBN 978-3-0343-1939-3. 296 pages. 2015.

Vol. 71 David Doolin: Transnational Revolutionaries: The Fenian Invasion of Canada, 1866
ISBN 978-3-0343-1922-5. 348 pages. 2016.

Vol. 72 Terry Phillips: Irish Literature and the First World War: Culture, Identity and Memory
ISBN 978-3-0343-1969-0. 297 pages. 2015.

Vol. 73 Carmen Zamorano Llena and Billy Gray (eds): Authority and Wisdom in the New Ireland: Studies in Literature and Culture
ISBN 978-3-0343-1833-4. 263 pages. 2016.

Vol. 74 Flore Coulouma (ed.): New Perspectives on Irish TV Series: Identity and Nostalgia on the Small Screen
ISBN 978-3-0343-1977-5. 222 pages. 2016.

Vol. 75 Fergal Lenehan: Stereotypes, Ideology and Foreign Correspondents: German Media Representations of Ireland, 1946–2010
ISBN 978-3-0343-2222-5. 306 pages. 2016.

Vol. 76 Jarlath Killeen and Valeria Cavalli (eds): 'Inspiring a Mysterious Terror': 200 Years of Joseph Sheridan Le Fanu
ISBN 978-3-0343-2223-2. 260 pages. 2016.

Vol. 77 Anne Karhio: 'Slight Return': Paul Muldoon's Poetics of Place
ISBN 978-3-0343-1986-7. 272 pages. 2017.

Vol. 78 Margaret Eaton: Frank Confessions: Performance in the Life-Writings of Frank McCourt
ISBN 978-1-906165-61-1. 294 pages. 2017.

Vol. 79 Marguérite Corporaal, Christopher Cusack and Ruud van den Beuken (eds): Irish Studies and the Dynamics of Memory: Transitions and Transformations
ISBN 978-3-0343-2236-2. 360 pages. 2017

Vol. 80 Conor Caldwell and Eamon Byers (eds): New Crops, Old Fields: Reimagining Irish Folklore
ISBN 978-3-0343-1912-6. 200 pages. 2017

Vol. 81 Sinéad Wall: Irish Diasporic Narratives in Argentina: A Reconsideration of Home, Identity and Belonging
ISBN 978-1-906165-66-6. 282 pages. 2017

Vol. 82 Ute Anna Mittermaier: Images of Spain in Irish Literature, 1922–1975
ISBN 978-3-0343-1993-5. 386 pages. 2017

Vol. 83 Lauren Clark: Consuming Irish Children: Advertising and the Art of Independence, 1860–1921
ISBN 978-3-0343-1989-8. 288 pages. 2017

Vol. 84 Lisa FitzGerald: Re-Place: Irish Theatre Environments
ISBN 978-1-78707-359-3. 222 pages. 2017

Vol. 85 Joseph Greenwood: 'Hear My Song': Irish Theatre and Popular Song in the 1950s and 1960s
ISBN 978-3-0343-1915-7. 320 pages. 2017

Vol. 86 Nils Beese: Writing Slums: Dublin, Dirt and Literature
ISBN 978-1-78707-959-5. 250 pages. 2018

Vol. 87 Barry Houlihan: Navigating Ireland's Theatre Archive: Theory, Practice, Performance
ISBN 978-1-78707-372-2. 306 pages. 2019.

Vol. 88 María Elena Jaime de Pablos (ed.): Giving Shape to the Moment: The Art of Mary O'Donnell: Poet, Novelist and Short Story Writer
ISBN 978-1-78874-403-4. 228 pages. 2018

Vol. 89 Marguérite Corporaal and Peter Gray: The Great Irish Famine and Social Class: Conflicts, Responsibilities, Representations
ISBN 978-1-78874-166-8. 330 pages. 2019

Vol. 90 Patrick Speight: Irish-Argentine Identity in an Age of Political Challenge and Change, 1875–1983
ISBN 978-1-78874-417-1. 360 pages. 2019.

Vol. 91 Fionna Barber, Heidi Hansson, and Sara Dybris McQuaid (eds): Ireland and the North
ISBN 978-1-78874-289-4. 338 pages. 2019.

Vol. 92 Ruth Sheehy
The Life and Work of Richard King: Religion, Nationalism and Modernism
ISBN 978-1-78707-246-6. 482 pages. 2019.

Vol. 93 Brian Lucey, Eamon Maher and Eugene O'Brien (eds)
Recalling the Celtic Tiger
ISBN 978-1-78997-286-3. 386 pages. 2019.